A Solid Foundation for Serious Astrologers

Astrology: Understanding the Birth Chart is designed to be useful to all students of astrology, from beginners to more advanced practitioners, and will help you develop an integrated, synthesized approach to understanding the birth chart. You will discover how classical astrology can enrich your understanding of the planets, signs, and houses. You will also learn how to identify key themes in the chart, and how to relate the different aspects and elements together to gain a holistic understanding of the birth chart—and of the individual.

Kevin Burk takes you step by step from the core basics to the finer complexities of chart interpretation. But what sets this book apart from so many others is that Kevin doesn't just give you the "hows" of astrology—he also gives you the "whys," without getting bogged down in obscure technicalities.

About the Author

Kevin Burk (California) holds a Level IV NCGR certification in astrological counseling and has practiced astrology in the San Diego area since 1993. His website (www.astro-horoscopes.com) has won several internet awards for design and content, and has hosted more than 700,000 visitors since its inception.

To Write to the Author

If you wish to contact the author or would like more information about this book, please write to the author in care of Llewellyn Worldwide and we will forward your request. Both the author and publisher appreciate hearing from you and learning of your enjoyment of this book and how it has helped you. Llewellyn Worldwide cannot guarantee that every letter written to the author can be answered, but all will be forwarded. Please write to:

Kevin Burk
℅ Llewellyn Worldwide
P.O. Box 64383, Dept. 1-56718-088-4
St. Paul, MN 55164-0383, U.S.A.
Please enclose a self-addressed stamped envelope for reply,
or $1.00 to cover costs. If outside U.S.A., enclose
international postal reply coupon.

Many of Llewellyn's authors have websites with additional information and resources. For more information, please visit our website at
http://www.llewellyn.com

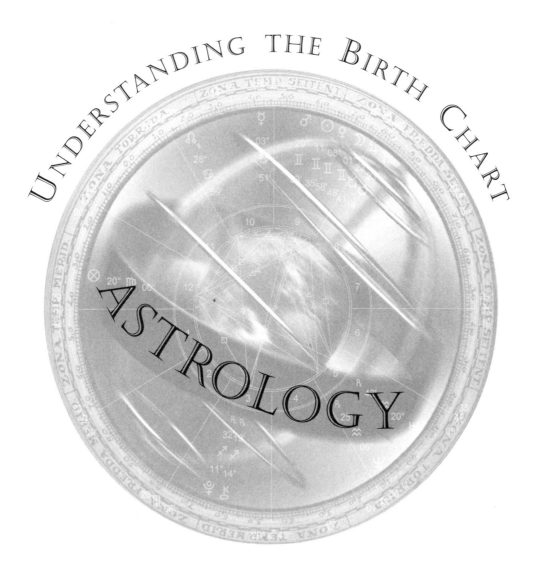

UNDERSTANDING THE BIRTH CHART

ASTROLOGY

A COMPREHENSIVE GUIDE TO CLASSICAL INTERPRETATION

KEVIN BURK

2002
Llewellyn Publications
St. Paul, Minnesota 55164-0383, U.S.A.

First Edition
Second Printing, 2002

Book design by Donna Burch
Cover design by Lisa Novak
Cover photo by Digital Stock
Editing by Andrea Neff

The material on calculating house systems in chapter 6 originally appeared in the *NCGR Education & Curriculum Study Guide Level II*, published by the National Council for Geocosmic Research, www.geocosmic.org. Permission to use this material is gratefully acknowledged.

All horoscope charts used in this book were generated using Win*Star © Matrix Software.

Library of Congress Cataloging-in-Publication Data

Burk, Kevin, 1967–
     Astrology : understanding the birth chart / by Kevin Burk.
          p. cm.
     Includes index.
     ISBN 1–56718–088–4
        1. Natal astrology. I. Title

BF1719 .B87 2001
133.5—dc21   00–052062

Llewellyn Publications
A Division of Llewellyn Worldwide, Ltd.
P.O. Box 64383, Dept. 1-56718-088-4
St. Paul, MN 55164-0383, U.S.A.
www.llewellyn.com

 Printed in the United States of America on recycled paper

Contents

Chapter 5
Interpreting Planets in Signs 93

Chapter 6
The Angles, the Houses, and the Part of Fortune 167

Chapter 7
Basic Interpretation 185

Chapter 8
The Aspects 201

Chapter 9
A Brief Look at Natal Retrograde Planets

Chapter 10
Eclipses, Lunations, and the Moon's Nodes

List of Figures

Acknowledgments

I couldn't have possibly written this book on my own. However, since there's only room on the cover for one name (mine), I want to take a moment to recognize and thank the people who truly helped make this book possible.

I want to thank Terry Lamb, who was my first astrology instructor, and who is therefore one of the people directly responsible for the book that you're reading right now because she gave me the foundation that enabled me to write this book. Terry's classes and instruction prepared me to complete my NCGR Level IV certification in Astrological Counseling. Terry is also the person who introduced me to the incredible power of Classical Astrology.

I also want to thank and acknowledge Dr. J. Lee Lehman, Ph.D., both on a personal level, for the invaluable information that I have received as one of her students, and on a professional level for the work that she has done to bring Classical Astrology techniques into modern usage. Her books, *Essential Dignities* and *Classical Astrology for Modern Living* are the bibles of classical astrology.

Jim Shawvan took on the daunting task of being my first reader and editor of both this volume and the companion math book. His feedback on both major issues (the astronomy facts are correct thanks to Jim) and minor issues (I'm embarrassed to remember how many typographical errors he caught) is greatly appreciated.

Andrea Neff, my editor at Llewellyn, picked up where Jim left off, and has helped me to smooth out the remaining rough edges. Never underestimate the value and importance of a good editor!

I also want to acknowledge and thank some other very important teachers (who just think that they happened to be my students at the time). Robyn Dennen and Lorraine Del-Rose actually helped me to complete this book, because I was teaching the material to them as I was writing it, and had to keep at least one chapter ahead of them at all times. Julie Braden, Patricia Ray, Diana

Wall, and Michael Zlocki gave me the chance to refine and revise the material, by asking me to teach it to them.

On a more personal note, I've been blessed with the love, wisdom, and support of many other teachers, who, while they didn't specifically teach me about astrology, certainly taught me how to work with astrology in a loving, healing, and compassionate way. Dorothy, Adam, and Argena, this book is dedicated to you.

1

Introduction and History of Astrology

What Astrology Is—And What It Isn't

What is astrology? If you ask most people today, they'll tell you that it has something to do with your date of birth, and probably also something to do with the daily horoscope columns you can find in most newspapers and magazines. Whether or not they profess to believe in astrology, most people know what their "sign" is (even if they don't understand what that means). Although the popularity of these types of columns (and books, too) has kept astrology at least near the mainstream of popular culture, they have nothing at all to do with real astrology.

Astrology is not a science, at least not by today's definition of the term. Portions of astrology do overlap with the realm of science, and as research astrologers have demonstrated time and again, astrological influences can be shown to have statistically significant results. By far the most famous studies were done by Francoise and Michel Gauquelin, showing how the planet Mars has a pronounced tendency to be strongly placed in the charts of successful professional athletes. Much of astrology, though, falls outside of the very limited realm of "science" into what is loosely termed "metaphysics."

Astrology is also not a religion. You don't need to believe in astrology in order to use astrology any more than you need to believe in a hammer to use a hammer. Astrology is a tool, nothing more, nothing less. It is an amazingly versatile tool with a wide range of applications, but it is a tool, nonetheless; and as is the case with any tool, its use is more appropriate in some situations than in others.

1

So astrology is not a science, not a religion, and has almost nothing to do with the daily horoscope columns in the newspapers. What is it then?

Astrology is the study of cycles. By observing the cyclical movements of the planets, we are able to gain a greater understanding of the cycles and patterns in our own lives. Astrology can be a powerful tool for healing and transformation, and it can be a key that can unlock a greater spiritual connection to the universe. Astrology can be applied in many ways to many different situations. Although astrology is not fortunetelling, when skillfully applied, astrology can be an extremely effective predictive tool.

On a personal level, astrology can be used to gain a deeper understanding of our individual life paths and life experiences. Exploring the natal chart (also known as the birth chart or horoscope) can give us insight into our personal issues, our patterns, our fears, and our dreams. We can gain insight into our purpose in life and gain a stronger sense of self. Astrology is a tool that can help us understand and unlock our highest potentials, and that can teach us how to live in harmony with the universe.

Before we explore how astrology can do all of this, let's take a look at its origins to see how astrology has evolved into its present form.

History of Astrology

Although humans have always been fascinated by the night sky, the first Western culture to actively take notice of the movements of the heavens was the Sumerian culture in the valley of Mesopotamia, as early as 6000 B.C. Around 2400 B.C., the Babylonians (also known as the Chaldeans) built on these observations, and recorded the first astrological tables. Over thousands of years, they developed the first system of astrology (which, by the way, was also astronomy—the two were synonymous until the 1800s) based on observations of the planetary cycles and how they related to important events in their civilization.

Babylonian astrology was quite different from modern-day astrology. The Babylonians certainly didn't have computers, and moreover, they also didn't have lists of the positions and motions of the planets. All they could do was observe the planets in the night sky, and track when the planets first appeared, when they appeared to change direction, and when they disappeared. The Babylonians first started to pay attention to the zodiac as we know it today around 700 B.C., although the oldest known Babylonian horoscope dates back only to 409 B.C.

When Alexander the Great conquered Chaldea in 331 B.C., the Greek culture inherited the Babylonian astrology, although it was not until the foundations of Greek medicine and science had been established that the Greeks began to take an active interest in astrology. Even if astrology came to the party late, the advances that the Greeks had made in the fields of mathematics, medicine, geometry, and philosophy not only advanced and enhanced the practical applications of astrology as a science, but also made it clear to the Greeks that astrology was in fact the core of the seven fundamental sciences in that it incorporated all the key elements of the other six sciences.

The modern names for the planets and the signs, as well as the foundations of our modern understanding of them, come from the Greek literature. By far the best-known person from this period is Ptolemy (Claudius Ptolemaeus), who published, in A.D. 140, the *Tetrabiblos*, one of the most famous works on astrology ever written. In this book, Ptolemy presents a system of astrology that employs planets, signs, houses, and aspects, and that is very much the heart of astrology as we know it today. Ptolemy was not, however, an astrologer himself— he was an encyclopedist, and simply created a comprehensive record of the philosophies and techniques that had been used at that time.

After the fall of the Roman Empire, Western astrology all but disappeared for almost 500 years. Fortunately, the Arabs became the caretakers of the Greek astrological knowledge (because during the height of the Greek and Roman civilizations, there was free and open trade between the West and the East, and this included a great deal of sharing of astrological knowledge between the two cultures), and the Arabs both preserved it and mixed it with their own systems of astrology. When the West finally started to pay attention to higher education again, Ptolemy was required reading for all scholars, and astrology was once more a cornerstone of Western education.

Astrology continued to evolve and develop through the Middle Ages and until the end of the Renaissance. Advances in mathematics and measurement opened the door for the creation of many of the modern house systems (the Greeks used whole-sign houses). Advances in timekeeping enabled astrologers to generate more accurately timed charts than ever before possible. Astrology was a fundamental part of the culture of the times, practiced by healers and physicians, as well as by court-retained royal astrologers. Any educated person of the time would have had a strong foundation in astrology, both in theory and in practice. Natal astrology became available to common people during this time period (in earlier days, only royalty were deemed important enough to have their natal charts calculated and analyzed).

One of the most important astrologers at this time was William Lilly, who in the mid-1600's published his astrological legacy, *Christian Astrology*. In addition to being an exceptional look at the types of astrological techniques that were used during this time period, *Christian Astrology* is one of the most detailed and comprehensive textbooks on horary astrology ever published. In addition to laying out the rules and techniques of horary, Lilly includes a number of examples of horary charts with his interpretations. Lilly's track record with predictive astrology was exceptional—and this got him in a lot of trouble! He predicted the Great Fire of London fifteen years before the plague and the fire; after the actual event, Lilly was investigated as a possible contributor to the fire! (He was acquitted, of course.) One of Lilly's students, Nicholas Culpeper, became one of the definitive experts on medical astrology and herbology.

With the Age of Reason, however, and the increased power and influence of the Church, the practice of astrology in the West once again fell into decline. Once esteemed members of the nobility and advisors to kings, astrologers were rapidly demoted to the rank of parlor magicians. In 1666, astrology was officially banished from the Academy of Sciences in France. Although general interest in astrology remained quite high, astrologers were no longer as respected or considered to be part of the mainstream.

During this time period, the discovery of the planet Uranus in 1781 caused a tremendous upset in the astrological community: this new planet forced the reevaluation of the entire system of Western astrology. Although Neptune's and Pluto's subsequent discoveries certainly caused stirs, Uranus was the planet that really shook things up.

Astrology didn't begin to rise in popularity again until the 1890s with the renewed interest in spirituality, mysticism, and the occult that was most prominent in England. Astrology was practiced more openly and with greater interest in Europe; notably, Carl Jung incorporated many of the symbols of astrology into his psychological work, particularly those relating to his concept of archetypes and the collective unconscious. England still had very strict laws against fortunetelling at the time, and Alan Leo, a prominent astrologer, attempted to change the focus of his approach to astrology away from fortunetelling and present it instead as a form of psychology. Although this ultimately didn't keep Alan Leo out of jail, it did mark the start of natal astrology as we know it today.

In the late 1960s and 1970s, as the astrological community in America began to grow and develop, new techniques were proposed and tested. One significant trend during this period was to move away from the frequently negative and fatalistic interpretations that had been used in classical astrology, and to look for more empowering ways to interpret a birth chart.

Also during this period, the Sun sign horoscope columns that first appeared in England in the 1920s saw a surge of popularity. Astrology was a part of popular culture again—or at least a watered-down, packaged version of it was.

In the past, one of the greatest challenges of astrology was the time and precision that calculating a chart required. Now that computers have made this a non-issue, modern astrologers have the ability to experiment with a wide range of classical techniques, both to rediscover our roots, and to discover how to translate the time-tested approaches to interpretation into a more modern context.

Branches of Modern Astrology

Modern Western astrology encompasses a wide range of different approaches and techniques. The three main branches of astrology, in chronological order of their evolution, are: mundane, interrogatory, and natal. What distinguishes these branches from each other goes beyond the fundamental differences in subject matter. Each branch has its own individual method of interpreting the elements of the astrological chart. In the language of astrology, each "word"—be it a planet, sign, or house—has a slightly different set of interpretations depending on the context of the chart and the techniques being used.

Mundane Astrology

The term "mundane" comes from the Latin word for "world," and mundane astrology is the astrology of world events. Mundane astrology was the first system of astrology to evolve, and it developed over thousands of years by people observing the cycles of the planets and recording the important events of their society. (At least initially, these events had much to do with when it was time to plant crops, and when it was time to harvest crops.) As the astrologers developed a better understanding of the planetary cycles and how they related to world events, the focus began to shift to the affairs of the kings and the growth, prosperity, and expansion prospects of the kingdoms.

Today, mundane astrology is used to predict and analyze world events, both politically and physically. Some mundane astrologers, for example, specialize in weather forecasting. Others pay attention to the economic or social factors that may be influencing a given country.

Financial astrology is a relatively recent offshoot of mundane astrology that is becoming increasingly popular today. Many financial astrologers are also professional investors, and they are able to use their understanding of the ebb and flow of economic cycles (as shown through the planetary cycles) to guide their investment choices.

Interrogatory Astrology

Interrogatory astrology is the branch of astrology that is concerned with events—in the past, the present, and the future. Horary astrology asks, "Will this happen?", electional astrology asks, "When is the best time to make this happen?", and event interpretation asks, "What happened?"

Horary Astrology

Horary astrology answers questions such as "Will I get the job?", "Where did I leave my checkbook?", and "Will I win the lawsuit?" The principle behind horary astrology is that when a question is truly asked, there is a connection between the individual asking the question (the querent) and the universe. The chart, for the moment and location in which the question was asked, then contains the entire essence of the question—including the outcome.

Electional Astrology

Electional astrology is very similar to horary astrology; the difference is that rather than asking how an event will turn out, the goal is instead to pick a time for the important event when the outcome is most likely to be favorable. Electional astrology can be used for everything from picking a date for a wedding, to deciding when to ask for a raise (or look for a new job), when to file a lawsuit, when to plan a surgery, and even when to file your taxes.

Event Interpretation

Event interpretation is what all horary and electional charts become after the fact—once you've asked a horary question, you can go back and compare the chart with what actually happened, and see how the outcome is reflected in the chart. Event interpretation can also be used to gain insight into the cause of an event. When interpreted properly, event charts will tell a very accurate story describing the nature and cause of the event, as well as the effects of the event. One area where event interpretation was used a great deal was in medical astrology: the astrologer would take the time of decumbiture (being sick to the point where the person could not get out of bed), and by interpreting that chart, could discern both the nature of the illness, and the individual's chances for recovery.

Natal Astrology

Something that most modern astrologers forget, or indeed, never learned, is that natal astrology was originally about making predictions, not about analyzing one's personality traits. Most of the techniques and approaches that are being rediscovered today focus on the primary concerns of the Middle Ages: length of life, health, children, and financial matters. We must remember that in the Middle Ages, even up to the last 150 years, one's life expectancy was significantly shorter (not to mention bleaker) than it is now. Although these types of predictions are a fundamental part of Jyotish astrology, the intrinsically fatalistic (and often quite negative) interpretations come as quite a shock to those who have primarily experienced the more modern, humanistic approach to natal astrology.

The idea that a natal chart could be used as a tool for self-understanding and spiritual and psychological enlightenment came about because Alan Leo was trying to stay out of jail. Leo was a very prominent astrologer in England near the turn of the century, and in the great tradition of astrologers, he was running afoul of England's laws prohibiting fortunetelling. Leo was arrested and tried several times, and acquitted each time; but he decided he didn't want to push his luck. Instead, he changed the titles of his astrology lessons, and maintained that his approach to astrology was not fortunetelling, it was instead a form of psychoanalysis. Unfortunately, the English courts didn't buy that argument, and Leo was ultimately put in jail. But his legacy survives to this day, and Alan Leo is unquestionably the father of modern natal interpretations.

Modern Natal Astrology and the Battle Between Fate and Free Will

For as long as humankind has sought to understand our place in the universe and our connection with a higher power, we have struggled with the question of whether our lives are predestined and planned out, or whether they are entirely of our own creation. The Fate vs. Free Will battle has gone on for centuries, although it was arguably brought into focus by the Church, since one of the cornerstones of the Church's power was the tenet that individuals had to make a conscious choice as to whether they wanted salvation or damnation. The Church does not have a history of playing nice with people who hold different belief structures; at various points in history, and with varying degrees of success, the Church has waged war on all things divinatory. Astrology has been a casualty of war many times; in fact, the Church was so effective in its campaign that Western astrology almost died out entirely in the Middle Ages.

Most of the time, astrology and other forms of divination seem to fall squarely in the "Fate and Predestination" camp. If we truly had free will, then how could people predict the future?

Today, of course, most New Age spirituality places great emphasis on our gift of absolute free will; that we make our own choices, and must learn to take full responsibility for the world that we have created for ourselves. If this is the case, then why can astrological predictions be so accurate? How can a birth chart show who we are if we are truly free to choose for ourselves?

The answer is this: we do have absolute free will; however, we almost never use it. This is why predictive astrology works, and this is also how natal astrology has evolved into such a powerful tool for self-discovery, understanding, healing, and transformation.

In the case of the interrogatory forms of predictive astrology, the story that the electional or the horary chart tells is based on the assumption that everyone involved is pretty much running on autopilot (as most of us are, most of the time). These charts show how the energy of the universe is flowing, and what the most probable outcome will be if we simply surrender to the tide of events. The person asking the question, though, has absolute free will and can significantly impact the eventual outcome by changing his or her individual role in the events.

In the case of natal astrology, the modern approach is to look at the birth chart as a map of the types of experiences that we need to have in order to be the most fulfilled in our lives. We are by no means required to follow the map, of course; and the map is not the actual terrain—we can choose from an infinite number of ways to experience the energies in our charts. We also have the ability to grow and to evolve, and to become more skillful in how we work with the energies in our charts and in our lives. While the birth chart is very much a starting point and a template for our lives, we are in no way limited by it (which would be a fatalistic approach). Instead, by taking an absolute free will approach, we can only limit ourselves.

How and Why Astrology Works

As we've already stated, astrology is the study of the cycles of the planets. Astrology does not claim that the planets have any direct impact on individuals in any way, shape, or form. Where the planet Jupiter is today in the sky has absolutely no effect on our existence. So why does astrology work? It works because the same force that moves the planets, also moves us. We are all part of the universe, and we all follow the same cycles and patterns. It's difficult, however, to discover the patterns in our lives directly; but by observing the regular cycles of the planets, we can understand the nature of the cycles, and learn how we, too, are a part of those universal cycles.

This is a demonstration of the Law of Correspondences, which states:

As above, so below.
As within, so without.
As the universe, so the soul.

The Law of Correspondences is one of the foundations of astrology, and one of the reasons why astrology works.

Astrology also follows the Law of Alchemy, which states that all the energies are inside of us: if we suppress or deny them, however, they will manifest outside of us. Ultimately, this means that we can choose how we learn our life lessons (much of the time, at least). If we choose to take personal responsibility for our actions, and make a conscious and spiritual effort to let go of our fears, then we have the ability to experience harmony and balance in our lives, both inside and out. Any lessons that we don't approach on a conscious level, however, will manifest in our lives as external forces that are far more difficult to ignore. The more we try to ignore or repress these energies, the larger the disruptions become.

One thing to remember about the Law of Alchemy and astrology is that just because we have a certain amount of influence as to *where* we experience certain life lessons, we can never avoid them entirely (much as we might like to). Some lessons we will simply have to experience both inside and outside. We must also ultimately accept that we experience challenges and lessons in certain areas of our lives because on some level we choose to experience that lesson in that particular arena. Eventually, we have to pick a corner, stand our ground, and accept our life lessons in whatever form they come.

Finally, astrology also operates based on the Law of Beginnings, which states that the beginning point of a thing contains the potential that will be fulfilled during the life cycle and beyond. In this book, the beginnings that we will be focusing on are the beginnings of our lives, as we learn how to work with an individual's natal chart and discover how this map of the positions of the planets is also a map of each individual's life path.

A Word about Astrology and Behavior

Astrology operates on the Ketheric level of existence: the level of a spiritual blueprint. There are seven planes of existence, which are (in descending order):

	Spiritual Mental = Ketheric
	Spiritual Emotional = Celestial
	Spiritual Physical = Etheric
(transition)	Astral
	Mental
	Emotional
	Physical

In order for astrology to get from the motivations and blueprint stages of the Ketheric level down to the physical level where things actually happen, the pure astrological motivations go through a series of filters. Motivation becomes Assumption, which becomes Belief, which becomes Attitude, which becomes Behavior (which is a hardened belief). Each of us has our own series of filters, which are influenced by our past experiences, our karma (past life lessons), and our dharma (present and future life lessons).

When we interpret birth charts, we are looking at spiritual blueprints for individuals—the Ketheric level. It is absolutely impossible to predict how individuals will experience their birth charts without their input. We can theorize, we can make up stories that describe how they *could* be experiencing their charts, but until we actually get to know the individuals and get their feedback, it is all theory. Part of the process of using astrology as a tool for self-awareness and healing is connecting the dots between the individuals' spiritual blueprints and their current reality. Once we understand both the underlying needs and motivations of the individuals, and how they expect to encounter these energies, we can begin to effect change and discover how to experience the same energies and motivations in a more conscious, constructive, and personally responsible manner.

Always remember that there are no "bad" planets, and that there is no such thing as a "bad chart." We have absolute free will, and part of the cost of that gift is that we must learn to take full responsibility for the world that we have created for ourselves. We choose how we work with and experience the energies in our birth charts—and if we aren't happy with the choices that we've made up to this point in our lives, we have the ability and the authority to make different choices from this point on.

2

The Planets

The planets are the most important part of astrology. Everything else in astrology relates to the planets, describes how they act and interact, and even modifies their expression; but without the planets, nothing happens. The signs only exist to describe where the planets are located. Aspects show relationships between planets. Even the houses, which can be interpreted without planets, are traditionally linked to the planets by rulership. That the planets are so fundamentally important may be a surprise to many people, particularly because a popular misconception about astrology is that the signs are the most important things—everyone wants to know "What's your sign?", not "Where are your planets?", right? Well, the thing to remember is that when people are asking "What's your sign?", what they're really asking is what sign your Sun (a planet) is in.

Now, technically and astronomically, of course, the Sun isn't a planet—it's a star. For that matter, the Moon isn't a planet, either—it's a satellite orbiting the Earth (which *is* a planet, but which seems to be conspicuously absent from astrology charts). For the purposes of astrology, though, the Sun and Moon (which are sometimes referred to as "the Lights") are included in the general term "planets."

The planets are like the actors in a play. The sign that a planet is in represents that planet's role, its costume, its motivation, if you will. The houses are the setting, the backdrop for the action. You can have an actor just being himself or herself and not playing a role (theoretically, at least), but the costumes, the scenery, and the plot cannot stand on their own without the actors.

Categories and Classifications of the Planets

Planets fall into many different categories, and as we will soon see, all planets are not created equal; some of them simply play more obvious and crucial roles in our lives than others.

Inner Planets versus Outer Planets

The most common distinction made between the planets is "inner planets" versus "outer planets." The term "inner planets" usually refers to the seven visible planets (although sometimes Jupiter and Saturn are not included in this category). This type of classification is very much a modern construct: before 1781, when Herschel discovered Uranus, there were only "inner" or "visible" planets—planets that were visible to the naked eye. (Of course the skies were a great deal clearer then!) These included the Sun, Moon, Mercury, Venus, Mars, Jupiter, and Saturn.

The "outer planets" are the planets that are only visible with a telescope: Uranus, Neptune, and Pluto. The asteroid Chiron functions as a bridge between the inner and the outer planets.

The distinction made between "inner" and "outer" planets is an important one. The inner planets move relatively quickly: Saturn, the slowest of the inner planets, completes a cycle of the zodiac every 29½ years. Even in ancient times, human life expectancy was long enough that we were likely to experience at least one complete cycle of all of the planets; today, we are expected to live well past our second Saturn return, and even to approach our third Saturn return. The more cycles of a planet that we live through, the more we are able to understand and master the energy and the lessons of that planet, so we have at least a fighting chance to gain a level of mastery with the energies of the inner planets.

The outer planets, on the other hand, have cycles that are considerably longer in duration. The fastest of the outer planets is Uranus, which takes about 84 years to complete a cycle of the zodiac. Today, it is not unusual for people to live past their Uranus return, and humans are gradually developing a greater understanding of the energy of Uranus. Neptune, on the other hand, takes 165 years to complete an orbit around the Sun, and Pluto takes 248 years. These planets generally represent forces that are beyond our control as individuals.

Personal Planets, Social Planets, and Transpersonal Planets

Another term you will hear is the "personal planets." Generally, the personal planets are the fastest-moving planets: the Sun, Moon, Mercury, Venus, and Mars. These planets are called "personal" because they are the ones that have the greatest impact on the expression of our personalities as individuals.

Jupiter and Saturn are sometimes classified as "personal" planets, but more often, they are considered to be "social" planets. Their longer orbits (twelve years for Jupiter, 29½ years for Saturn) are said to have more impact on how we as individuals relate to society.

The "transpersonal planets" are, of course, the outer planets by another name. The outer planets are also sometimes referred to as the "generational planets" because their positions by sign (each spends at least seven years in a given sign) can be said to define a generation.

Straight Talk About Sect

"Sect" is a word that comes from the Latin word *seco*, which means "to cut" or "to divide." In astrology, sect refers to the division between diurnal (day) planets and nocturnal (night) planets. Each of the seven visible planets was classified as either diurnal or nocturnal by nature, and then the planet's condition in the overall chart was evaluated based on the position and sect of the chart. Although sect hasn't turned out to be too impressive a technique when it comes to chart interpretation, it is an incredibly valuable tool in understanding the fundamental nature of the planets.

The most important concept to understand about sect is the balance between "showing forth" and "appearance." "Showing forth" means expressing the true nature of a thing with no guile or deception; it is a "what you see is what you get" situation. "Appearance," on the other hand, is just the opposite, because looks can be deceiving. The more diurnal a planet is, the more it "shows forth," and the more nocturnal a planet is, the more it "appears."

Obviously, the two extremes on the scale are the two sect rulers: the Sun for diurnal, and the Moon for nocturnal. As the most diurnal planet, the Sun is entirely "showing forth." The Sun can never be anything other than exactly what it is—and the Sun expresses its true nature with blazing and blinding intensity.

The Moon, on the other hand, is all appearance: it has no light of its own, and only reflects the light of the Sun. While the Sun is constant, and never changes from day to day, the Moon changes its appearance every night.

The ranking of the planets by sect is as follows:

DIURNAL	Sun
	Jupiter
	Saturn
NEUTRAL	Mercury
	Venus
	Mars
NOCTURNAL	Moon

Mercury, the master of ambivalence, is considered to be entirely neutral, equal parts appearance and showing forth.

Be careful about confusing diurnal and nocturnal with other polarities, in particular with the concept of "masculine" and "feminine," or "active" and "receptive." Diurnal and nocturnal certainly have much in common with these other classifications, but they are not the same. Nocturnal planets are by no means fundamentally passive or receptive (remember, Mars, which is arguably the most active and aggressive planet of all, is a nocturnal planet—and Mars is most definitely a masculine energy).

As we meet each planet in turn, we'll take some time to explore how each planet's sect expresses as a part of that planet's fundamental nature.

The Sun

Glyph: ☉	The Circle of Spirit, with no beginning and no end, whole and complete. The dot in the center is the spark of life; we are part of the whole spirit, but we are a spark of that spirit: the point where the infinite manifests into finite form. The entire symbol depicts the realization of infinite potential through a specific point—the individual.
Orbital Cycle:	One year (365.25 days).
Retrograde Cycle:	Not applicable. The Sun is always direct in motion.

04 Sect:	Most diurnal (defines diurnal sect).
05 Qualities:	One-pointed. Focused. Yang energy. Altruistic.
06 Represents:	Light; consciousness; our will; our power; our sense of purpose. Masculinity; fatherhood; experience of father figures. Willpower, vitality, how and where we want to succeed.
07 Expression:	Shines. Attempts to have an influence. Resists efforts to make it what it is not.
08 Psychology:	The libido; the basic drive to do anything at all.
04 Urge:	To be. To create.
10 Need:	To be recognized. To express the self.
11 Health:	Heart, upper back, spleen, circulatory system, sperm, right eye of male/left eye of female, spine, general vitality and physique, thymus gland.
12 Symbols:	Hero; father, or experience of the father; men in general, and kings and rulers in particular; leaders; teachers; God.

The Sun is the heart of the solar system. It is the source of all light, energy, and life in our universe, and likewise, the Sun in an astrological chart is the source of all energy, health, and vitality. We are able to see the other planets in the solar system because they reflect the light of the Sun. In the same way, in our charts, the Sun is our fundamental life force. The Sun is our vitality; when our Sun is strong and well cared for, we are full of strength and energy. When we do not "feed" our Suns, we grow weak, lethargic, and depressed.

The Sun represents how we want to be a hero, and the archetypal journey of the Sun is the hero's journey. The hero is born at sunrise, when the Sun is on the Ascendant in the chart, and sets out into the world. In the outside world, he brings order out of chaos through the use of his will at midday, when the Sun is on the Midheaven in the chart. He undergoes trials to prove his strength and worthiness, and ultimately dies at sunset, when the Sun is on the Descendant. He descends into the underworld and proves his right to be reborn at midnight, when the Sun is on the *Imum Coeli* in the chart. Then the hero prepares to be reborn again at the next sunrise. (The Ascendant, Midheaven, Descendant, and *Imum Coeli* are the four angles in the chart, and we'll define and explain them in great detail when we look at the houses in chapter 6.)

On a more practical level, the Sun is our conscious sense of self, of who we are as individuals. To use a more modern term, the Sun is our "personal power." The Sun only operates in the present moment, and the true expression of the Sun involves using our will to take action, to create some expression of our true selves, and of our individuality.

We do not automatically express our Sun; in fact, we have to earn our Sun by making conscious choices, by pursuing the types of activities and experiences that enhance our sense of individuality, and that express our personal creative forces. When we experience our Sun, we are not aware of anything except the present moment; we are focused, centered, and have no sense of self-awareness or self-reflection, because all of our energy is directed at simply being who we truly are, as hard as we possibly can.

Anytime we are confronted with a completely new experience, we access our Sun; once we have a frame of reference for something, however, the Moon takes over to a large extent.

The Sun is the most diurnal planet, which means that it can only ever express its true nature. The Sun is entirely incapable of any kind of deception or disguise. The Sun is also the most masculine energy in the chart; it is one-pointed and wants to express itself in a focused, directed manner. The Sun is also the most yang planet in the chart; it is entirely expressive and outgoing, and not at all receptive.

While the Sun's focused nature gives us the ability to take action—actually to take any kind of action at all—the Sun lacks perspective, adaptability, and flexibility. The Sun operates in the realm of absolutes and has no ability to deal with ambiguity.

Just as the Sun is quite literally the star of our solar system, the Sun in our charts shows where and how we want to be a star. The Sun represents the way that we want to be known, the things that we want to express and to be recognized for. By looking at the sign position of the Sun, we learn the motivations that we have for self-expression, and see the why and the how of expressing our Sun.

The Sun wants to have an influence, and it always seeks a greater expression of itself. The Sun represents our integrity, and is the key to how all the other parts of ourselves, all our many facets, hang together to make a whole and integrated being. Once again, remember that the Sun, being entirely diurnal, can only express its true nature. The Sun will resist any attempts to make it what it is not, by shining brighter and with greater intensity until its true nature cannot be denied.

In order to stay healthy and happy, we must make sure that we are "feeding" our Sun! We must make a conscious effort to seek out the types of experiences that will reinforce our Sun. To a great extent, this means that we absolutely have to have fun in our lives—on a daily basis if at all possible. Anything we truly enjoy doing feeds our Sun; these activities recharge us on a very tangible level.

The Moon

Glyph: ☽	The Crescent of the Soul: the soul receives and holds the spirit.
Orbital Cycle:	Approximately 27.33 days.
Retrograde Cycle:	None.
Sect:	Most nocturnal (defines nocturnal sect).
Qualities:	Yin. Receptive. Responding.
Represents:	Femininity; women; motherhood; the past, source, heredity, and subconscious.
Expression:	Where we feel and experience emotions. Memory, the past, habits and conditioning. Responsible for day-to-day actions that do not require conscious thought.
Psychology:	Our unconscious nature; feminine archetypes; anima.
Urge:	To feel inner support and nurturing. To be comforted.
Need:	Emotional tranquility and a sense of belonging.
Health:	Stomach, lymph nodes, breasts, body fluids, all containers and linings of the body. Fluid balance of the body, digestion, glandular secretions, left eye of male/right eye of female.
Symbols:	Women; the public; change.

The Moon is the second most important planet in the chart—and it's a very close second. While the Sun represents the archetypal masculine principle, the embodiment of yang energy, the Moon is its perfect complement: the archetypal feminine principle and the embodiment of yin energy. The Moon gives shape and form to the expression of the Sun. The Sun represents the spirit; the Moon is the soul, which receives and holds the energy of the spirit. The Sun *gives* motivation and the Moon *receives* it.

The Moon represents our unconscious, receptive, responsive, emotional side. The Moon is the container that gives form to the Sun's energy and expression. As such, the Moon is our memory. All our past experiences, all our hopes, fears, patterns, and expectations are represented by the Moon. The Moon is the caretaker of our soul's memory—and this includes not only our past experiences in this lifetime, but our memories and experiences from past lives as well.

We've already mentioned that we don't automatically experience or express our Sun; instead, most of us spend most of our lives living through our Moon. We usually go through life unfocused in time, remembering past experiences and using these to make sense of our present. We project what our future will be like, again, based on our expectations and experiences in the past. In many cases, this is absolutely essential to our ability to function. Thanks to the Moon, we are able to remember our patterns, create habits, and let portions of our lives run on automatic. For example, without the Moon, every time we got into a car, we would have to learn how to drive again! Thanks to the Moon, we usually don't have to put our full attention toward such routine activities. Of course, we can also lose ourselves a bit too much—if you've ever arrived home from work and realized that you didn't remember a single thing about your commute, or if you've ever missed your exit on the way to work because you just weren't paying attention, you know what this feels like. The people who are closest to us and know us well know us best through our Moon, not our Sun.

While the Sun is the most masculine energy in the chart, the archetypal male, the Moon is the most feminine energy in the chart, and represents the archetypal female energy. The Sun, being the most diurnal planet, is all substance, and constant in nature. The Moon, being the most nocturnal planet, is all appearance, and constantly changing in nature. The Sun is the most yang energy in the chart, while the Moon is the most yin, representing the power of waiting, receiving, encompassing, and responding.

The earliest mythologies associated with the Moon link it to the triple-goddess archetype of women: Maiden, Mother, and Crone, which relates directly to the waxing or growing phases of the Moon (Maiden), the full phase (Mother), and the waning or diminishing phases (Crone). The Moon, perhaps more than any other planet, embodies the cyclical and changing nature of the universe, playing out the natural cycles of birth, growth, death, and rebirth each month in the night sky.

The Moon rules all containers—and this includes our physical bodies (which are nothing more than containers for our spirits). The Moon shows how comfortable we are with our physical bodies. The Moon is the caretaker of all our needs while we are incarnate in a physical body; the Moon shows where and how we want to be nurtured and cared for, and how we are motivated to nurture and care for others. Even though the Moon represents all women, the Moon's energy resonates the most strongly with motherhood, without question. The Moon in the chart represents our experience of and attitude toward motherhood.

The Moon also represents our family—including our families of origin, families of choice, and our ancestors and heritage. The Moon's need to belong, to nurture, and to protect, is ultimately a need to return to the source, to once again experience our interconnection with everything in the universe. The Moon remembers what we are required to forget when we incarnate on Earth: that all separation is an illusion; that we are an integral part of all creation; that because we are one with all that is, our fears are also illusions, and our needs are already met.

The relationship between the Sun and the Moon in the birth chart is extremely important. Among other things, it illustrates the relationship between our conscious, rational, logical nature, and our unconscious, emotional, and spiritual nature. A harmonious relationship between the Sun and the Moon may make it easier for us to express our needs, and to integrate our individuality with our need for community and emotional support. Challenging relationships between the Sun and the Moon can set up a fundamental struggle: a lifelong struggle to reconcile our conscious and unconscious selves, which can lead us to new discoveries and a deeper understanding of our true selves.

Backing Up to Look at Retrograde Planets

That the Earth is not the center of the universe is hardly a surprise to most of us today. But before Copernicus came along and developed his Sun-centered (heliocentric) model of the solar system, everyone assumed that the Earth was the center (geocentric) and that the planets, including the Sun and the Moon, all revolved around the Earth.

One thing that the ancients observed was that all the planets other than the Sun and the Moon would periodically slow down, stop, and then change direction for a time, either moving backward through the zodiac (retrograde motion) or returning to their forward (direct) movements. The retrograde cycles of the planets were extremely important; in the centuries before systems of mathematics and measurement enabled astrologers to describe a planet's precise position in the sky, the most important things that could be observed about the planets were when the planets first appeared in the night sky (rising), when they last appeared in the night sky (setting), and when they appeared to stop (station) and change direction (retrograde).

We know now, of course, that the planets never change direction; they all orbit the Sun, they never slow down, and they certainly never back up. Retrograde motion is an illusion caused because we're observing the planets orbiting the Sun from a vantage point (the Earth) that is also orbiting the Sun, at a different speed.

Mercury and Venus, who orbit between the Earth and the Sun, retrograde more frequently and for different reasons from the rest of the planets, Mars through Pluto, whose orbits are outside of the Earth's. Illustrations of the different types of retrograde motion are shown in figures 1 and 2.

A quick and dirty way to tell if a superior planet (outside of the Earth's orbit) is about to change direction is to see if it is trine the Sun (a 120° aspect or angular relationship that will be covered in detail in chapter 8). Any time an outer planet is opposite the Sun, it is retrograde. The inferior planets (inside the Earth's orbit, i.e., Mercury and Venus) are a bit different. Since these planets are inside of the Earth's orbit, they must appear to be very close to the Sun at all times. Mercury can never be more than 28° from the Sun, and Venus can never be more than 46° from the Sun. Any time you see either of these planets reaching the limit of their distance from the Sun, they're getting ready to change direction.

Inferior Planet in Direct Motion

Inferior Planet in Retrograde Motion

Figure 1. Inferior Planets in Direct and Retrograde Motion

Superior Planet in Direct Motion

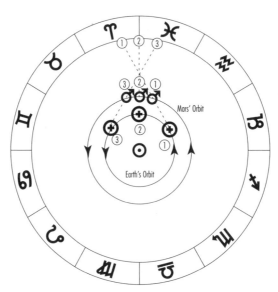

Superior Planet in Retrograde Motion

Figure 2. Superior Planets in Direct and Retrograde Motion

All this astronomy is well and good, but how do we go about interpreting retrograde planets? Well, we'll go into detail about that later on (in fact, all of chapter 9 is devoted to understanding natal retrograde planets). For now, let's just say that retrograde planets generally don't function in the same way that direct planets do. Traditionally, retrograde planets are thought to have a more "internal" expression, while direct planets are "outwardly" expressed. Individuals with retrograde planets often feel that they have very personal issues related to that planet, and these planets are often the focus of much of their attention.

Mercury

Glyph: ☿	The Crescent of the Soul linked to the Cross of Matter by the Circle of Spirit. The spirit links the soul and matter through Mercury. This implies receptivity to higher energies that come into the wholeness and become integrated in the person and then manifest on the physical plane.
Orbital Cycle:	88 days.
Retrograde Cycle:	Approximately a four-month cycle; retrograde for three weeks, every four months.
Sect:	Neutral.
Qualities:	Neutral: equally yin and yang. Quick, changeable, dual-natured.
Represents:	The Messenger; the connector. Logical and reasoning capabilities. Left brain, logical processes. Communication, transportation, movement, dexterity, writing, thought, transportation, movement, language, ambiguity, and ambivalence.
Expression:	Makes connections between different concepts. Bridges the gap. Explores duality.
Psychology:	Linear, logical thought. The left-brain functions.
Urge:	To express perception and intelligence through skill.
Need:	To connect and to learn.

Health:	Nervous system, organs of perception, thyroid, metabolism, or sense of time. Hands, arms, general ruler of all hormones.
Symbols:	Keys, children, movable objects, messengers and messages, all vehicles and forms of transportation, and all forms and instruments of communication (telephones, fax machines, computers, and so on).

In mythology, Mercury was the messenger of the gods, renowned for his speed, and relied upon as the primary source of communication and transmittal of information. The planet Mercury, likewise, is responsible for processing information for us on all levels. Mercury rules communication, logic, and our mental faculties. Mercury is our ability to perceive, to reason, and to make sense of the world.

The essential nature of Mercury has to do with making connections. Language, essentially, is the use of symbols for things that allow us to reference them; in other words, the language connects the words (symbols) with the things that the words describe. Mercury also rules all forms of physical connections, including any kind of travel or movement.

We must not take Mercury's functions lightly: Mercury not only shows how we communicate with others, but it also shows how we communicate with ourselves. Before we can begin to connect with the outside world, before we can begin to form the ability to use language, we must first learn how to make sense of our perceptions. The first language we learn is the one we speak to ourselves to help us interact with the outside world. We take our perceptions for granted, but we would do well to remember that our ability to understand reality relies entirely on our ability to explain, decipher, map, and integrate our individual perceptions and experiences of reality.

Mercury is the only truly neutral planet; it is equally diurnal and nocturnal, and represents the balance between yin and yang energy. Mercury receives input from the Sun and the Moon, our conscious and unconscious selves, and integrates these different perspectives into a unified understanding. Mercury is the epitome of duality and of ambiguity; it strives to understand all possible sides of an issue, and is perfectly capable of balancing two opposing and conflicting concepts simultaneously. Mercury is notoriously unstable, and will bounce between the two sides of an issue with great abandon, reveling in the paradox and the duality. This demonstrates one of Mercury's lesser-known roles: that of the trickster.

Mercury's condition in the birth chart and placement by sign will show our motivation to communicate, as well as our preferred methods of communication. This applies to both how we tend to express ourselves, and to how we are most comfortable taking in new information. A well-placed and dignified Mercury can certainly be a sign of intelligence, or at least of a very quick mind; however, it is not possible to determine a person's intellectual ability by looking at his or her Mercury. A retrograde Mercury, or a Mercury in poor condition, in no way indicates a lack of intelligence or the presence of learning disabilities.

Other than the Moon, Mercury is the fastest-moving body in the solar system. Because of this, the planet Mercury also functions as a "messenger" of the other planets, and is frequently involved in the timing of events, and in connecting or bringing together the energies of different, often conflicting planets.

Venus

Glyph: ♀	The Circle of Spirit over the Cross of Matter. (Spirit presides over matter.)
Orbital Cycle:	225 days.
Retrograde Cycle:	One year, seven months; retrograde for six weeks during this time period.
Sect:	Moderately nocturnal.
Qualities:	Yin energy. Harmony. Beauty. Love. Balance. Values.
Represents:	Love, attraction, beauty, balance, harmony.
Expression:	The forces of attraction and adhesion; like attracting and holding to like.
Psychology:	Our relationship functions and issues, both interpersonal and spiritual. Our desire and need to find balance and unity. What we value and how we relate to it.
Urge:	To relate; to connect.

Need:	To feel connected; to join with a partner and experience unity.
Health:	Parathyroid, physical beauty, kidneys, throat, pancreas, female sex organs, chin, cheeks, sense of taste, venous blood circulation, sensory organs of the skin.
Symbols:	Women, beauty, art, music, mirrors, love, relationships, money.

Venus was the Roman goddess of love and beauty, and the planet Venus rules these forces of attraction. Venus represents the power of cohesion: like things attracting like things, and holding them together through a natural affinity. We also refer to this force as love.

In classical astrology, Venus was called the "Lesser Benefic," and was second only to Jupiter in overall wonderfulness, and truly, Venus is a pretty fun planet to spend time with. Venus, in the chart, shows what we value, what we enjoy, and the ways that we experience all forms of pleasure. Venus relates to physical pleasures, as well as to the less tangible ones, and is associated with all forms of beauty. But most of all, Venus is about how we relate to the things we value.

Venus is a moderately nocturnal planet, which means that it is more appearance-oriented than showing forth. Venus was known as "the light that beckons." What this generally means is that when we're under the influence of Venus, we tend to overlook the flaws in the object of our affection, and overemphasize the wonderful qualities. In relationships, Venus is what helps make our partner's little quirks "endearing" rather than "annoying."

Venus shows the types of things that are important to us—what we value in life. These are the romantic ideals that we strive for, and the qualities that we look for in others and hope to embody in ourselves. Venus is a very fertile and creative energy and seeks expression through the fine arts and through music, as well as through crafts, gardening, pottery, and so on. More than anything, though, Venus has to do with relationships.

Venus seeks perfection through unity, and embodies the idea that the whole is more than the sum of its parts. Nowhere is this more evident than in our natural desire to find companionship in its many forms. Venus shows both how we express love and affection, and also how we want to receive it from others.

When experiencing the energy of Venus, we would do well to remember that Venus operates best on a higher, spiritual level. Ultimately, Venus is where we seek to reconnect with the rest of the universe, to rediscover our relationship to all creation. Too frequently, though, we become obsessed with the more tangible, physical aspects of Venus, and lose sight of its higher nature.

Mars

Glyph: ♂ (☌)	The original symbol for Mars was the reverse of the symbol for Venus: the Cross of Matter over the Circle of Spirit (matter presides over spirit).
Orbital Cycle:	688 days (One year, eleven months).
Retrograde Cycle:	Retrograde for about 2½ months, every two years.
Sect:	Very nocturnal.
Qualities:	Yang energy. Active. Focused. Single-minded. Self-centered.
Represents:	Our ability to act based on our desires. The ability to remain who we are in the face of the pressure to change; to maintain our true nature against threats.
Expression:	One-pointed, direct, forceful. How we go after what we want, and how we defend ourselves from threats. Fight-or-flight instincts.
Psychology:	Aggression and self-assertion.
Urge:	To act. To expend energy in a focused manner.
Need:	To survive and to challenge.
Health:	Muscles and movement, kinetic energy, irritations and inflammations, fevers, surgeries, accidents. External reproductive organs, head and face, red blood corpuscles, motor nerves, bladder, adrenal glands.
Symbols:	Surgeons; metals and metal workers; butchers; police in forceful situations; soldiers; men; brothers; uncles.

Mars was the Roman god of war, and the planet Mars (so named because of its fiery red color) symbolizes our aggressive nature. Mars represents how we go about getting the things we want; how we assert ourselves and our independence; and how we defend ourselves when we are under attack. Mars is the complement to Venus, and both planets have to do with the mechanics of desire and attraction. While Venus is the force of adhesion (like attracting like), Mars is the force of cohesion (different elements attracting each other). Mars is yang energy to Venus' yin, but unlike the Sun, Mars is entirely self-centered in its approach and expression. The Sun has an element of altruism and generosity to it; Mars is only concerned with looking out for number one.

Mars, in many ways, is like the engine of our car. It represents raw power and force; it needs to be harnessed and channeled in order to be productive. If misused, it can be exceptionally destructive. Ultimately, Mars doesn't really care who's doing the driving, so long as it's expending energy and taking some kind of action. Mars is not happy unless we're doing something—preferably something that takes a great deal of energy, focus, and concentration.

One of the most important keys to understanding the nature of Mars is that Mars is a nocturnal planet. This means that Mars is significantly more appearance-oriented than showing forth; in other words, Mars can be extremely deceptive. While Venus was considered to be "the Light that Beckons," Mars is "the Light that Commands." Mars gets us to do things by making us want something—so badly that we're willing to do almost anything to get it; and because Mars is so appearance-oriented, Mars doesn't feel particularly bound to be honest when getting us to want something. In fact, Mars can often operate like a used-car salesman, promising us whatever we want to hear if only we'll get up off the couch and do something.

The ancients considered Mars to be the "Lesser Malefic," and rarely had nice things to say about Mars. To some extent this is understandable; Mars is certainly responsible for more than its fair share of trouble—it is, after all, the planet that rules our aggressive, argumentative, and violent tendencies. To be fair, though, Mars only gets us into trouble when we become ego-involved. Remember that Mars is the engine of our car, and it doesn't really care who's driving. From time to time, every one of us has turned the car keys over to our ego and gone for a little joyride. We usually end up regretting it, of course. When the ego does the driving, we get into arguments attempting to prove our worth or our independence, and friendly games become more about winning at any cost than about enjoying the challenge. When we are able to stay aligned with our higher selves and keep the ego in the back seat where it belongs, Mars is the energy that makes it possible for us to achieve our goals, and to express and assert our individuality.

Jupiter

Glyph: ♃	The Crescent of the Soul moving to the Cross of Matter— the soul entering and working through matter.
Orbital Cycle:	Twelve years.
Retrograde Cycle:	One year; retrograde for approximately four months during this one-year period.
Sect:	Very diurnal.
Qualities:	Expansive. Generous. Optimistic. Enthusiastic. Freedom-loving.
Represents:	Our desire for growth, freedom, faith, and spirituality.
Expression:	Expansion of consciousness, humor, philosophy, travel.
Psychology:	How we grow and expand our understanding of the world. How we experience faith and grace.
Urge:	To contribute to a larger order. To connect with something greater than the self. Growth.
Need:	Faith, trust, confidence. To improve oneself.
Health:	Arterial blood circulation, liver, thighs, hips, feet, right ear, upper forehead, glycogen and fatty tissues, pancreas.
Symbols:	Teachers; travelers; permissive father figures.

Jupiter is by far the largest planet in the solar system; is it any wonder then, that the ancients associated Jupiter with all forms of growth, expansion, prosperity, and abundance? Jupiter in classical astrology is often referred to as the "Greater Benefic," and you'll have to look long and hard through the ancient literature to find a single negative or uncomplimentary statement about Jupiter.

Jupiter is about growth and expansion; it's about connecting to something bigger than the self. This includes all forms of physical and tangible abundance and prosperity, as well as spiritual and philosophical pursuits. While

Mercury rules the "lower mind," Jupiter is in charge of the "higher mind," which is one of the areas where we get in touch with our spirituality. Jupiter is a very diurnal planet and radiates warmth, generosity, and love, much like the Sun does.

Jupiter is the planet that says "Yes!" to just about everything; it's about breaking out of our limitations and exploring new territory. Jupiter is the planet that convinces us that we can accomplish anything we want, and that's certainly a potent and wonderful feeling; but Jupiter is also rather prone to exaggeration and overconfidence. Sometimes rules and boundaries exist for a reason. Freedom and independence are very important to Jupiter. Jupiter craves new experiences and new information, and loves travel and exploration of all kinds: physical, mental, and spiritual. Jupiter contributes greatly to our sense of humor and of fun, as well as to our ability to be compassionate.

Jupiter is the first of the "social planets." Along with Saturn, Jupiter has a very strong influence on how we relate to society as individuals. Jupiter is always striving to understand the big picture, and part of that big picture includes discovering and exploring our roles as individuals within the larger structures of society. Jupiter is also the planet that relates to our experience of religion. Again, this involves exploring our relationship as individuals with the universe. Jupiter is all-consuming. It learns by growing and encompassing things, making them a part of it.

Jupiter's fundamentally cheerful and optimistic view of the world is a result of its absolute and unshakable faith in the perfection of the universe. When we have faith, we do not need to worry about anything. When we truly believe that whether or not we personally understand the reasons for the events in our lives, that everything is divinely guided and in our highest and best good, we have no room in our lives for fear. All the wonderful qualities and experiences related to Jupiter boil down to a question of faith in our true, spiritual, universal, and eternal natures. When we step into faith, our fears of separation and lack disappear, and we experience an endless flow of happiness, joy, and abundance. We grow and expand because we begin to remember that we are far more than our illusions of individuality—we are, in fact, a part of all creation.

However important faith is, we cannot survive simply by believing that everything will work out for us according to divine plan. We must learn to ground our faith in reality and experience it in our daily lives, not use it as a way to avoid and escape our responsibilities in the physical world. To paraphrase an old Arabian saying, "Trust in God, but tie your camel." This is an important lesson for Jupiter.

Saturn

Glyph: ♄	The Cross of Matter rising through the Crescent of the Soul—form and structure coming out of the soul.
Orbital Cycle:	29½ years.
Retrograde Cycle:	One year; retrograde for approximately 4½ months during this one-year period.
Sect:	Moderately diurnal.
Qualities:	Restrictive. Limiting. Firm. Solid. Tangible. Structured.
Represents:	Laws, structures, responsibility, authority figures.
Expression:	Makes things tangible; physical manifestation of ideas and concepts. Sets up boundaries and structures.
Psychology:	Our experiences with authority, both internally and externally. Our perceptions of the rules of society and the world, and how we respond and react to those rules.
Urge:	To make things tangible and structured. To manifest in the physical realm. To limit and protect.
Need:	Self-reliance, self-discipline, responsibility.
Health:	Bones, teeth, aging process. Skin, ligaments, knees, left ear and auditory organs, gall bladder, parathyroid glands, body protein.
Symbols:	Authority figures; teachers (strict ones); father figures; older men.

Saturn has one of the worst reputations in astrology. The ancients called Saturn the "Greater Malefic," and saddled it with all things miserable in life. While Saturn doesn't deserve all the centuries of bad press that it has received, even the most generous astrologers would be hard-pressed to call Saturn "fun." Saturn is necessary; Saturn is a valuable teacher; but Saturn is rarely if ever fun.

The essence of Saturn is limitation. Saturn is about structure (or the illusion of structure). Saturn is about restrictions, and about all forms of responsibility, from individual to societal. Saturn is the "Lord of Karma," and one of the reasons that we tend not to like Saturn too much is because Saturn is absolutely fair; with Saturn we get exactly what we deserve. Jupiter is like the teacher we had in school who gave us an "A for effort" and never assigned homework on weekends. Saturn, on the other hand, is like the teacher who everyone hated: the one who assigned the most homework, the one who never accepted any kind of excuse for anything, the one who graded fairly (read: brutally!). But in the end, which teacher did we learn the most from?

Saturn is the complement to Jupiter. Jupiter represents the urge to jump, but Saturn provides the foundation that we need to push against in order to be able to jump in the first place. Saturn's contracting, restricting force is the complement and the balance to Jupiter's ever-expanding nature. While Jupiter relates to how we respond to the more pleasant and expansive elements of society, Saturn relates to how we respond to the structures, authority figures, rules, and responsibilities that come with being a member of society.

Saturn lessons are some of the hardest for us to learn, and they take the longest for us to begin to master. Astrologically, we do not even become adults until we have experienced our Saturn return—a complete cycle of Saturn through our charts, which happens at about age 29½. Saturn, perhaps more than any other planet, embodies the Law of Alchemy in that until we learn how to discover and integrate Saturn's energy in ourselves, we will continually experience Saturn's influence in the outside world. We must learn how to discover our own boundaries and limitations, and we must learn to take responsibility for our lives and our actions. When we have done this, we discover a wonderful freedom: since we have limited ourselves, we do not have to worry about being limited by others, and we can safely enjoy ourselves. Unfortunately, we usually don't reach this point until we've spent many years experiencing Saturn from the outside.

Saturn represents all authority figures—everyone who sets rules and limitations for us. Our first experience of Saturn comes from our parents, who tell us "no" and prevent us from doing the things we want to do. As children, we are far too young to understand that our parents are simply protecting us from harm. But no matter how unpleasant we find the experience, the experience of being told "no" is also a very liberating one. Boundaries not only limit us, but they also define us. Part of Saturn's function is to crystallize and define things through exclusion. Saturn defines what we are not, and this in turn helps us discover what we truly are.

Saturn's lessons are hard, but they are also some of the most important lessons for us to learn. Saturn is about growing up and taking on responsibility both on an individual level and on a group level. We learn which types of behavior are appropriate, and what kind of behavior other people expect from us. We learn that the universe is about balance, and that for everything we take, we must contribute something in return. The most important and often the most difficult lesson with Saturn is learning to move beyond the fear and the illusions of Saturn.

Most of us have had a number of unpleasant encounters with authority figures over the course of our lives, and as a result of those experiences, we may be carrying around beliefs about the world and our place in it that are fear-based and extremely limiting. We created these beliefs and built these walls to make sure that we would never put ourselves in that particular painful situation again; and because these beliefs make us feel safe, we often become attached to them. These beliefs, however, are illusions, and eventually, the outer planets will come along and break them down. If we do not learn to give up our attachments, our additions to Saturn's illusion of structure, life can become very challenging for us.

We live on Earth, which is a learning planet; and the three-dimensional plane is ruled by Saturn. While we are here, we must abide by Saturn's rules and pretend that the boundaries, structures, and perceptions that we have about this world are real. However, we are also eternal, spiritual beings, who, on some level, can remember that Saturn doesn't, by any means, have the last word about everything. The ultimate goal in working with Saturn is to learn how to play the game, but not to become attached to the outcome. We must learn to be in the world, but not of it. The more we learn to respect Saturn, but not to cling to it, the more we will also discover how many of the rules that we thought were so fundamental to the way our world works, we created ourselves. When we discover that we've made up most of the rules we live by, we also remember that we have the power to create new ones.

Chiron

Glyph: ⚷	A key. An "O" and a "K" for "Object Kowal," the original designation for Chiron.
Orbital Cycle:	51½ years.
Retrograde Cycle:	One year; retrograde for approximately five months during this one-year period.
Sect:	None.
Qualities:	Somewhat neutral—similar to Mercury in that it carries the light energy of the outer planets.
Represents:	Where we encounter and have the opportunity to accept spirituality in the chart. This often comes through the wound—the weakest point in the chart. Through our efforts to heal this wound, we are able to transcend the wound and experience a true spiritual connection.
Expression:	Triggers initiation by carrying and translating the light, energy, and lessons of the outer planets.
Psychology:	Our core wound carried into this lifetime. The area of life where we have the greatest pain and the greatest fear.
Urge:	To heal; to transcend the bounds of the physical (Saturn-based) reality and connect with the truth of the universe.
Need:	To carry the light; to allow the light energy of the outer planets to enter the physical body and begin the process of spiritual and physical transformation.
Health:	Chronic and severe health crisis, usually accompanied by the activation of the Kundalini energy.
Symbols:	Healers, astrologers, clairvoyants, and others using divinatory skills; ecologists; crystal users. People involved in dealing with transitions such as hospice counselors, spiritual counselors, and gurus as guides. People using their hands as a focal point for their work such as healers, hairdressers, palmists, and chiropractors.

Chiron is an asteroid (officially designated as a "planetoid" and suspected to be a captured comet) that was discovered in 1977 by astronomer Charles T. Kowal.

One of the many things that makes Chiron unique is that its orbit, which is wildly erratic, takes it from inside the orbit of Saturn at the point closest to the Sun, to outside the orbit of Uranus at the point farthest from the Sun. Chiron, therefore, serves as a bridge between the inner and outer planets, and can assist us in making the transition from the known to the unknown.

Chiron was named after the centaur who was a renowned healer and teacher in Greek mythology. Although the stories disagree on the actual events, Chiron was accidentally wounded, in some fashion, by one of Hercules' poisoned arrows. Because Chiron was immortal, he could not die; but he also could not heal his wound, and suffered in agony as a result. Prometheus, who stole fire from the gods and gave it to humankind, was still being punished by Zeus for his actions, and would continue to be punished until a god willingly gave up his immortality to free him. Chiron agreed to take Prometheus' place, and Zeus was forced to free Prometheus. Zeus was then moved to end Chiron's suffering, and transformed him into the constellation of Sagittarius.

The myth of Chiron reveals many key archetypes that show the nature of Chiron. Chiron is the "Wounded Healer," and Chiron in our charts represents our core wound—the wound that we believe is unhealable. In the myth, Chiron is transformed by his wound, and ultimately transcends it as he ascends to the heavens. In the same way, Chiron in our charts shows how we must learn to work through our fears and our pain, and in doing so, how we will be transformed by the power of our own spirituality.

In practice, Chiron often seems to be to the outer planets what Mercury is to the inner planets: Chiron often carries forward the light of the outer planets, and is responsible for the timing of our initiations.

Where we find Chiron in our charts is where we will have the opportunity to experience our true spirituality, and to discover our unique healing gifts. This process takes courage, because in order to explore our wound and attempt to heal it, we will have to experience it and allow ourselves to be purified and transformed by that experience. Chiron's wound cannot be healed without opening ourselves up to our individual spiritual truths. In the process of exploring and attempting to heal our Chiron wounds, we move beyond the realm of Saturn, and connect with the higher truths that are the realm of the outer planets.

Uranus

Glyph: ♅   "Venus upside-down with wings."

Orbital Cycle: Eighty-four years.

Retrograde Cycle: One year; retrograde for approximately five months dur-
                    ing this one-year period.

Sect: None (functions as diurnal).

Qualities: Yang. Focused. One-pointed. Instantaneous. Sudden.
                    Unexpected.

Represents: The unexpected and disruptive—both accidents and mir-
                    acles. The process of spiritual awakening. The level be-
                    yond cause and effect. Revolutions and disasters.

Expression: Sudden, unexpected, unconventional, and frequently dis-
                    ruptive. Instantaneous and fleeting. A flash of lightning.

Psychology: The sudden flash of creative inspiration. The experience
                    that forces us to reevaluate all the beliefs and foundations
                    in our lives. When and how the walls come tumbling
                    down—and whether we are freed from prison, or exposed
                    and threatened as a result.

Urge: To change and disrupt structure without regard for indi-
                    vidual experiences or emotions.

Need: To exert an egoless and unpredictable force.

Health: Accidents, threats to bodily integrity.

Symbols: Inventors; innovators; revolutionaries; agents of change.
                    Scientists and those who strive to change and break open
                    our concept of reality.

At this stage in human evolution, we live in a Saturn-ruled world, and we must play by Saturn's rules. The outer planets exist to help us see beyond the illusions of Saturn, to remind us that the universe is eternal, and that as integral parts of the universe, we, too, are eternal. Because we have not yet evolved to the point where we are able to master the energies of the outer planets, we tend to experience them in relationship to our experience of Saturn—and how successfully we are able to work with the lessons and energies of the outer planets is directly related to how well we have mastered Saturn's lessons and energy.

Uranus is the first of the outer planets, and its sole purpose is to disrupt Saturn's structures. Saturn represents the cosmic egg: the physical universe that we can see, hear, feel, and touch. Uranus, then, is the crack in the cosmic egg—the first and often traumatic realization that there is far more to the universe than we believed.

The energy of Uranus is a flash of lightning with often devastating repercussions. Uranus is unexpected, instantaneous, and fundamentally disruptive—but ultimately neutral in nature. Uranus is equally responsible for accidents and miracles; and often the only difference between the two is one of perspective. When Uranus strikes, for a moment we are given a blinding flash of insight; a glimpse of a bigger truth that shatters our old perceptions and limitations; and then just as fast as it appears, it goes away, and we're left waiting for the dust to settle.

How we experience Uranus depends on how tightly we cling to the illusions of Saturn. If we have learned to master Saturn's energy, and to hold lightly onto its rules and structures, then when Uranus comes along and shakes things up, it can be an energizing and refreshing experience; hence, Uranus' frequent association with freedom and liberation. By the same token, if we're clinging to ideas and structures that no longer serve us, if we have invested in them and have bought into the illusion of Saturn, then when Uranus comes along, it can feel like our world is coming to an end; hence, Uranus' equally frequent association with unforeseen disasters.

More than anything, Uranus teaches us to become aware of our attachments in life—an important lesson, because Uranus is followed by Neptune and Pluto, and these two planets are not nearly as forgiving in their lessons! Uranus shows us where we need to learn to let go, to be flexible and open to change. Uranus is where the walls of our world begin to crack and start to tumble down. If we are not attached to these walls, if the walls were starting to feel like a prison, then Uranus is the sudden, unexpected chance at freedom. If, on the other hand, we were using the walls to hide and to protect ourselves from harm, then when Uranus comes along and the walls start to crack, it can be a frightening and threatening experience.

Uranus also operates on the level of the collective unconscious, symbolizing the new and innovative changes that await us. When individuals have a close connection between Uranus and one of their personal planets, they naturally tap into this new idea, and become responsible, at least in part, for bringing it into the world. The first thing that a new and innovative idea meets, of course, as it moves toward manifestation, is Saturn—and this usually translates into resistance from the rest of society (or at least from those who do not have such a close connection to the energy of Uranus and the new idea). Individuals with strong Uranus energy in their charts often have a rebellious streak in them, a need to follow their own path, and not to conform to the current standards of society. Eventually, as more and more people begin to express the new idea, the resistance to it fades, and it becomes an accepted part of our consciousness.

Of course, oftentimes the first place where this new energy finds resistance is within ourselves—and the first Saturn energy that must be converted is our own.

Neptune

Glyph: ♆	The Crescent of the Soul descending to the Cross of Matter.
Orbital Cycle:	165 years.
Retrograde Cycle:	One year; retrograde for approximately five months during this one-year period.
Sect:	None (functions as nocturnal—all appearance).
Qualities:	Yin. Receptive. Glamorous. Deceptive. Unfocused. Changing.
Represents:	The truth that reality is an illusion; the ultimate creative force; the ultimate potential for creation and creativity in the universe.
Expression:	Dissolves all boundaries and structures. Reveals the truth that anything is possible. Often experienced as fantasy and escapism, or as delusions.
Psychology:	Our ability to fantasize, to dream, to try to connect and comprehend the infinite potential of the universe.

Urge: To dissolve all structures and reveal the ultimate truth.

Need: To merge with the One.

Health: Allergies and infections; drugs, alcohol, poisons. Antibodies. The ductless glands (endocrine system). Pineal gland.

Symbols: Artists; dancers; musicians. Martyrs and victims. Photographers; filmmakers; clothing and costume designers; make-up artists. Social workers; psychologists; nurses; addicts.

Neptune is the second of the outer planets. After Uranus has opened us to the understanding that our Saturn-based reality is not the end of the road, that something lies beyond it, Neptune comes along and shows us just what that something is: everything. Saturn is the illusion that what we perceive as reality is true; Neptune, on the other hand, is the truth that everything we know, everything we perceive to be real, is nothing more than an illusion.

Neptune represents the ultimate creative force; the unlimited and unimaginable possibilities of the universe. Neptune tells us that not only do all these different realities exist, they all exist simultaneously. This is not the type of concept we're terribly well equipped to grapple with during our human experience. We need our boundaries and our structures; we rely on the illusions of Saturn because they help us define ourselves and maintain a sense of individuality. Neptune's energy completely denies all of this and blithely dissolves all boundaries and structures. Neptune shows us where our walls are the thinnest, where we have the weakest hold on what we like to consider "reality."

Neptune's vibration is extremely high, and very few of us are able to actually experience it for any length of time without losing touch with our physical bodies. For the most part, we experience different aspects of Neptune in the form of glamour, illusion, fantasy, and escapism. Individuals who do not work well with Neptune often become dependent on drugs and alcohol, seeking a way out of the harsh illusions of Saturn, but this is not the true path of Neptune. More constructive contact with Neptune can result in talent in music, dance, photography, and film, as well as a dedication to spirituality and religious pursuits.

Once again, how well we are able to handle Neptune's energy depends entirely on our level of mastery with Saturn's energy. Uranus is the first test of Saturn's hold over us; but Uranus is quick and sudden, and although it can be very disruptive, at least we are usually able to cope with it. Neptune's effects are far more subtle and disorienting, and much harder to ignore. Neptune dissolves everything it contacts; we lose all sense of ourselves as individuals and begin to tap into the cosmic group consciousness. If we are not addicted to Saturn, this type of experience can be entirely mystical and transforming. If we are attached to our illusions of structure, however, Neptune's influence can make us feel as if we're falling apart and out of control.

Neptune is associated with both mystical and spiritual experiences, as well as with psychic abilities. Where Neptune is found in our charts is where we are the most in tune with the higher realms. Again, the line between visionary and schizophrenic is often quite thin, and in order to access and integrate Neptune's energy into our lives, we must make sure that we are firmly grounded in the physical. Neptune is not meant to represent an escape route, although many individuals experience it as such.

On a social level, Neptune represents the collective dream: the desires and hopes that the members of society value, and work on an unconscious level to bring into reality. Individuals who have Neptune closely aspecting personal planets will naturally tap into this energy; those who are able to channel it constructively are frequently drawn to the arts, and through their personal creative expression, they begin to shape the collective dream, give it form, and bring it to the level of conscious awareness.

Pluto

Glyph: ♇ (♇)	The Crescent of the Soul connecting the Circle of Spirit and the Cross of Matter.
Orbital Cycle:	248 years.
Retrograde Cycle:	One year; retrograde for approximately five months during this one-year period.
Sect:	None.
Qualities:	Somewhat yang. Oppressive. Heavy. Slow. Inescapable.
Represents:	Death and rebirth. The ultimate destructive force of the universe.

Expression:	Where we fear our lack of control and where we try to exercise control. Transformation and change. Destruction. Burning away of unnecessary aspects of life.
Psychology:	Power and control issues.
Urge:	Change and evolve. Fulfill cosmic or soul purpose.
Need:	To let go; to let something die. To work to hasten the birth of the new.
Health:	Life-threatening illnesses.
Symbols:	The Phoenix; powerful and destructive forces; dictators; death and rebirth; psychologists and psychotherapists.

Pluto is the last of the outer planets. It is the slowest-moving planet, taking over 248 years to complete an orbit around the Sun, and it is also the most recently discovered planet. We have only begun to understand the true nature of Pluto, and we have many more lifetimes to go before we will reach the point of mastery.

Pluto represents the process of death and rebirth. Pluto represents the ultimate threat to the ego, because Pluto entirely obliterates the ego. Uranus shakes it up, and Neptune denies it, but Pluto is the final death of the ego. Since most of us still grapple with our relationship to the ego, and often find it very difficult to let go of, we tend to experience a great deal of fear and apprehension around Pluto. Pluto is an unstoppable force; we can do nothing to avoid it. Out of fear, we instinctively try to exercise control in order to avoid or protect ourselves from Pluto's energy. Although Pluto has no fundamental association with control and power, because of our fears, control issues are almost always present when Pluto is involved.

Pluto is the single most destructive force in the universe: the force of unconditional love. This statement may seem a bit strange at first—how is unconditional love a destructive force? Most of us can safely agree that love is extremely powerful: "Love conquers all," and that sort of thing. True love, unconditional love, is so powerful that it destroys everything in its path that is not real; the purity, the energy of unconditional love is so intense that no illusion can withstand it.

What we have to remember here is that when we incarnated on Earth, we learned to put a great deal of faith in our illusions—such as the illusion that we are separate individuals, and not connected to each other and to everything in the universe; and the illusion that we are not all-powerful, eternal, spiritual beings. Neptune may make the walls transparent so that we can see that our beliefs are not nearly as real as we would like to think, but Pluto is where the walls come tumbling down.

Now, Pluto doesn't always start out by destroying our fundamental perceptions of reality, but it does show the areas of our lives where we will have to learn to surrender control, to let go of our need to cling to our illusions, and to allow ourselves to be completely transformed.

Individuals who have personal planets in close contact to Pluto will naturally tap into this energy, and become agents of change and transformation. Pluto most certainly represents raw power, and individuals who carry Pluto's energy are drawn to arenas where they will be in positions to influence others. (Many politicians have a strongly placed Pluto in their charts.) The danger with Pluto is succumbing to the demands of the ego and attempting to use Pluto's energy for personal gain. This always leads to the destruction of the individual, and Pluto's energy will still fulfill its original purpose.

The only way to work with Pluto's energy is to surrender to it. We must learn that the areas of our lives that we feel the most need to control are the areas that we must learn to release entirely. We must trust that when we experience Pluto's energy, we will not lose anything real; that everything Pluto is tearing down has served its purpose and is no longer of use to us. By surrendering to Pluto, we free up a vast reserve of energy that we can then use to build new structures that will support us and help us through the next phase of our journey.

3

The Signs

The signs are perhaps the best-known parts of astrology and, at the same time, the least understood. Much of the confusion stems from the fact that the signs were named after constellations of fixed stars, and most people simply assume that the signs and the constellations are one and the same. This is not the case, nor has it ever been the case. In astrology, the signs are first and foremost units of measurement: they are equal to 30° of arc along the ecliptic, which is the plane of the Sun's apparent orbit around the Earth, and which is also really the Earth's orbit around the Sun. The equator is tilted approximately 23½° to the ecliptic. We measure the relative positions of the planets based on where they appear along the ecliptic, the orbital plane.

Now, the constellations that share the names of the twelve signs of the zodiac do cross the ecliptic, which is one of the reasons that the signs were named after them; but the constellations have never divided the ecliptic into equal segments. Furthermore, as most astronomers are more than happy to point out, there are actually at least thirteen constellations that cross over the ecliptic. Ophiuchus actually crosses the ecliptic in between Scorpio and Sagittarius. This does not mean that astrology is "wrong" or that there are now thirteen signs. There are, and always have been twelve signs, each representing an equal, 30° division of the ecliptic.

Even though the signs are fundamentally units of measurement, they are also much more than that. The ancients observed that when planets were in different signs, they behaved differently; so in addition to the signs being a measurement of a planet's longitudinal position along the ecliptic, the signs also color how the planets express themselves.

As we've said before, the planets are the actors, and the signs are the roles the actors play. The signs are classified by element and modality, and also by polarity (although polarity is really a subset of the elements: earth and water signs are more introverted, yin, receptive, and classified as part of the "feminine" polarity, while fire and air signs are more extroverted, active, yang, and classified as part of the "masculine" polarity). The elements and modalities are the building blocks of the signs, and we'll look at these first, before we explore the individual signs on their own terms.

The Elements

The elemental balance of the zodiac comes from the ancient Greek philosophical concept of the universe: that everything was made up of a combination of the four basic elements of fire, earth, air, and water. Each element has qualities associated with it that are unique to that element. The qualities of each symbolic element are very much derived from the qualities of the physical manifestation of that element.

Fire

The fire signs are Aries, Leo, and Sagittarius. The element of fire represents the energy of life and of spirit. Fire is outgoing, energizing, and transforming, and is the most self-motivated of the elements. Fire signs are concerned with the question of identity, and they also tend to be more action-oriented than the other elements. Fire signs are intense: they usually radiate great warmth and light, but in close quarters, they can also burn.

Fire signs are very focused in the moment, although, in the same way that a fire will spread quickly from one place to another, fire signs have a tendency to follow a train of thought rather than sticking with one idea or concept and seeing it through to completion. One quality of fire that is usually overlooked in the Western traditions (but is a fundamental quality of the Eastern element of fire) is that fire is clinging and dependent. Fire can only exist as long as there is fuel; once the fuel has been consumed, the fire dies.

When we think of the word "fire" we also think of terms like "passionate." Fire signs are very prone to intense emotions; however, the emotions that fire signs are the most comfortable with are either intense joy or intense anger.

Fire signs must learn how to experience the full range of emotions and not to limit themselves to these two extremes.

Fire is also a very masculine, one-pointed energy in that it has a strong "all or nothing" tendency. When a fire sign takes action it instantaneously runs on all eight cylinders. When fire signs go, they GO! By the same token, when they stop, it's usually a dead stop: they run out of fuel and drop from exhaustion. An important lesson for fire signs to learn is moderation.

Fire signs are extremely honest. It never occurs to them to express anything other than their true nature, and they have little tolerance for dishonesty in others.

Fire signs recharge through physical activity, especially physical activity outdoors and in the sun, which is ultimately the strongest representation of the element of fire. People with an emphasis in fire in their charts may also find that they enjoy sitting in front of the fireplace, tending to campfires, or dining by candlelight. Short of direct physical exertion or intense emotional outbursts, simply being near actual flames can be a nurturing and energizing experience.

Earth

The earth signs are Taurus, Virgo, and Capricorn. The element of earth represents substance and physical form. The Earth does not move: it stays in one place. Earth is practical, substantial, and material, and is concerned with matter and our need to interact with the physical world. Earth is passive and receptive; it must be acted on and formed by external energies. Earth is the most stable of the elements. Earth signs are concerned with the physical, the material, and with issues of worth and value.

Earth is the slowest-moving of the elements; in fact, earth almost seems not to move at all. Earth signs have the most even temperaments, and are the most difficult to provoke to take action—but don't forget that inertia works both ways! Yes, it takes a lot to get earth signs moving, and yes, they tend to move rather slowly when they do, but the sheer weight and mass that earth signs carry with them can be a formidable power to experience. Steamrollers don't move particularly fast—but they aren't to be trifled with.

Earth signs are first and foremost concerned with what is practical. Earth signs relate primarily on the physical, tangible level, and often struggle with understanding more abstract concepts. Individuals with a strong emphasis in earth tend to be very sensual, and very anchored in the physical. These individuals communicate best through their sense of touch, taste, and hearing. They are far more likely to rely on what their physical bodies tell them than on any information they receive on the mental, intellectual, or verbal levels. Earth signs experience the full range of emotions, although they are frequently so grounded that they do not appear to be feeling much of anything.

Earth signs have a tendency to become addicted to the illusions of the physical plane. It is a very short step from simply enjoying the material world and the creature comforts and pleasures that come with it, to identifying with these trappings and losing sight of our true, spiritual purposes. Earth signs can become so grounded that they have difficulty accepting that the unseen, spiritual world has any validity at all. The lesson of earth signs is to discover how to ground the spiritual energy in the material world.

Earth signs recharge through connecting with the Earth. Individuals with a strong emphasis in earth in their charts often find that they enjoy gardening, caring for their lawns, and anything that puts them in direct contact with nature.

Air

The air signs are Gemini, Libra, and Aquarius. The element of air represents the mental and social realms. Air moves horizontally across the surface and with great speed, forming connections between all that it encounters. Air signs are the most comfortable in the realm of abstract ideas and concepts, symbols, and communication.

Air signs are the most objective, and are capable of having the greatest amount of perspective of all the signs. The element of air is a member of the "masculine" polarity and is therefore more extroverted and active, and operates on the conscious, external level. All the air signs are double signs, rooted in duality and able to understand and appreciate all sides of an issue simultaneously. Air signs are also fundamentally concerned with relationships and understanding our place in the universe. Gemini relates the individual to his or her environment; Libra relates the individual to other individuals; and Aquarius relates the individual to society.

Because air is the element that relates to the mental plane, the element of air is rational and logical. This also means that air signs are not very comfortable with emotions in general, and with intense emotions in particular. Air signs will often try to distance themselves from emotions and retreat to the mental, abstract realms where they are the most comfortable. Remember, air moves along the surface; it does not like to go too deep.

Individuals with a strong emphasis in air often have extremely vivid imaginations. They are so attuned to the energies of the mental plane that they are able to discover new ideas and concepts, and build on old ones by discovering new connections or different perspectives. While air signs are full of wonderful ideas, they are not terribly successful at actually implementing these ideas. Air signs are thinkers, not doers—they leave the implementation of their ideas to the earth signs.

Air signs recharge through social and mental activity, but also through direct experience of air. This can include everything from deep breathing, to kite flying, to riding a motorcycle or roller coaster and feeling the rush of the wind. Air signs enjoy abstract challenges, and can energize through working puzzles and riddles, through research or debate, or simply by socializing with friends and meeting new people.

Water

The water signs are Cancer, Scorpio, and Pisces. The element of water relates to the emotional and spiritual plane. Water signs operate entirely on the level of feelings—but not just any feelings. The element of water relates to our deepest, most primal emotions, as well as to the needs and longings of our soul. These feelings are buried deep in our unconscious and subconscious minds, and many times we would like to keep them locked up there and even forget that they exist because we are frightened by the power and intensity that they carry.

Water is a "feminine" energy, receptive, responsive, and fluid. Water sinks, always seeking the lowest and deepest point, and water will continue to flow until it is contained. Water has no shape or structure of its own, and instead takes on the characteristics and form of its container. The element of water is irrational, instinctive, emotional, and entirely right-brained.

Like air signs, water signs also seek to make connections, only water seeks to connect on deep, transformational levels that air would never consider exploring. Water signs are concerned with healing and with the power of emotional release, and water signs are the most comfortable with any kind of emotion, so long as it is intense. Something that water shares with fire is a tendency to exaggerate and to be overly dramatic.

Water signs are perhaps the most retentive of all the elements. Water remembers each and every emotional experience, no matter how painful. At times, it almost seems that water enjoys exploring the painful memories and emotions the most of all, as they are frequently the most intense experiences. One of the hardest lessons for water signs is learning how to let go, to truly release the pain and the negativity and allow the true healing process to complete itself.

Water signs feel the most deeply of any of the elements. They may not always be able to communicate the depth of their feelings, the extent of their pain and joy, because words do not come easily to water signs. Water signs have an ongoing struggle with finding ways of communicating and expressing their feelings that truly encompass the intensity of the experience. Ultimately, words are inadequate; some things can only be communicated through direct emotional, energetic connections.

Because the element of water has no structure of its own and must be contained, water signs tend to have the most difficulty accepting and respecting interpersonal boundaries—particularly emotional ones. Water signs must learn to respect the emotions and the comfort level of others, and that not everybody is able to bare their soul and share their deepest feelings five minutes after being introduced. This can be a very difficult and painful lesson.

Water signs recharge through intense emotional connections, as well as through proximity to water. Individuals with an emphasis in water in their charts can clear their emotional bodies of the accumulated negativity by spending time in and near water. These individuals often find that they are happiest living near lakes, rivers, or oceans; otherwise, they may be attracted to rainy climates. Even if easy access to a body of water isn't available, taking long, hot showers, or soaking in a warm bath can have the same energizing and clearing effect.

The Modalities

Cardinal

The cardinal signs are Aries, Cancer, Libra, and Capricorn, and in the tropical zodiac, they correspond to the beginning of the seasons of spring, summer, fall, and winter in the Northern Hemisphere. Cardinal signs initiate, and focus on new beginnings. Cardinal signs are also fundamentally concerned with the question of identity.

The focus of cardinal signs is on new beginnings. Cardinal signs are trail-blazers and pioneers. They have a tremendous amount of initiative, and are extremely self-motivated. Cardinal signs are often associated with leadership, although they come by this accidentally, for the most part; they don't have a fundamental desire to lead, per se, but they do not want to be led themselves. If people follow them, or learn from their example, that's fine, but it's not their primary motivation for acting.

Cardinal signs seek to express and define individual identity; their tremendous energy and drive is necessary to break free of the collective and establish a sense of individuality. Each cardinal sign is concerned with a different aspect of identity, depending on the element involved. Aries, the cardinal fire sign, is concerned with simply creating and expressing an individual identity; Cancer, the cardinal water sign, is concerned with establishing and expressing an emotional identity; Libra, the cardinal air sign, is concerned with one's social and intellectual identity; and Capricorn, the cardinal earth sign, is concerned with creating a physical and tangible manifestation of identity.

While cardinal signs tend to be very dynamic, charismatic, direct, and impulsive, they also have some lessons to learn as well. First and foremost, cardinal signs are only concerned with starting new things: they care little for seeing a new venture through to completion, and tend to lose interest quickly. As soon as something becomes routine, cardinal signs become bored and start looking for something new to start. Cardinal signs must learn the art of impulse control; they tend to act as soon as they get a new idea, and rarely if ever take the time to think things through, or create an organized plan of action.

When pressured, the first reaction of a cardinal sign is to defend itself by counterattacking. Cardinal signs are the embodiment of the phrase, "Shoot first, ask questions later."

Fixed

The fixed signs are Taurus, Leo, Scorpio, and Aquarius. The fixed signs correspond to the middle of each season, when the changes in the weather are well established, and the steady rhythm of life has reasserted itself. Fixed signs follow the cardinal signs, and are concerned with sustaining and maintaining what was initiated by the cardinal signs. Fixed signs are fundamentally concerned with the question of self-worth.

Fixed signs are concerned with stability and structure; they want things to last. Fixed signs generally possess tremendous stamina and reserves—they aren't known for their speed (cardinal signs are the sprinters of the zodiac), but fixed signs are the marathon runners. Fixed signs, much like the element of earth, represent slow-moving but incredibly powerful forces. Fixed signs do not like change, and they will tend to hold onto and follow their original course of action regardless of whether or not this is the wisest choice at the time.

Fixed signs are concerned with the question of self-worth; they build on the identity issues established through the cardinal signs, and are concerned not simply with expressing an identity, but with making sure that that identity has value and substance. Taurus, the fixed earth sign, is concerned with our material and physical worth; Leo, the fixed fire sign, is concerned with our value and worth as individuals; Scorpio, the fixed water sign, is concerned with our emotional and spiritual worth; and Aquarius, the fixed air sign, is concerned with our social worthiness.

Fixed signs have stamina and persistence, and this makes them very formidable to deal with. They are also exceedingly stubborn, and one of the most important lessons for fixed signs to learn is flexibility and openness to change. Because fixed signs are focused on issues of self-worth, they have a tendency to become invested in their ideas and actions—any suggestions that changes should be made are instinctively perceived as a personal affront or attack on their worth as individuals. The first response of fixed signs when confronted is to dig in their heels and resist. This is not to say that fixed signs abhor any kind of change; however, the idea to make a change has to come from within, not from without.

Mutable

The mutable signs are Gemini, Virgo, Sagittarius, and Pisces. Mutable signs correspond to the end of each season, when the weather is preparing to change and transform into the next step in the cycle. Mutable signs are flexible and adaptable, and are concerned with change and with the completion of one cycle and the start of the next cycle. Mutable signs are all about change, adjustments, and tying up loose ends. In classical astrology, mutable signs were also known as "common" signs; they fall in between the haste of the cardinal signs, and the methodical plodding of the fixed signs, and generally represent events happening in the natural flow and in their own time. Mutable signs are the most aware of the dynamics of the complete cycle of birth, growth, death, and rebirth, and they strive to keep events moving smoothly along the wheel.

Mutable signs are fundamentally concerned with completion, healing, and becoming whole. They follow and build on the work sustained and maintained by the fixed signs, and represent the universal law that in order for one cycle to begin, the previous one must end. Gemini, the mutable air sign, is concerned with completing our social and intellectual selves; Virgo, the mutable earth sign, is concerned with completing and perfecting the physical plane; Sagittarius, the mutable fire sign, is concerned with completing our individual identities; and Pisces, the mutable water sign, is concerned with completing and healing our emotional and spiritual natures.

Mutable signs are known for their flexibility and their ability to adapt to and handle just about any situation in order to keep events moving toward their ultimate completion. Mutable signs, however, also have a tendency to be too flexible, too easily influenced by external forces, and too scattered to effect any kind of change. When a mutable sign is confronted, its first response is to change its nature, to adapt, to avoid, to do anything it can, in fact, to avoid an actual confrontation. What mutable signs must learn more than anything is focus: they tend to be concerned with so many different details at one time, that as a result their energy dissipates and becomes ineffective.

Aries

Glyph: ♈	The Ram's Horns, or the Fountain of Life
Planetary Ruler:	Mars
Planetary Exaltation:	Sun
Element:	Fire
Modality:	Cardinal
Polarity:	Masculine
Category:	Personal

Key Concepts:	Identity; expressing the self; taking impulsive action
Rules:	Head
Symbol:	The Ram

Aries is the first sign of the zodiac and represents the first stage of human evolution. The function of Aries is to begin, to pioneer, to create new life. Aries seeks to create with a pure and intense passion, and is the quintessential expression of raw, unharnessed energy. Aries breaks away from the collective consciousness of Pisces when the infinite connection to everything becomes too limiting. In order to be able to continue to evolve, a part of the infinite separates and forms the illusion of an individual identity: this is the process of Aries. Aries is a trailblazer because it must push past all boundaries and shatter all limitations. Aries is a leader because Aries is not comfortable being led or limited by others. Aries is courageous, inspirational, enthusiastic, original, and independent. Aries' overwhelming need to express its true self prevents it from ever acting falsely or deceitfully.

Aries is a cardinal fire sign. As a cardinal sign, Aries is involved in the initial creative process and is concerned with initiating and with taking action, and is also fundamentally concerned with the question of identity. As a fire sign, Aries is also concerned with the question of identity—a double emphasis! Fire signs express their energy dynamically and intensely and tend to operate in the present moment. In short, Aries is concerned with creating and initiating an individual identity, and with being allowed to express this energy freely, impulsively, and without limitation.

Aries is ruled by the planet Mars, and, in fact, while Mars was the Roman god of war, Ares was the Greek god of war. (Aries comes from the Latin word for "ram.") Like the planet Mars, Aries is about taking action in a direct and focused manner. Unlike Mars, however, which is a nocturnal planet and therefore somewhat deceptive by nature, Aries energy is always completely honest and forthright.

The main lessons that Aries needs to learn tend to deal with taking other people into consideration. One of the keywords for Aries is "I Am!", and if you picture that being shouted from a mountaintop, you'll get a feel for Aries energy. Unfortunately, Aries is as likely to shout in a library as it is from a mountaintop. It's not that Aries energy tries to be rude; it's just that Aries energy is completely unaware that there are any other individuals in the world. It is so focused on gathering the energy required to break away and express its own individuality, that it has no ability to understand or perceive that its actions will affect others. Aries can be aggressive and combative, at times, not out of viciousness, but simply because it sees the shortest path to a goal and tends to take it—regardless of whoever else might be in the way.

Aries is the most impulsive energy in astrology, and Aries energy must learn the art of delayed gratification and impulse control. Aries has a tendency to take immediate action without thinking things through. Being both a cardinal sign and a fire sign, Aries energy will tend to burn out the fastest.

Planets in Aries are motivated to discover and express the self. Aries is the sign that is the most strongly concerned with the question of identity and individuality. Planets in Aries become more impulsive and action-oriented, and more single-minded in their manifestation. Although these planets will tend to express themselves more honestly and directly (even the more nocturnal planets), they also will tend to lose a great deal of perspective. Planets in Aries also run the risk of becoming very ego-oriented. Planets in Aries tend to lose any inherent stamina that they may have.

The emotional planets, the Moon and Venus, seem to have the most difficult time in Aries both because Aries encourages them to act immediately (which is not always the wisest move when we're listening to our emotions), and because the only emotions that Aries, as a fire sign, is really comfortable with are extreme joy and extreme anger.

Taurus

Glyph: ♉	The Bull's Head, or the Cosmic Womb
Planetary Ruler:	Venus
Planetary Exaltation:	Moon
Element:	Earth
Modality:	Fixed
Polarity:	Feminine
Category:	Personal

Key Concepts:	Stability, structure, building and creating things of value and use
Rules:	Neck, throat, voice
Symbol:	The Bull (the Cow)

Taurus is the second sign of the zodiac and represents the second stage of human evolution. Taurus gives form and structure to the new identity that Aries has created, and picks up where Aries runs out of steam, to sustain and maintain what Aries has initiated. Taurus provides the container for the masculine and yang energy of Aries. Aries and Taurus taken together represent the animation of the physical body. Taurus is motivated to ground things in the physical, to create tangible representations of lasting beauty and value.

Taurus is a fixed earth sign. As a fixed sign, Taurus is concerned with sustaining and maintaining, and also with the question of self-worth. As an earth sign, Taurus operates on the physical and the material plane. Like Aries, Taurus gets a double dose of many qualities since the element of earth and the fixed modality share much in common. Taurus is therefore concerned both with sustaining and maintaining the physical and material aspects of life, and with our sense of physical and material self-worth.

Taurus is by far the slowest-moving sign, and arguably the one that carries the greatest amount of inertia, so once Taurus gets moving, it's very difficult to stop it again. In the Northern Hemisphere, where astrology developed, Taurus relates to the middle of springtime, when the world has settled into a calm routine of steady growth, and this is very much what Taurus likes: slow, steady, progressive growth.

As an earth sign, Taurus is extremely sensual—something that is also supported by Venus, the planet that relates to pleasure, ruling Taurus. Taurus is the most grounded in the physical of all the signs, and communicates best through touch and direct physical experience. Taurus is steady, loyal, and determined. Taurus energy has a cooling and calming effect. Taurus energy is extremely creative, although it tends to relate more to crafts than to fine art.

The most important lesson for Taurus to learn is to let go of its natural attachment to the physical. Taurus energy can very easily begin to identify with the physical aspects of life. We are not our bodies; our bodies are simply containers that carry our soul and our spirit for a short time. Our bodies are temporary, but our spirit is eternal. When Taurus becomes too attached to the physical, it begins to identify with the material plane, rather than with its true self. Taurus' sense of self-esteem and self-worth becomes dependent on its appearance. It becomes obsessed with the accumulation of things in an effort to build up its sense of self-worth and to protect itself, and the pursuit is entirely pointless, because nothing on the physical plane is real or lasting. Taurus must learn that its true worth, its true identity, has nothing to do with physical trappings.

As a fixed earth sign, Taurus is also the single most stubborn of all the signs. None of the fixed signs particularly like the idea of change, but Taurus can actively fear it. This is a side effect of becoming too attached to the material plane—any attempt to make a change is perceived as an attack on its physical security and self-worth, even a threat to its fundamental ability to survive. Taurus must learn how to become more flexible, and to welcome change as a natural part of life.

Planets in Taurus become much slower and more deliberate. They become more grounded in the physical and often seek a more tangible means of expression than they would elsewhere. While this is a very supportive and balancing energy for planets like Venus and the Moon, planets that are by nature quick, such as Mercury and Uranus, have a more difficult time in Taurus.

Gemini

Glyph: ♊	Crescents above and below representing the lower and higher mind, joined through the recognition of duality. The pillars are the transmission lines between the minds, and the way through Gemini is to follow the middle path.
Planetary Ruler:	Mercury
Planetary Exaltation:	None (North Node)
Element:	Air
Modality:	Mutable
Polarity:	Masculine
Category:	Personal

Key Concepts:	Duality, communication, connecting lower mind and higher mind
Rules:	Arms, shoulders, hands, lungs, nervous system
Symbol:	The Divine Twins, Castor and Pollux

Gemini is the third sign of the zodiac and represents the third stage of human evolution. Gemini follows Taurus, and is the point where we first begin to realize that our bodies are separate from the rest of the world. Things exist that are not a part of us, that are separate from our sense of self. Gemini seeks to explore and understand our relationship to the rest of the world.

Gemini is a mutable air sign. As a mutable sign, Gemini is concerned with completion, healing, and becoming whole. As an air sign, Gemini operates on the mental plane, and is most comfortable with abstract ideas, notions, and symbols. Gemini is therefore concerned with healing and completing our mental facilities; with pursuing a comprehensive understanding of the world of ideas. Gemini is arguably the most mutable of the signs; it is certainly the quickest in motion, and the one that is the most prone to change. Gemini expresses the fundamental nature of duality, and pursues its understanding of the world by exploring the two extremes of any situation, and forming a connection between the opposite ends of the spectrum.

As an air sign, Gemini moves quickly across the surface, exploring everything and attempting to map the terrain. Gemini energy is by far the most curious and inquisitive of all the signs. It delights in new experiences and has a sincere desire to try absolutely everything at least once. Ruled by the planet Mercury, Gemini is motivated to understand, to explore, and to communicate. Gemini ultimately seeks to connect the higher and the lower mind (although in order to do this, Gemini must also work with its opposite sign, Sagittarius). Gemini is extremely flexible and versatile. Gemini's genuine interest in almost everything lends it a great deal of charm, and Gemini is almost always at ease in social situations. Meeting new people, starting up conversations with strangers— well, this is just another way of discovering more pieces to the puzzle of life, something that Gemini embraces with a passion.

What Gemini must learn, however, is to focus. None of the air signs are particularly comfortable with deep emotions, but Gemini tends to be the most uncomfortable of all. Gemini can be so flexible and adaptable that it will either avoid obstacles, or if that isn't possible, it will change in order to prevent any kind of confrontation, any situation that might slow it down, or force Gemini to put down roots and explore an issue on a deeper level. Gemini's curiosity and fascination can be charming, certainly, but Gemini's insatiable curiosity is often accompanied by an extremely short attention span. Ultimately, Gemini must learn to slow down, and to step back so that it can begin to see the big picture. Gemini tends to focus entirely on the details, and can, as they say, miss the forest for the trees.

Planets in Gemini become much quicker in their action, and often more playful. Gemini emphasizes the abstract, and planets in Gemini will tend to operate more in the mental realm. Planets that are steady and focused as a part of their nature will become more flexible and open in their expression, but they will also lose much of their focus. Planets like the Sun and Mars, who rely on being able to take direct action, have difficulty in Gemini, because they are always given at least two different courses of action to choose from. Planets that express emotion and sensitivity also have a difficult time in Gemini because they are not able to be as emotional as they need to be.

Cancer

Glyph: ♋	A mother's arms embracing a child, or the claws of the crab
Planetary Ruler:	Moon
Planetary Exaltation:	Jupiter
Element:	Water
Modality:	Cardinal
Polarity:	Feminine
Category:	Personal
Key Concepts:	Nurturing, belonging, forming emotional bonds to others; identifying with the source
Rules:	Stomach, breasts
Symbol:	The Crab (also the Tortoise, the Scarab, the Cat, the Crawfish . . .)

Cancer is the fourth sign of the zodiac and represents the fourth stage of human evolution. Cancer is the first sign where we encounter the full range of emotions and feelings, and the first sign where we can begin to rediscover our soul connection to all creation. In Gemini we begin to explore our surroundings, discover that we are separate from the objects around us, and learn how to navigate and relate to the physical world. The transition from air to water is always jarring, and perhaps the most jarring is the transition from the mutable air of Gemini to the cardinal water of Cancer, for in Cancer we discover our emotions, the first of which is a profound and crushing sense of isolation and loneliness. Through Gemini we define our separation from our environment, and in Cancer we experience the pain of this separation. We experience this pain because in Cancer we also begin to remember that we once experienced a tremendous emotional and soul connection with all creation, and we long to experience this feeling of safety and acceptance again.

Cancer is a cardinal water sign. As a cardinal sign, Cancer is involved in the initial creative process and is motivated to take action and to initiate. As a cardinal sign, Cancer is also fundamentally concerned with the question of identity. As a water sign, Cancer operates on the level of emotional, psychic, and soul connections; in the unconscious, feminine and feeling realms. In short, Cancer is concerned with creating an emotional and soul identity.

Ruled by the Moon, Cancer is an inherently nurturing and protective sign, and very focused on protecting and preserving the family; in fact, Cancer nurtures and protects in order to strengthen emotional connections and to maintain its true connection to the source of all creation. Because Cancer remembers our ultimate connection to all creation, on the highest level Cancer understands that when we nurture others, we are also nurturing ourselves, and when we are being nurtured, we are also nurturing others. Because there are truly no boundaries between us, when we give love we are also receiving it simultaneously. Cancer, however, does not always manifest on the highest level, and all too often it forgets the truth of our connection to each other. When this occurs, Cancer can become obsessed with having its personal emotional and security needs met.

When Cancer feels threatened, or when it fears that its needs will not be met, Cancer can become needy and clinging, possessive, and helpless. Mothering and nurturing can quickly become smothering. Cancer can look for emotional security in physical objects, and has a tendency to become attached to substitutes for the love and affection it craves. As Cancer rules the stomach, food is one of the more popular choices; when Cancer feels hurt and alone, comfort food, a warm blanket, and familiar surroundings are often its first line of defense. Cancer can try to build a cocoon—or perhaps more accurately, a hard outer shell—to protect itself from the pain of the outside world. Ultimately, Cancer must learn how to be more self-reliant and self-sufficient. Cancer must learn that while the connections to and support of others certainly form an important part of life, we must also have enough strength and courage to be able to go out into the world on our own, as individuals.

Planets in Cancer are placed in an emotional bath. They become extremely sensitive to feelings, and to unconscious and subconscious manifestations. Planets in Cancer become entirely subjective and lose most, if not all, of their perspective. The planets that have a fundamentally emotional and nurturing nature such as Venus, the Moon, and Jupiter, all do well in Cancer (although the Moon can become a bit too emotional in Cancer!). Planets that rely on objectivity, such as Mercury and Saturn, have a more difficult time dealing with Cancer's energy.

Leo

Glyph: ♌	The Lion's Mane; the Heart and Circulatory System
Planetary Ruler:	Sun
Planetary Exaltation:	None
Element:	Fire
Modality:	Fixed
Polarity:	Masculine
Category:	Interpersonal
Key Concepts:	Gaining acceptance and approval from others; being recognized and appreciated for our individuality and specialness
Rules:	Heart, chest, upper back; the brain
Symbol:	The Lion

Leo is the fifth sign of the zodiac and represents the fifth stage of human evolution. Leo follows the sign of Cancer in which we discover our emotional nature, our family connections, and more than that, in which we discover that there is a collective consciousness that we are a part of. In Cancer, we also discover that to a large extent, we are dependent on this collective consciousness to meet our needs. Leo evolves from Cancer's fear of not being nurtured, and Leo seeks to win the approval of the group by being special. Leo is the first of the "interpersonal" signs, and is the first sign where we have a complete sense of individual identity, and where we begin to explore our relationship to the group.

Leo is a fixed fire sign. As a fixed sign, Leo is involved in sustaining and maintaining what has been created and initiated before. As a fixed sign, Leo is also fundamentally concerned with the question of self-worth. As a fire sign, Leo is concerned with the question of identity. Fire signs express their energy dynamically and intensely and tend to operate in the present moment. In short, Leo is concerned with sustaining and maintaining a sense of individual identity, and with being allowed to express this energy freely.

Ruled by the Sun, Leo energy wants to shine, to express itself, and above all, to be the center of attention. It its highest expression, Leo comes entirely from the heart, and expresses a tremendous warmth and generosity. Leo is extremely creative and attracted to all forms of self-expression—in fact, Leo is attracted to any activity that will enable it to demonstrate to others that it is special, giving, creative, generous, and worthy of attention and appreciation. As a fire sign, Leo is extremely honest and forthright; everything that Leo undertakes is an expression of the true self, and Leo desperately wants to be acknowledged and appreciated for its true self. Leo will give of itself openly and freely, but Leo's love and generosity is not completely unconditional: Leo gives, but Leo wants to be acknowledged and recognized for its gifts—and Leo's fundamental need for the approval and attention of others can sometimes become the true motivation for Leo's generosity.

Although Leo is very aware of the importance of being accepted by others, Leo does not have any perspective on the dynamic of the group. Leo is only aware of the group as an entity, and does not yet understand that the group is made up of other individuals who are just as special, and who each are entitled to their own time in the spotlight. This is a very difficult lesson for Leo, and while it is learning this lesson, Leo has a tendency to act out in order to ensure that it is always the focus of attention. Leo's childlike innocence and openness can quickly become childish behavior. Temper tantrums? Leo invented them. Leo is the original "drama queen," combining fire's tendency to do things in a very big way, with the desire to make sure that everyone understands just how special Leo is. Leo must learn that one's true sense of self-worth comes from within; it must learn how to be secure in its own identity, and not to rely so completely on the approval and recognition of others. This overwhelming need for approval can make Leo a very easy target for manipulation.

Planets in Leo become more open, generous, expressive, and creative, but they also become extremely self-centered. The Sun and Jupiter are the happiest in Leo; they resonate very strongly with Leo's expansive energies, and both the Sun and Jupiter like to give of themselves. Planets that benefit from perspective and objectivity have a harder time dealing with Leo's energy. In particular, Mars and Saturn are very prone to ego-involvement when combined with Leo energy. Emotional planets like the Moon and Venus are able to express themselves in Leo, but they must be careful not to use their emotional expression (and outbursts!) simply as a means to get attention.

Virgo

Glyph: ♍	A Bound Sheaf of Wheat
Planetary Ruler:	Mercury
Planetary Exaltation:	Mercury
Element:	Earth
Modality:	Mutable
Polarity:	Feminine
Category:	Interpersonal
Key Concepts:	Perfection of the physical; being of service to others
Rules:	Lower intestine
Symbol:	The Virgin: She Who Has No Master

Virgo is the sixth sign of the zodiac and represents the sixth stage of human evolution. In Virgo, we seek approval from the collective by being of service.

Virgo is the first sign where we are able to put the needs of others ahead of our own personal needs. Although Virgo still does not recognize individuals as such (Libra is the first sign in which we understand that the "group" is made up of other individuals like ourselves), Virgo is where the seed of this idea is planted.

Virgo is a mutable earth sign. As a mutable sign, Virgo is involved in the processes of healing, adaptation, and change, and is fundamentally concerned with completing things and becoming whole. As an earth sign, Virgo operates in the realm of the physical, of the material, and of the practical. Virgo, then, is concerned with completing and perfecting the physical plane. In the Northern Hemisphere, where astrology originated, Virgo is associated with the time of the harvest, and indeed, the virgin that Virgo is associated with is the Vestal Virgin. The Vestal Virgins (dedicated to the service of the goddess Vesta, the keeper of the flame) were responsible for sorting through the harvest each year and selecting the best grains, the finest seeds to be held back and protected until they could be planted for the next year's harvest.

The planet Mercury both rules and is exalted in the sign of Virgo, making Virgo by far the most mental and intellectually oriented of the earth signs. Mercury represents the ability to think, to reason, to apply logic, to make connections, and to discriminate. Mercury also represents dexterity and speed, both of thought and of action. Virgo has the ability to quickly assess any given situation, and to perform complex analyses and evaluations. With Virgo, details are everything. Virgo energy is extremely efficient and precise, and is the very embodiment of the idea of constant, never-ending improvement. Virgo has a tendency to become too focused on the little things, however, and, like Mercury, has a difficult time seeing the big picture. Virgo paints with a very fine brush, but sometimes broader strokes are more appropriate for the job.

The stereotypical embodiment of Virgo energy is the Felix Unger character from Neil Simon's play *The Odd Couple:* a fussy, obsessive neat-freak who absolutely could not sleep at night if he thought someone had neglected to vacuum under the sofa cushions in the guest bedroom. This is certainly not a typical expression of Virgo energy, although it is one example of what can happen when Virgo energy gets out of control. One thing that many people with a strong Virgo emphasis in their charts will tell you is that they're not necessarily very good housekeepers. Just because they are acutely aware of how disorganized their physical environment is doesn't mean that they have the drive to actually do anything about it!

Criticism is a natural expression of Virgo energy, and when the criticism is given with compassion, and when it's constructive (and most importantly, when it is asked for in the first place!), it can be extremely helpful. Virgo doesn't miss much; but Virgo can easily become overly critical, both of the self and of others, and offer advice when it's not welcome. If Virgo falls into this trap of criticizing everything, then Virgo loses the ability to enjoy or appreciate anything at all. The hardest and most important lesson for Virgo to learn is that perfection is a process, not a destination. We can always improve, but we must also take the time to appreciate our accomplishments along the way.

Not surprisingly, planets in Virgo become extremely precise and efficient. Planets in Virgo also become far more focused on the physical plane, as well as significantly more left-brained. Virgo may be an earth sign, but it still operates in the mental realms. Emotional planets, such as the Moon and Venus, gain stability and perspective, but also lose some of their freedom to express emotions. The planets that have the most difficulty in Virgo are the planets that lean toward the spiritual and the metaphysical. Jupiter in particular has a difficult time in Virgo: the planet that represents our ability to have faith is not very comfortable in the sign that is motivated by the need to have proof.

Libra

Glyph: ♎	Balance Scales; Setting Sun
Planetary Ruler:	Venus
Planetary Exaltation:	Saturn
Element:	Air
Modality:	Cardinal
Polarity:	Masculine
Category:	Interpersonal
Key Concepts:	One-to-one relationships; expressing beauty and harmony in the world
Rules:	Lower back, kidneys
Symbol:	The Scales

Libra is the seventh sign of the zodiac and represents the seventh stage of human evolution. Libra is the first sign that recognizes others as individuals with the same feelings, drives, wants, and needs as ourselves. Although we recognize that there is a collective group that is distinct from our sense of self through the signs of Leo and Virgo, not until Libra do we begin to realize that this group is made up of other individuals. Libra seeks to reconnect to the source through balance and harmony.

Libra is a cardinal air sign. As a cardinal sign, Libra is involved in the initial creative process and is concerned with initiating, and with taking action. As a cardinal sign, Libra is also fundamentally concerned with the question of identity. As an air sign, Libra operates in the mental and social realm. Libra is therefore concerned with expressing our mental and social identity. Libra, like all air signs, is a double sign and fundamentally understands the concept of opposites. The ability to always see both sides of a situation lends air signs in general, and Libra in particular, a great deal of objectivity.

Ruled by Venus, Libra is strongly motivated by both beauty and relationships. Libra seeks to answer the question of identity through one-to-one relationships, and more importantly, through finding a balance and a harmony within these relationships. Libra's need to relate to something isn't limited to other individuals, either. Libra can relate to art, music, mathematics, science, and also to Libra's personal connection with the creator and the universal source.

Saturn, the planet of limitations, structure, and responsibility, is exalted in the sign of Libra, and this shows that Libra also has a fundamental sense of justice that connects strongly with Libra's need for balance and harmony. With the realization that there are other individuals in the world, Libra also accepts a great deal of personal responsibility. Always aware of how the actions of others (or of the collective) affect us, Libra now understands that our individual actions also have effects on other individuals.

Libra is truly the diplomat of the zodiac. No other sign has such a refined understanding of the laws of balance and harmony, or such a true appreciation of the astounding beauty that lies within all things harmonious and balanced. Libra seeks to create, with others, a greater sense of beauty and harmony in the universe. Libra's desire for relationship can, however, lead to dependence on others, and Libra's need for balance and harmony can sometimes lead to either being manipulated or manipulating others. Because Libra is an air sign, this type of behavior may seem to be the most logical and reasonable approach; Libra is not particularly in touch with the emotions that would often disagree with this line of thinking. What Libra must learn more than anything is that the only way to find true balance and harmony in a relationship is to maintain and express our own individuality to the fullest extent, and to have our partner do the same. Libra energy often seems to feel that it is incomplete, and needs a relationship in order to become whole. Libra must learn that it does not need to rely on others in order to be whole.

Planets in Libra become more balanced in their expression, and show more of a tendency to compromise in order to maintain peace and harmony. Planets in Libra are able to see both sides of any issue, which can be difficult for planets like Mars or the Sun, who need to be able to take direct, focused action. Venus in Libra displays Venus' more objective, less emotional side. The Moon in Libra has difficulty expressing deep emotions, and may look to relationships for a sense of security and safety.

Scorpio

Glyph: ♏	The Scorpion
Planetary Ruler:	Mars (modern astrology: Pluto)
Planetary Exaltation:	None
Element:	Water
Modality:	Fixed
Polarity:	Feminine
Category:	Interpersonal
Key Concepts:	Experiencing deep, transformational emotional connections; death and rebirth
Rules:	Reproductive organs, bowels
Symbol:	The Scorpion

Scorpio is the eighth sign of the zodiac and represents the eighth stage of human evolution. In Libra we realize that there are other individuals in the world who are just like ourselves, and we began to explore how to balance and relate to others on a one-to-one basis. In Scorpio, we begin to take this relationship to a deeper level. We realize that if these other individuals are exactly like ourselves, then they too must have the same emotions, feelings, and needs; they, too, must experience the loneliness and pain of being separated from the source of all creation. By connecting with these individuals on a deep, emotional level, Scorpio seeks to experience union once more. Scorpio is the sign where we seek to merge with another individual, to lose all sense of individuality; to die, for a moment, and to be reborn again. On a physical level, one way of experiencing this death and rebirth, this union and transformation, is of course through sex, and Scorpio is very much the "sex symbol" of the zodiac. But it is important to remember that Scorpio is not simply about sex: Scorpio is about death, rebirth, and transformation.

Scorpio is a fixed water sign. As a fixed sign, Scorpio is concerned with sustaining and maintaining, and is also concerned with self-worth. As a water sign, Scorpio operates through the realm of emotions and feelings. Scorpio is therefore concerned with our emotional and spiritual self-worth. "Fixed water" is, essentially, ice, and Scorpio at times may appear to be cold and reserved. Scorpio, however, has more to do with icebergs than with ice: there is much more going on underneath the surface than meets the eye. Scorpio operates on such a deep and unconscious level that it is not always easy to express its feelings. Scorpio experiences emotions more intensely than any other sign of the zodiac.

Traditionally, Scorpio is ruled by the planet Mars, but most modern astrologers associate the planet Pluto with Scorpio because of the similarities between the two. We'll talk more about rulerships, both traditional and modern, in the next lesson. Although Scorpio and Pluto certainly share a fascination with transformation and the cycles of death and rebirth, Pluto does not have the emotional component that is such a fundamental part of Scorpio's nature. Mars, however, is a planet that is very comfortable with intense emotions, and is unquestionably the ruler of Scorpio. Scorpio brings out the feminine, receptive, and unconscious energy of Mars. Scorpio energy is most frequently directed inward, always searching through the unconscious, uncovering our fears, our wounds, our hidden desires; in short, Scorpio energy is about confronting our demons, and acknowledging them. Mars is the planet that enables us to pierce the veil of illusions; Scorpio is a sign that is not at all interested in how things look on the surface. Scorpio wants to get to the heart of the matter, to bare its soul; and more than that, Scorpio wants to share the experience of baring its soul with another individual. Ultimately, Scorpio energy is about healing ourselves and our spiritual wounds by connecting with other individuals on a soul level.

Sex is certainly one way that we can encounter the experience of death and rebirth, and it's also a way to experience very intense and powerful emotional connections with other individuals. But Scorpio is by no means the only sign that can express itself sexually, nor is sex the primary manifestation of Scorpio's energy.

Scorpio energy, being ruled by Mars, is very susceptible to the traps and pitfalls of the ego; and when Scorpio gets ego-involved, Scorpio gets dangerous. When threatened, confronted, or otherwise challenged, Scorpio energy will attack in order to defend itself; and being so fundamentally in tune with the emotional realm, Scorpio energy has an uncanny instinct for finding the most painful spot and focusing its considerable force on that point. Scorpio, like the scorpion, will only attack when it feels threatened, but when Scorpio attacks, it's deadly. Scorpio's attacks can seem to come out of nowhere because Scorpio, like all water signs, tends to hold onto old pain and emotional issues, picking at the scabs and keeping the anger alive, although buried very deep beneath the surface. One of the most important lessons for Scorpio, the sign concerned with transformation and change, is (ironically) to learn how to let go. Scorpio energy must also learn how to relax and enjoy life; often Scorpio is so focused on change and transformation, on tearing down the old to make way for the new, that it never allows time for the new to manifest.

Planets in Scorpio gain depth and intensity, and become agents of change and transformation. Emotional planets become even more emotional, and have a tendency to focus on heavier, darker issues. Planets that rely on their communication or social skills, such as Mercury and Venus, often have a difficult time in Scorpio: Scorpio is about probing the psyche; it's not built for small talk.

Sagittarius

Glyph: ♐   The Hunter's Arrow

Planetary Ruler: Jupiter

Planetary Exaltation:	None (South Node)
Element:	Fire
Modality:	Mutable
Polarity:	Masculine
Category:	Transpersonal
Key Concepts:	The Quest for Truth
Rules:	Hips, thighs
Symbol:	The Archer

Sagittarius is the ninth sign of the zodiac and represents the ninth stage of human evolution. Sagittarius is the first of the "transpersonal" signs, where humans begin to explore their relationship to the larger social structures of society and ultimately of the universe. In Scorpio, we experience the death of the ego when we merge, at least for a brief moment, with another individual on a fundamental and emotional level. We lose all sense of self and we reconnect with our soul memories of being connected to everyone and everything in the universe. At the end of this process, we are reborn, and once again buy into the illusion of separation and of individuality.

Sagittarius begins at this point: we have just been reborn, and we take with us the new understanding that every other individual has similar hopes, needs, dreams, and emotions. This is an eye-opening experience, to say the least! Until this point, we are only marginally aware of other individuals and of our relationships to them. Once we connect on an emotional level through Scorpio, however, we fully understand that we are part of something far greater. Sagittarius wants to explore this, and seeks to discover how we fit in as individuals in the larger scheme of things.

Sagittarius is a mutable fire sign. As a fire sign, Sagittarius is concerned with the question of identity. As a mutable sign, Sagittarius is concerned with healing and completion. In short, Sagittarius is about the completion of our identities. Sagittarius is ruled by Jupiter, the planet of growth and expansion, and Sagittarius is always seeking new experiences and new information. It is important to remember that the mythological figure associated with Sagittarius is the centaur: half-man, half-horse. Part of the process of Sagittarius searching for an understanding of our place in the universe involves reconciling our animal nature with our divine nature. Sagittarius energy is as comfortable exploring philosophy, spirituality, and religion as it is exploring physical pleasure and activity, and ultimately one of the lessons of Sagittarius is to learn how to integrate the two.

Sagittarius is ruled by Jupiter, the planet of expansion, growth, and freedom. Like Jupiter, Sagittarius is only concerned with the Big Picture, and often has little patience for the details. Jupiter's influence makes Sagittarius want to experience the world. Sagittarius loves travel and exploration, and meeting new people. Like Jupiter, Sagittarius tends to absorb new ideas and concepts. Although Sagittarius does have a tendency to be idealistic and quite attached to its beliefs (an unusual trait for a mutable sign), Sagittarius is also willing to modify and adjust its belief system to accommodate new information, because this will help Sagittarius get closer to understanding the ultimate truth. Sagittarius energy benefits from Jupiter's influence by demonstrating a tremendous amount of enthusiasm and an overall love (and lust) for everything that life has to offer.

Sagittarius, however, can tend to be a bull in a china closet, and its enthusiasm and energy often make it less aware of the needs and feelings of other people. Sagittarius is notorious for its lack of tact—something that stems from Sagittarius' absolute devotion to the truth. Sagittarius doesn't suffer bruised feelings easily, although it must learn that this is not the case with everyone! Sagittarius also has a tendency to overlook the details, and can become so invested in its beliefs that it won't even entertain ideas that contradict them. Sagittarius' need for freedom can sometimes manifest as an unwillingness to compromise in order to maintain a relationship. When Sagittarius is confronted with a situation that doesn't conform to its beliefs, it can be happy to simply leave and go off on its own, rather than stay and be forced to adjust.

Planets in Sagittarius become both more independent and more changeable. The Moon and Venus in Sagittarius find it very difficult to express compassion; they must learn how to access and express their emotional nature through trial and error. Jupiter and the Sun generally do very well in Sagittarius because of their connection to the exuberance and identity issues of the element of fire.

Capricorn

Glyph: ♑	The Sea Goat
Planetary Ruler:	Saturn
Planetary Exaltation:	Mars
Element:	Earth
Modality:	Cardinal
Polarity:	Feminine
Category:	Transpersonal
Key Concepts:	Responsibility, structure; protecting the integrity and security of society
Rules:	Skeleton, knees
Symbol:	The Sea Goat

Capricorn is the tenth sign of the zodiac and represents the tenth stage of human evolution. In Sagittarius, we begin to explore our roles as individuals within the greater arena of the universe and the microcosms of society. Sagittarius seeks an understanding of universal truth. Capricorn begins to take this understanding of truth and uses it as a foundation to create laws and structures that will help protect the integrity of society. Capricorn is where we begin to take on a sense of personal responsibility to the group. Sagittarius explores the philosophical ideas of our relationship to society; Capricorn takes these theories and creates governing laws and guidelines from them, bringing them into tangible manifestation.

Capricorn is a cardinal earth sign. As a cardinal sign, Capricorn is involved in the initial creative process and is concerned with initiating and with taking action. As a cardinal sign, Capricorn is also fundamentally concerned with the question of identity. As an earth sign, Capricorn operates in the realm of the physical, the material, and the practical. Capricorn, then, is concerned with creating a tangible, durable, and concrete representation of its individual identity, ideally one that will show how Capricorn contributed to the overall health and safety of society. Capricorn defines itself in terms of what it has accomplished.

Ruled by Saturn, the planet of limitations, structure, and responsibility, Capricorn can be a very serious sign. Capricorn has a fundamental respect for authority, and a need to both understand the rules and boundaries in any given situation, and to support, uphold, and enforce them. This is not to imply that Capricorn necessarily responds to traditional authority figures; quite the contrary. However, Capricorn will respond to and obey whatever it chooses to recognize as an authority (and Capricorn *always* has some perception of authority). These boundaries, rules, regulations, and limitations are how Capricorn is able to define its sense of individual identity. Saturn defines things by what they are not rather than by what they are; Capricorn looks at the boundaries and structures that surround it, and knows that these define who Capricorn is.

Capricorn is without a doubt one of the hardest-working signs of the zodiac. This comes both from the Saturn influence, which says that everything that we have must be earned, and also from the influence of Mars. Mars is exalted in the sign of Capricorn, and this demonstrates Capricorn's ability to focus on a goal and to pursue that goal with a single-minded determination. The Mars influence also means that Capricorn can easily become ego-involved, which can lead to ruthlessly ambitious behavior at times.

The hardest lesson for Capricorn is learning how to let go and relax. It has been said that Capricorns have to learn how to play, and that they frequently grow younger as they grow older. The reason for this is that Capricorn is very susceptible to the ego-based fear that it will not be able to survive without clearly defined rules and boundaries. Ideally, the understanding of what is practical and acceptable behavior gives Capricorn the freedom to create, explore, and fully express itself within these parameters. When the ego becomes too active, however, Capricorn can become attached to the rules, laws, and boundaries, and can even identify with them. Any attempt to change these rules, any attempt to shift or expand the boundaries, even if they no longer serve their original purpose, may be viewed as a threat to Capricorn's very existence. Capricorn's tendency to pursue power and control comes from this fear. Capricorn must learn how to experience perfect freedom and grace within the accepted boundaries.

Planets in Capricorn become more focused, practical, and ambitious. They carry a strong awareness of their burdens and responsibilities, and generally try to live up to what they perceive to be their highest potential. Planets in Capricorn also become very independent and self-reliant, and tend to resist forming strong connections to others. Obviously, the planets that rely on being able to form emotional connections, such as the Moon, Venus, and to some extent, Jupiter, are not very comfortable in Capricorn. They don't lose their fundamental need for these connections, they just have a difficult time initiating and maintaining them. Mars and Saturn are both extremely well placed in Capricorn; Mars in particular is channeled quite well by the structured and restrictive energy of Capricorn.

Aquarius

Glyph: ♒	Electricity transmitted through waves of ether
Planetary Ruler:	Saturn (modern astrology: Uranus)
Planetary Exaltation:	None
Element:	Air
Modality:	Fixed
Polarity:	Masculine
Category:	Transpersonal
Key Concepts:	Protecting and preserving the needs of the group; seeking perfection of society; understanding the role of the individual in the group
Rules:	Ankles, circulatory system
Symbol:	The Water Bearer

Aquarius is the eleventh sign of the zodiac and represents the eleventh stage of human evolution. Aquarius follows the sign of Capricorn, where we seek to build structures and create laws and customs that will support the integrity of the group. Aquarius is where we begin to look at these laws and structures and evaluate whether they do, in fact, serve the best interest of the group. Any structures that no longer serve the group, any laws or rules that restrict personal freedom rather than protecting those that they serve, are torn down by Aquarius and replaced with new rules that both enhance personal freedom and protect the integrity of the group.

Aquarius is a fixed air sign. As a fixed sign, Aquarius is involved in sustaining and maintaining what has been created and initiated before. As a fixed sign, Aquarius is also fundamentally concerned with the question of self-worth. As an air sign, Aquarius operates in the intellectual, mental, and social realm; Aquarius is idea-oriented and abstract. Aquarius, then, is concerned with establishing a sense of social, mental, and intellectual self-worth. The sense of social self-worth is derived from membership in groups of our own choosing; in other words, Aquarius finds validation through acceptance by one's peers.

Although modern astrologers consider the planet Uranus to be the ruler of Aquarius, and support this because of Aquarius' tendency to be revolutionary and unconventional, Aquarius is traditionally ruled by the planet Saturn, which governs all limitations, structures, and responsibilities. Aquarius is, in fact, particularly concerned with the rules of society, or at least with the rules and structures that define a given group. Aquarius is not by nature revolutionary. Although Aquarius will fight to the death for personal freedom, that personal freedom must be supported and protected by rules and social structures. We must remember that anarchy is not the same thing as freedom. The energy of Uranus is an expression of anarchy, and exists simply to disrupt any and all structures, to break up Saturn manifestations and illusions. Aquarius only seeks to disrupt those structures that do not support personal freedom and equality; it will fight to support and preserve those structures that do.

Aquarius defines itself through group association. Because Aquarius places more importance on group identity than on individual identity, Aquarius can be a truly selfless sign. Although Capricorn will work within the group to support the group, Capricorn also seeks individual recognition for its efforts. Aquarius can identify with the group rather than with an individual identity, and can therefore be truly a "team player," and also truly humanitarian. Where Capricorn seeks prominence in the group, Aquarius seeks absolute equality in the group and draws strength and support from membership in a collective.

Being an air sign, Aquarius can tend to live in a theoretical and philosophical world rather than in a practical one. Aquarius will often fight for a utopian ideal and be unable to translate it into something workable. Although Aquarius can have great compassion for humanity (which comes from the head),

Aquarius can also have great difficulty in feeling any kind of compassion for individual humans (which comes from the heart). This is again a symptom of living in a mental ideal and being unable to translate it to a practical level. Although Aquarius is a great supporter of personal freedom and equality, this freedom and equality can often be limited to members of whatever group Aquarius belongs to. As a fixed sign, Aquarius can be exceptionally stubborn and resistant to change, and one of the lessons that Aquarius must learn is how to become more flexible and open to the ideas of others, even when they do not agree with its own.

Planets in Aquarius gain a tremendous amount of perspective and objectivity. They are inclined to operate in the theoretical and mental realms, rather than to take direct action. Planets in Aquarius also become focused on the group dynamic rather than on an individual level. Mental planets such as Mercury and Jupiter tend to be very comfortable in Aquarius, although they may tend to embrace rather unusual ideas. Mars in Aquarius expends much of its energy on the theoretical and planning stages, and may have difficulty in taking action on the physical plane. Both the Sun and Mars have difficulty in Aquarius because Aquarius energy does not easily acknowledge the individual, and the Sun and Mars are only comfortable expressing themselves on that level. Emotional planets such as the Moon and Venus lose their ability to express and experience emotions on a deep level. They tend to manifest a great deal of compassion, but can be uncomfortable when a general feeling of compassion becomes too specific or personal.

Pisces

Glyph: ♓	Two halves of the circle of spirit, cut, but linked through the being, connecting the higher and lower self; the two fish, large (marine mammals, all-knowing, and wise) and small (gilled fish, live in schools, follow instincts only)
Planetary Ruler:	Jupiter (modern astrology: Neptune)
Planetary Exaltation:	Venus
Element:	Water

Modality:	Mutable
Polarity:	Feminine
Category:	Transpersonal
Key Concepts:	Returning to the source; healing and transmuting negativity; remembering our spiritual connections to each other and to the universe
Rules:	Feet
Symbol:	The Fish

Pisces is the twelfth sign of the zodiac and represents the twelfth stage of human evolution. In Aquarius, we explore our relationship to society by identifying with the group consciousness. In Pisces, we complete the cycle of evolution and begin to dissolve the ego, to release the illusion of separation from the source, and to merge once again with the universe, integrating all we have learned through experiencing the previous signs. Aquarius identifies with the group, but Pisces seeks to merge with the group completely. Pisces represents the final stage and also the new beginning; as one cycle ends, the next one begins.

Pisces is a mutable water sign. As a mutable sign, Pisces is concerned with adapting, changing, and completing. As a water sign, Pisces operates in the realm of emotions and feelings. In short, Pisces is concerned with healing and completing on the emotional and spiritual plane. The motivation of Pisces is to absorb negative emotions from others and to transmute them. Pisces can be tremendously sensitive and caring. Because Pisces has a fundamental understanding that we are all part of the same universe, that truly there is no separation between us, Pisces has the ability to express unconditional love freely. Pisces tends to be psychic because it is able to pick up instinctively on the connections that we each share with everyone and everything in the universe.

Pisces is ruled by the planet Jupiter, and while it shares Jupiter's tendency for expansion (Pisces has a great deal of difficulty with boundaries since it tends not to recognize any), Pisces embodies the more spiritual elements of Jupiter. Pisces energy is about faith, for without faith, we would not be able to surrender the ego, to let go of the illusion of our individuality and merge with the universe. If Pisces didn't have the faith that we were truly eternal, spiritual beings, it wouldn't be able to let go of the physical with such ease. Pisces is perhaps the most compassionate of all the signs. It shares Jupiter's desire for the truth, but Pisces also knows that the truth is very subjective at times, and that sometimes the unseen is even more important than that which can be measured in the physical realm. Modern astrologers associate the planet Neptune with Pisces, and both Neptune and Pisces share a foglike quality, and a sensitivity to higher, spiritual vibrations.

Pisces energy has a tendency to embrace the martyr archetype, however, and despite what Pisces might think, this is very much a manifestation of its ego, not of its higher self. Yes, Pisces does a great and necessary service by absorbing and transmuting the negative energy and emotions of others, and yes, this is a powerful healing experience; but Pisces must learn that it doesn't need to suffer in order to serve the spirit. Rather than holding onto the negativity that Pisces collects, Pisces is perfectly capable of releasing it, and experiencing little or no discomfort in the process. Pisces energy also has a tendency to attempt to escape the physical through fantasy, as well as through chemical means. This can be fueled both by a need to avoid the pain and negativity that Pisces carry with it and either chooses not to release, or doesn't understand how to release, and also by an ego-driven belief that leaving the body through drugs and alcohol is a way of experiencing spirituality. Pisces must learn that its purpose is not to leave the physical, but instead to bring spiritual energy into the physical realm. In order to do this, Pisces must learn how to stay grounded and in its physical body. By connecting to the Earth, Pisces will naturally discharge the negativity it collects, and be able to move beyond the ego traps and martyr games.

Planets in Pisces lose their ability to take direct action; Pisces energy can be very disorienting, and planets in Pisces often act atypically. Planets in Pisces become extremely sensitive and receptive to the spiritual and emotional realms, and become less focused on and aware of boundaries. The Moon in Pisces in particular can have difficulty separating other people's feelings from its own. Venus in Pisces becomes very romantic, artistic, and creative. Planets that require direct action or structure, such as Mars and Saturn, tend to be uncomfortable in Pisces.

4

Essential Dignities

We now come to the first elements of astrological interpretation: combining the planets and the signs. Remember our earlier analogy that the planets are the actors, and the signs are the roles that they play. Needless to say, actors are far more comfortable and convincing in certain roles than they are in others. The more a given role fits an actor's "type," the more comfortable the actor is playing that role, and the more effective and compelling the performance.

Unlike actors, the planets never lose themselves in their roles. Mars is always Mars, no matter what sign it is in, or where it is placed in the chart. No amount of makeup and costuming could ever make us mistake Jupiter for Saturn. For example, take Sylvester Stallone, the action hero actor. He's the most convincing when he's playing Rambo, blowing things up and saving the day—that's the type of role that best fits his image, and he's by far the most comfortable in those roles. To cast Stallone as Hamlet, for example, or even worse, as Juliet, would be a grave mistake. (O.K., I know *I* would buy a ticket to see him play Juliet, but that's not the point.) By the same token, we wouldn't expect to see Shirley Temple playing an action hero. Most actors are lucky enough to only play roles that suit them and that will allow them to show off their strengths. The planets, on the other hand, aren't nearly as lucky.

In astrology, we have twelve different roles—the twelve signs of the zodiac. Eventually, each planet has to step into each and every role, no matter how miserable they may be playing the part, or how terribly miscast they may seem to be.

So how can we tell how convincingly a planet is going to play a given part? We do that by evaluating a planet's overall strength, or essential dignity, in a particular sign.

Introduction to Essential Dignities

Essential dignities were a fundamental part of classical astrology—one that has been largely forgotten or misunderstood by most modern astrologers. Thanks largely to the work of *Project Hindsight, ARHAT (the Archive for the Retrieval of Historical Astrological Texts)*, and in particular to classical astrologers like Rob Hand and Dr. J. Lee Lehman, Ph.D., modern astrologers can now begin to understand the nature and quality of the dignities, and discover how working with them makes interpreting and delineating the planets both much easier and far more accurate.

A table of essential dignities is shown in figure 3, courtesy of J. Lee Lehman, Ph.D., and her book *Essential Dignities.*

In Ptolemy's table, there are five essential dignities (rulership or house, exaltation, triplicity, term, face), and two essential debilities (detriment, fall). You will also notice that only the "inner" planets through Saturn are included in the table. The use of essential dignities predated the discovery of the outer planets by almost two thousand years. The outer planets can have no essential dignity or debility. Some of these terms may be very familiar: in particular, the concepts of "rulership," "exaltation," "detriment," and "fall" have also survived into modern astrology, although few astrologers seem to understand exactly what they mean or how to work with them.

All degrees indicated in the table are rounded to the next whole degree: that is, 12°01' (twelve degrees, one minute) would be rounded up to 13°. The degrees also represent the last degree that a planet rules. For example, Jupiter in Aries is in terms from 0°00' Aries to 5°59' Aries, but at 6°00' Aries, Venus takes over.

Rulership

The definition of rulership is the single biggest difference between classical astrology and modern astrology, and the cause of more verbal brawls at astrology conferences than I even want to think about. In classical astrology, there

SIGNS	RULERSHIP	EXALTATION	TRIPLICITY		TERMS					FACE			DETRIMENT	FALL
			DAY	NIGHT										
♈	♂	☉	☉	♃	♃ 6	♀ 14	☿ 21	♂ 26	♄ 30	♂ 10	☉ 20	♀ 30	♀	♄
♉	♀	☽	♀	☽	♀ 8	☿ 15	♃ 22	♄ 26	♂ 30	☿ 10	☽ 20	♄ 30	♂	
♊	☿	☊	♄	☿	☿ 7	♃ 14	♀ 21	♄ 25	♂ 30	♃ 10	♂ 20	☉ 30	♃	☋
♋	☽	♃	♂	♂	♂ 6	♃ 13	☿ 20	♀ 27	♄ 30	♀ 10	☿ 20	☽ 30	♄	♂
♌	☉		☉	♃	♄ 6	☿ 13	♀ 19	♃ 25	♂ 30	♄ 10	♃ 20	♂ 30	♄	
♍	☿	☿	♀	☽	☿ 7	♀ 13	♃ 18	♄ 24	♂ 30	☉ 10	♀ 20	☿ 30	♃	♀
♎	♀	♄	♄	☿	♄ 6	♀ 11	♃ 19	☿ 24	♂ 30	☽ 10	♄ 20	♃ 30	♂	☉
♏	♂		♂	♂	♂ 6	♃ 14	♀ 21	☿ 27	♄ 30	♂ 10	☉ 20	♀ 30	♀	☽
♐	♃	☋	☉	♃	♃ 8	♀ 14	☿ 19	♄ 25	♂ 30	☿ 10	☽ 20	♄ 30	☿	☊
♑	♄	♂	♀	☽	♀ 6	☿ 12	♃ 19	♂ 25	♄ 30	♃ 10	♂ 20	☉ 30	☽	♃
♒	♄		♄	☿	♄ 6	☿ 12	♀ 20	♃ 25	♂ 30	♀ 10	☿ 20	☽ 30	☉	
♓	♃	♀	♂	♂	♀ 8	♃ 14	☿ 20	♂ 26	♄ 30	♄ 10	♃ 20	♂ 30	☿	☿
	+5	+4	+3		+2					+1			–5	–4

Ruler　Exaltation　Detriment　Fall

Figure 3. Ptolemy's Table of Essential Dignities and Debilities as shown in *Essential Dignities* by J. Lee Lehman, Ph.D.

Set Janus to Lilly triplicity + custom terms (there are some differences between this table + the presets for Lilly or Ptolemy).

were only seven planets, and the sign rulers were neatly divided with each planet ruling a pair of signs, and the Sun and Moon each ruling one. This was perfectly acceptable until 1781 when Uranus showed up and, true to its nature, shook everything up. No longer did the planets and the signs match up neatly. And the subsequent discoveries of Neptune and Pluto made things even messier. Modern astrologers decided to change the system of sign rulerships to include these new planets.

This was only possible because at the time, the link between classical techniques and modern astrology had already been severed, and few astrologers either used or understood the true meaning of the essential dignities. Instead, they reassigned the rulerships based not on how strong a planet was in a given sign, but on how much they felt a planet was like a given sign. Aquarius was taken away from Saturn and assigned to Uranus; Pisces was taken away from Jupiter and assigned to Neptune; and after a long dispute between Aries and Scorpio, the general consensus decided that Scorpio is ruled by Pluto, not Mars. The modern usage of the term "rulership" is really a system of "affinities" and has nothing whatsoever to do with "rulership" as an essential dignity.

When we talk about a planet in a sign that it rules, it is an evaluation of that planet's strength in that sign. How well can that planet play the role that it's been given? Well, a planet in a sign that it rules is playing the role for which it is most famous—the signature part that turned it into a $20 million-plus, A-list star. This is a planet that can do whatever it wants, and doesn't have to answer to anyone or anything. It is the master of its own destiny. This is wonderful for the planet, but it's not always the best thing for the individual! Just like an A-list Hollywood star, no one is going to say "no" to a planet in rulership—no matter how stupid, self-centered, dangerous, or potentially destructive its ideas happen to be.

On an esoteric level, planets in the signs of their rulership are operating on the highest plane of existence: the level of pure being. In their own sign, planets are able to express their true nature, their highest purpose in its purest form. We have the opportunity to begin to understand and work with the planet on this level after the age of sixty.

Exaltation

Exaltation is a term that has more or less survived into the modern literature, but with little or no information on exactly what it means. Planets in the sign of their exaltation are treated like honored guests: things are done on their behalf by others, and with the best of intentions; but no matter how comfortable and pampered these planets may be, they ultimately do not get to choose their own agenda. They are bound by certain standards of acceptable behavior, and kept in check.

Planets in exaltation are very strong—and in many ways much easier to deal with than planets in the signs they rule. As honored guests, planets in exaltation tend to be on their best behavior; they strive to be gracious and to express their higher nature. On an esoteric level, planets in exaltation are operating on what we would call the spirit or soul level (what the Greeks called *Nous*), which is where we connect with our higher selves and our guides. We are able to access and experience planets in exaltation on this level from the ages of forty-five to sixty.

Triplicity

Triplicity is a moderately strong essential dignity; it is not nearly as strong a placement as exaltation or rulership, but a planet with dignity by triplicity is still quite fortunate; in fact, "fortune" and "luck" seem to be the best ways to describe a planet in triplicity. These planets just seem to be lucky. They have a knack for being in the right place at the right time, and receiving benefits because of this. Their strength, then, does not seem to come from any inherent talent or ability, merely from good timing. Think of triplicity as an actor who comes off well in a performance because of strong direction, good production, and outstanding material—in other words, an actor in a role that would be very difficult to screw up. Luck is a tricky thing, though, and with planets in triplicity (as with so many other things), luck has a nasty habit of running out just when we begin to rely on it. To some extent, we can relate this to the fact that triplicity is usually determined by the sect of the chart: a planet that would be dignified by triplicity in a diurnal (day) chart, may have no dignity at all at the same position in a nocturnal (night) chart. Note that a chart is diurnal (a day chart) when the natal Sun is positioned above the horizon in houses seven through twelve, and is nocturnal (a night chart) when the natal Sun is positioned below the horizon in houses one through six.

Term

A planet with dignity by term is one that makes a valiant effort at the part it's playing, but is simply out of its league. William Lilly described dignity by term as representing a planet that was in very declining fortunes; someone who was struggling to make ends meet, and was perhaps only a short while from being turned out onto the street. Planets with dignity only by term have an interest in the matter, but not enough strength, skill, or luck to have much of an impact or to accomplish their goals. More than any other quality or dignity, William Lilly used the terms to assign physical descriptions to people.

Face

Face is by far the weakest of the essential dignities: in fact, it is hardly a dignity at all. A planet that only has dignity by face has a great deal of anxiety about its situation. Because fear and anxiety about something give them focus, planets in face at least have an interest in the situation—but they are in no position to have any kind of an impact on it whatsoever. This is an actor who probably stepped into the part at the last minute, had no time to prepare, and knows that his career depends on his performance. The only thing that can be said about face is that it will keep a planet from being classified as peregrine (without any essential dignity at all). The fear and anxiety keeps the planet focused on the goal, but in no way gives the planet the resources or ability to reach the goal.

Detriment

A planet in a sign opposite of the sign that it rules is in the sign of its detriment. Planets in detriment are classified as debilitated, but this does not mean that they are necessarily weak. In fact, planets in detriment are actually quite strong; however, they tend to use their strength in ways that are inappropriate to their current situation, and as a result, end up in some very difficult positions. Planets in detriment are in poor condition because of their own actions. A planet in detriment is like Sylvester Stallone playing Juliet on Broadway because he insists that playing Juliet will be the best thing for his career. No one is going to tell him he can't do it, but this doesn't mean he's going to do well in the part.

On an esoteric level, planets in detriment are operating on the mental/emotional plane, and are most challenging to us between the ages of fifteen to forty-five. In practice, individuals with planets in detriment tend to worry too much about the affairs of that planet, and are often exceedingly self-conscious about how they express the energy of that planet.

Fall

A planet in the sign opposite the sign of its exaltation is said to be in fall. Planets in fall are not in quite as bad a situation as planets in detriment. Planets in fall are weak because they are in a place where they have no influence—sort of like being stranded in a foreign country where you don't speak the language and don't understand the local customs. Planets in fall are debilitated through no fault of their own. To continue with the actor analogy, a planet in fall is Sylvester Stallone playing Juliet on Broadway because his agent got him into the contract, and he can't break it.

On an esoteric level, planets in fall are operating on the physical plane, and are most prominent from birth to age fifteen. When we are not able to express the energy of a planet in fall, when we experience difficulties and challenges with the planet, these will tend to manifest in our physical bodies as illnesses and injuries.

Peregrine

A planet with no essential dignity is called peregrine, which means "wandering." Peregrine planets have no affinity, strength, talent, or resources; but at the same time, they do not have any essential debilities either. Peregrine planets in natal charts are very different from peregrine planets in other forms of astrology. In horary and electional astrology, a peregrine planet is in very bad shape; in natal astrology, where we have the ability to work with our understanding of the planets over the course of our lives, peregrine planets are simply less predictable and less typical in their expression. This is not necessarily a bad thing, and it also does not mean that peregrine planets can't express themselves. However, peregrine planets do seem to take a very roundabout way of getting from point A to point B. A peregrine planet in a natal chart is like an actor who has been cast against type in a role; the actor's approach to the part is unusual, and not at all what we would expect, and it takes some time to get used to it and to accept the actor's performance—but the actor still has a fighting chance of turning in an acceptable performance in the end. A table showing the peregrine degrees for all the planets is shown in figure 4.

This table requires some explanation. What it represents are the degrees where a given planet is peregrine. Each block represents 10°. The Sun, for example, is peregrine for the first 20° of Gemini. Where degree numbers are listed in a block, these degrees again represent where the planet is peregrine. As in the essential dignity table, the degrees are rounded to the nearest whole degree. Venus, for example, is peregrine from 14° to 20° of Aries, but not from 6° to 14° of Aries.

A Word About Classical Interpretations

One adjustment that modern astrologers who use classical techniques must often make involves translating the very fatalistic and frequently negative interpretations assigned to the planets to a more supportive, enlightened, and empowering format. A planet in debility is not a bad thing. It does not mean that the individual will have a bad experience with that planet, nor does it limit what that individual can accomplish with his or her life—including the areas of life impacted by the debilitated planet. Essential dignities are so valuable in natal interpretations because they can help us understand how a planet is likely to express itself in a given sign, and, even more importantly, *why* a planet is likely to express itself in that way in a given sign. The challenges presented to a debilitated planet represent some of the most important growth and life experiences for the individual. By the same token, having a natal chart filled with strongly dignified planets presents its own set of challenges. The more strongly a planet is allowed to express its own nature, the more essential it becomes that we learn how to master the energy of that planet and keep it in its proper perspective in our charts and in our lives.

How the Outer Planets Fit In

One of the fundamental differences between modern astrology and traditional astrology boils down to how the newly discovered outer planets fit in

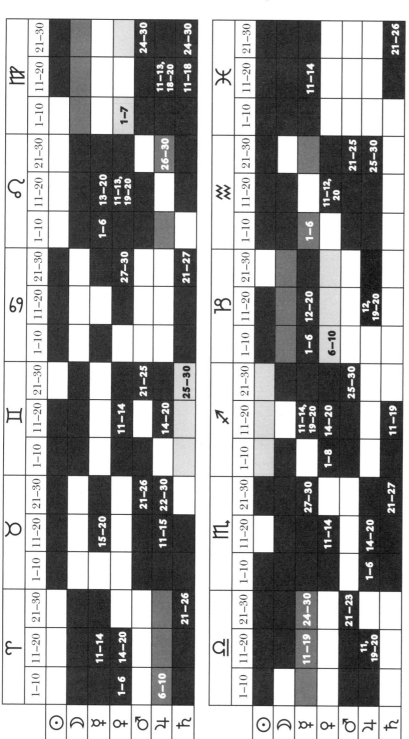

Figure 4. Peregrine Degrees for Traditional Dignities

with the traditional systems of rulership and dignity. True to its nature, when Uranus was discovered in 1781, the very neat and symmetrical system of essential dignities was challenged and upset for the first time in history. Here was a planet that didn't have a place in the existing scheme of things. Astrologers scrambled to understand the energy of this new planet, and also to reevaluate the fundamental tools of astrology.

The fact that new planets were discovered (Neptune in 1846, and Pluto in 1931) at a time when the practice of astrology (and formal instruction in astrology) was in serious decline opened the door to the modern "rulerships," which are not evaluations of a planet's strength, but instead are indications of how alike the planet and the sign seem to be. Other than in horary astrology, essential dignities fell out of favor in general practice until very recently, so the new system of rulerships was not challenged too frequently (beyond the lingering debate about what the modern rulership of Pluto should be: some astrologers still insist that Pluto rules Aries, not Scorpio).

In her book *Cosmic Astrology,* June Wakefield proposes what I believe to be the most elegant solution, one that takes into account not only the outer planets, but also, by extension, the modern rulerships associated with Uranus, Neptune, and Pluto. Wakefield sets up her theory by establishing a few key assumptions:

- The Sun, as we use it in the chart, is not the true Sun; instead, it is the Earth/Moon dyad.
- The true Sun is the source of all life, energy, and light; its energy is expressed on the material plane through all the planets and all the signs.
- The outer planets, Uranus, Neptune, and Pluto, operate on a higher plane than the visible planets. These three planets act as "secondary Suns," and bring the energy of the true Sun closer to the material plane. Each of the three outer planets rules a different plane of existence: Uranus rules the Plane of Matter, Neptune rules the Plane of the Mind, and Pluto rules the Plane of Life. Each of these "secondary Suns," in turn, expresses through a pair of visible planets, and each of those planets rules and expresses through two signs.

I find this system to be exceptionally elegant—and it answers the question of the modern "rulerships" very nicely. Uranus rules Aquarius? It sure does. Since Uranus, the ruler of the Plane of Matter, expresses itself through Saturn and the Earth/Moon dyad, Uranus not only ultimately rules Aquarius, but also

Capricorn, Cancer, and Leo. Does Pluto rule Scorpio or Aries? Why quibble! Pluto, the ruler of the Plane of Life, expresses itself through Mars and Venus, so Pluto rules both Scorpio and Aries, as well as Taurus and Libra. Furthermore, Neptune, the ruler of the Plane of Mind, expresses itself though Mercury (lower mind) and Jupiter (higher mind) and rules not only Pisces, but also Sagittarius, Gemini, and Virgo. Since all four elements are needed in order for anything to manifest on the physical plane, it's nice that each of the outer planets "rules" four signs: one each of fire, earth, air, and water.

Now, I still don't teach that the outer planets directly "rule" any signs: that is, they don't have any essential dignity or debility; but I certainly believe that they must somehow fit into the overall scheme of things. Since there's no question about the fact that the outer planets do not operate in the same way as the visible planets do, I'm very open to the idea that they operate on an even higher plane, and express themselves, at least in part, through the visible planets.

Dispositor Trees

The simplest way of working with the essential dignities involves looking at the hierarchy of rulerships in a natal chart. Rulership means just what it sounds like it means—the planet that rules a sign actually rules or governs any planets that are in that sign. When a planet rules another planet, it is said to be the *dispositor* of that planet's energy. The Moon, for example, rules all planets in Cancer—it is the dispositor of any planet in Cancer in the chart. Planets in Cancer will look to the Moon for guidance on how they can express themselves. The ruling planet is thought to impose form and structure on the expression of the planet ruled. Of course, the quality of the guidance, and the nature of the form and structure imposed, are going to depend entirely on the location and position of the ruling planet. Mars in Cancer, for example, will tend to be more grounded and practical in its expression if the Moon is in Taurus, and more scattered and quick to react if the Moon is instead in Gemini.

We can create a diagram of how the planets in the chart relate to each other based on their rulerships, called a dispositor tree. Dispositor trees are extremely helpful in uncovering the themes of a natal chart because they quickly and obviously reveal which planets are the bosses, and which planets must do the bidding of the ruling planets.

When creating a dispositor tree, we always begin with planets in their own rulership: these planets will be at the top of the tree because they are their own rulers. We then work through the rest of the planets in the tree, starting with the planets that are directly ruled by the planet in rulership, then moving down to the next level by looking for the planets ruled by these planets, and so on. Although the outer planets will be included in the dispositor tree, they do not rule anything themselves; they are only ruled.

First, let's look at a relatively simple dispositor tree for Liza Minelli. Every single planet in Liza's chart can be traced back to her Moon in Cancer. Because her Moon in Cancer effectively rules or disposes her entire chart, it is called the sole dispositor or final dispositor, which in interpretation would mean that just about everything in her life gets filtered through her Moon. In other words, the boss of Liza's chart is her Moon.

Sometimes instead of a planet in rulership being at the top of a tree, we will find a pair of planets in mutual reception by rulership. This is the case with another actress, Meryl Streep, who has her Moon in Taurus and her Venus in Cancer. (Mutual receptions will be covered in more detail in chapter 8). We'll be examining Streep's chart in detail in later chapters, but for now, let's take a look at her dispositor trees. Notice how Streep's chart is split between the planets that "report" to her Mercury in Gemini, and the planets that "report" to her Moon/Venus mutual reception. Right away we can tell that Streep has a very clear division between her emotional and feeling nature and her intellectual approach to the world, something that will prove to be a key theme in her chart.

Not all dispositor trees are as neat and tidy as these two examples. Often, we end up with a chart where three or more planets are linked to each other, and they in turn rule the rest of the chart, as is the case with Sylvester Stallone (whose chart we will also be looking at in greater detail in chapters 6 and 10).

In Stallone's case, his Sun in Cancer is ruled by his Moon in Libra; his Moon in Libra is ruled by his Venus in Leo; and his Venus in Leo is ruled by his Sun in Cancer. Every other planet in his chart reports to one of these three planets. Stallone's chart, then, is not ruled by a single planet, but rather by a committee made up of the Sun, Moon, and Venus; and since none of these three planets have any real autonomy in the chart, since they each answer to the others, this has the potential to set up an inherent struggle for Stallone. Every choice, every action, every decision that he makes will first have to meet with the approval of the committee. Like any governing body, each member of the committee has its own agenda, and since each member of this particular committee is also peregrine, we're not looking at a terribly efficient process.

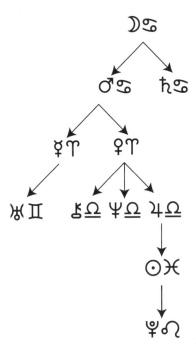

Figure 5. Liza Minelli's Dispositor Tree

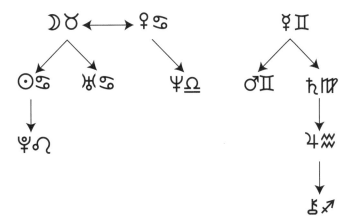

Figure 6. Meryl Streep's Dispositor Tree

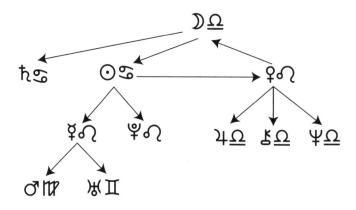

Figure 7. Sylvester Stallone's Dispositor Tree

5

Interpreting
Planets in Signs

Now that we have a basic understanding of the essential dignities, we can begin to work with them and understand how to interpret the planets in the signs, and discover the types of performances each actor is likely to give in each role. The reason for learning how to evaluate the relative strength of a planet in a sign through the essential dignities is that this can help us to come up with more detailed, accurate, and well-reasoned interpretations. Most importantly, with practice, this can make the difference between being able come up with our own individual interpretations of the planets in the signs, and having to look up someone else's interpretations in an astrological "cookbook." At the end of the chapter, we will spend a little time on the outer planets in the signs, but since the outer planets define generations and not personality traits, interpreting them requires a different approach.

Basic interpretation is relatively simple: we simply combine the core essence and expression of the planet with the motivation and style of the sign. For example, the Sun in Aries is motivated to express individuality (the Sun) through taking impulsive, direct, and pioneering actions (Aries). Taking a planet's essential dignity into account helps to understand more about how a planet is likely to express itself in a given sign—what the planet's core motivation is, and how easily it can discover its goals and move toward achieving them. This is what we're going to look at next.

The Sun

Rulership: Leo

Exaltation: Aries

Triplicity: Fire (day)

Detriment: Aquarius

Fall: Libra

Peregrine: Taurus, Cancer, Libra, Sagittarius (by night), Aquarius, Pisces, Gemini (1° to 20°), Virgo (11° to 30°), Scorpio (1° to 10°, 21° to 30°), Capricorn (1° to 20°)

The nature of the Sun is diurnal, yang, one-pointed, focused, and expressive. The Sun is obviously going to be stronger and give a more convincing performance in signs (or roles) that embody and support this energy.

The Sun in Fire Signs

The Sun is the triplicity ruler of fire during the day, and the expressive, focused, intense energy of fire can certainly support the Sun in its expression—but not all fire signs are created equal, as we are about to see.

Sun in Aries

The Sun in Aries is very well placed, as Aries is the sign of the Sun's exaltation. Aries is, of course, the most focused and single-minded of all the signs, and the most concerned with identity. These motivations are very familiar to the Sun, and resonate well with the Sun's nature. In Aries, the Sun is motivated to express individuality and identity through taking direct and impulsive action. When a planet is in exaltation, it doesn't get to set its own agenda, but things are done for it on its behalf. It is treated like an honored guest, and is generally on its best behavior. Aries sets a full schedule of activities for the Sun, with a strong focus on starting new projects and taking direct action. Aries, however, doesn't really care about recognition for its work, and the Sun in Aries is not really able to sit back and be appreciated in the way that it can in Leo. As with Leo, the Sun in Aries tends to be far more lucky in a day chart than in a night chart; in a day chart, the Sun is far more likely to enjoy the agenda set by its host than it will in a night chart.

Sun in Leo

Unquestionably, the Sun's starring role (literally) is in Leo. The Sun in Leo is motivated to express individuality and identity through creating and giving to others from the heart. When the Sun is in Leo, it gets to express its true nature, to shine, to give warmth and light, and to be a unique and creative individual. During the day, the Sun gets an extra boost in Leo by also being in its own triplicity. This is an important distinction! Remember, when a planet is in the sign it rules, it is its own boss—and no one is going to dare to tell it "no" under any circumstances. This means that planets in the signs they rule can often get themselves into some pretty unfortunate circumstances. Since dignity by triplicity generally means that a planet is lucky, that they have a knack for being in the right place at the right time, the Sun in Leo in a day chart may be less likely to shoot itself in the foot. Triplicity rulership doesn't make the Sun in Leo any less prone to ego attacks and prima donna behavior, the traps and pitfalls of Leo, but it does mean that the things the Sun decides it's going to do have a way of turning out much better than they have a right to.

Sun in Sagittarius

Finally, we have the Sun in Sagittarius, the last of the fire signs. The Sun in Sagittarius is motivated to express its individuality through exploring our relationship as individuals to the universe. The only dignity that the Sun has in Sagittarius is triplicity rulership, and that's only in a day chart. In a night chart, the Sun is peregrine in Sagittarius. Why is Sagittarius so different from Leo and Aries? Sagittarius is focused on the relationship of the individual to the universe; Leo and Aries are focused entirely on the expression of individual identity. Sagittarius is motivated to explore things that are bigger than our own sense of self, concepts with which the Sun is neither too familiar nor too comfortable. In a day chart, the Sun in Sagittarius is lucky: it is able to maintain a focus on the expression of individual identity, while it explores the vast unknown territories of the universe. In a night chart, however, the Sun in Sagittarius is peregrine: it tends to wander, exploring the cosmos, focusing on the big picture and hoping to discover its individuality by working from the outside in.

The Sun in Air Signs

While the Sun is usually quite comfortable in the focused, one-pointed energy of the fire signs, the Sun is equally as uncomfortable in the dual-natured energy of the air signs. The Sun needs to express individual identity, while the air signs all operate in terms of relationships, not of individuals.

Sun in Gemini

The Sun in Gemini is not quite as uncomfortable as it is in Libra and Aquarius. In Gemini, the Sun expresses and explores its individual identity through communication, thought, logic, and exploration of duality. Since Gemini is about our relationship to the environment, not to other individuals, the Sun isn't actively discouraged from self-expression; but Gemini is still an air sign, and the embodiment of duality. The Sun is the most comfortable when it can take direct action. Gemini, however, always offers a choice. The Sun is peregrine for most of Gemini, only having dignity by face for the last 10° of the sign. What is the most challenging for the Sun in Gemini is that Gemini has such difficulty focusing on anything, and is so changeable. In order for the Sun to express itself effectively, it requires focus. The Sun in Gemini, however, finds it very difficult to focus on one thing at a time, and ultimately ends up trying to create a single, integrated identity from a multitude of different facets. The Sun in the last 10° of Gemini has some conscious awareness of this, and the fact that it tends to worry about its lack of constancy gives it some direction, which at least is enough to stop the wandering effect of being peregrine.

Sun in Libra

The Sun in Libra is in the sign of its fall, and the Sun is peregrine throughout Libra as well. Libra is not quite as difficult an energy for the Sun to deal with as Aquarius energy. The Sun in Libra expresses its individual identity through harmony, balance, and one-to-one relationships. The Sun in Libra is not necessarily weak, it is simply in a situation where it is not able to express itself in the way that it would like. Planets in fall are the victims of circumstances beyond their control. Libra, of course, is the sign that is about one-to-one relationships between individuals. The Sun is uncomfortable in Libra because Libra makes the Sun constantly aware that every time it tries to express its individuality, it has an impact on other people. The Sun is entirely self-centered and isn't naturally aware that there even *are* other people, so it's in very unfamiliar territory here. Ultimately, Libra energy is about learning how to express individuality completely, while maintaining good boundaries with other people; unlike Aquarius, at least Libra does acknowledge the individual. The Sun in Libra can learn how to express itself fully, but because the Sun is peregrine in Libra, it is in completely unfamiliar territory. The Sun in Libra discovers the rules of relationships through trial and error, but ultimately, it can gain enough of an understanding of them to function quite well.

Sun in Aquarius

The Sun in Aquarius is in the sign of its detriment, and the Sun is also peregrine throughout Aquarius. Why is Aquarius such a difficult energy for the Sun? Aquarius energy is entirely focused on the group consciousness and has tremendous difficulty in even acknowledging that the group is made up of individuals, each with their own unique needs. The Sun in Aquarius is motivated to discover and express its individual identity through identifying with the group consciousness, and putting the needs of the group ahead of the needs of any individual in the group. For the Sun in Aquarius, the process of learning how to express itself consists of peeling away layers of the group consciousness and discovering what parts of the group consciousness support the Sun's individual identity, and what parts do not.

The Sun in Earth Signs

The Sun is not terribly comfortable in earth signs, either, because they are too slow and plodding in their expression. The Sun needs freedom to express itself; it wants to be able to radiate, not to have to worry about how practical things are.

Sun in Taurus

The Sun is peregrine through all of Taurus, the slowest of the earth signs. In Taurus, the Sun is motivated to express individual identity through exploring and experiencing the physical plane. While it's quite easy for the Sun in Taurus to identify with our bodies and our possessions, our true identity is in fact the energy that animates our bodies, not the physical body itself. Certainly, given enough time and enough digging, it is possible to uncover our spirit, our spark of life and individuality at the center of our physical forms; but this is hardly an obvious or a direct path to take, as evidenced by the peregrine status of the Sun in earth signs. Taurus energy is the most focused on the status quo, and in this fixed earth sign, the Sun has to struggle to get beyond the comfort zone of the physical. The Sun in Taurus expresses its light in a slow, steady, comfortable manner. Individuals with the Sun in Taurus are energized and supported by following a well-established routine, and prefer to move through life at a leisurely, if somewhat methodical, pace.

Sun in Virgo

The Sun is peregrine for all but the first 10° of Virgo, where it has dignity by face. The Sun in Virgo expresses its individual identity through being of service and of use to others. The Sun in Virgo defines itself based on how useful it is, and is always striving to perfect and improve the physical realm; but Virgo is still an earth sign, and the Sun in Virgo will still tend to look only as far as the physical for its expression. Virgo's dedication to service to others often feels incompatible with the Sun's fundamental need to express individuality, and the Sun in Virgo can often attempt to define and express itself in terms of how it helps others. The analytical energy of Virgo provides a compass for the Sun during the first 10° of Virgo, so here the Sun at least can try to analyze its way through the physical to discover its true self. For the last 20° of Virgo, however, the Sun is again peregrine, focusing perhaps too much on the details to be able to see the big picture, and is too concerned with assisting others to acknowledge the needs of the individual self.

Sun in Capricorn

In Capricorn, the Sun is motivated to create a physical representation of individual identity—but for the first 20° of Capricorn, where the Sun is peregrine, the approach tends to be to work from the physical end first; rather like starting with a block of marble and a chisel without having a clear picture of what you are trying to sculpt. You can certainly end up with a thing of beauty when you're done, but it's going to take a long time, and be a rather confusing and winding process. Of all the earth signs, the Sun in Capricorn perhaps has the easiest time because Capricorn is a cardinal sign, and by nature is active, outgoing, and expressive. The challenge, of course, is that Capricorn is focused entirely on the physical plane, and the Sun in Capricorn may tend to base its sense of self on its accomplishments and achievements in the world.

The Sun in Water Signs

The Sun is mostly peregrine in water signs (Cancer, Scorpio, and Pisces, except from 11° to 20° of Scorpio, where it has dignity by face). Water signs operate on a deep, emotional level, while the Sun is the most comfortable when it is allowed to express itself freely. Water signs have the most difficulty communicating on a surface level, and the Sun in water signs often has to struggle to shine through.

Sun in Cancer

The Sun in Cancer is motivated to form emotional connections with others, and motivated by the need for these emotional connections. Cancer energy can be very difficult for the Sun because the Sun needs to feel self-reliant, and Cancer energy often believes that it cannot survive without the support of others. Cancer is a cardinal sign and, like the Sun, is concerned with the question of identity; but the Sun in Cancer tries to define itself in terms of its emotional connections with others. In this respect, the Sun in Cancer faces many of the same challenges as the Sun in air signs: to learn how to discover and express its individual identity directly, rather than in the context of a relationship. The Sun in Cancer wanders until it can discover the truth that we can meet our own emotional needs, that we are whole and complete in and of ourselves.

Sun in Scorpio

The Sun in Scorpio wants to get to the bottom of things, and is motivated to explore what is hidden, dark, and forgotten. Scorpio energy has the most difficulty of all the signs with outward expression. One of the key Scorpio processes involves the death of the ego, which enables us to merge with another individual on a fundamental, emotional, and spiritual level. The ego, however, is instrumental in helping us define, establish, and express our individual identities. In order for us to discover our true selves, we must be willing to let go of our egos; however, the Sun usually finds it quite useful to at least be able to work with the ego initially to define some boundaries and get a feel for the shape of our individual identities. The Sun in Scorpio would rather skip this process and instead try to get right to the heart of the matter—Scorpio doesn't have time for small talk. Because of Scorpio's single-mindedness and determination to discover what is hidden, the Sun is not peregrine for the middle 10° of Scorpio: it has direction and knows that it can ultimately find its true core essence if it just digs deep enough. For the rest of Scorpio, however, the Sun will tend to wander, exploring its emotional and soul connections and unconscious nature in search of its true self, but without a strong reference point in the more conscious world.

Sun in Pisces

Sun in Pisces is placed in the sign that is motivated to dissolve all boundaries, including our sense of individuality and separation from the source. Needless to say, this is not comfortable for the Sun, and it must learn how to discover and express its individual essence, even though that essence is beginning to merge with the universe. Whereas Scorpio energy pursues the death of the ego and wants to merge with another individual, Pisces energy completely dissolves the ego and wants to merge with all creation. Pisces energy is completely without structure or boundaries, and ultimately, we at least need the illusion of these boundaries in order to maintain an individual identity. The result is that the Sun in Pisces is motivated to express its individuality by dissolving and denying the very things that defined it in the first place. This tends to have a Zen quality to it, and ultimately requires a very delicate balance; while the Sun in Pisces can shine through by expressing compassion for others, it must be careful not to sacrifice itself in the name of helping others.

The Moon

Rulership: Cancer

Exaltation: Taurus

Triplicity: Earth (night)

Detriment: Capricorn

Fall: Scorpio

Peregrine: Aries, Gemini, Leo, Virgo (by day), Scorpio, Capricorn (by day), Pisces, Libra (11° to 30°), Sagittarius (1° to 10°, 21° to 30°), Aquarius (1° to 20°)

The nature of the Moon is nocturnal, yin, receptive, and containing. The Moon gives form to the Sun's expression, and represents our emotional, unconscious, feeling, and soul nature. The roles that we know and love the Moon to play are the ones where the Moon is allowed to express its full emotional range, in all its infinite subtlety, as well as roles that provide good structure and grounding to support, contain, and focus the Moon's emotional nature. Even though the Moon would seem to be the most comfortable in water and earth signs (and indeed, it is), the Moon is more comfortable in some signs than in others.

The Moon in Water Signs

Being of such a fundamentally emotional nature, the Moon is naturally associated with the element of water; and at least in Cancer, the Moon is at its most powerful. But Cancer is, in fact, the only water sign where the Moon has any dignity at all.

Moon in Cancer

When the Moon is in rulership in Cancer, it becomes the embodiment of the universal mother energy. It is able to feel and express the full range of emotions, to hold and preserve the memory of all experiences. The Moon in Cancer, motivated to establish and express our emotional and soul identity, truly understands the universal longing to be nurtured and protected, to return to the source. As Cancer is the signature role for the Moon, it will always give a powerful, emotional performance in this sign. In Cancer, the Moon does not usually feel the need for any kind of restraint—it's not so much a question of overacting, but more one of overreacting. Everything is a big deal to the Moon in Cancer, and each and every scene must demonstrate the Moon's full emotional range. Its feelings are true, but they're not always entirely appropriate at the time they're being expressed. The Moon in Cancer has to learn that it is not the only actor, and that it is not the focus of every scene. While the Moon in Cancer feels very safe and comfortable expressing and sharing emotions, the Moon in Cancer can also reach a point where the *only* time it feels safe is when it is expressing and sharing emotions with others. The Moon in Cancer is always focused on its core emotional and survival needs, and if these needs aren't being met, the Moon in Cancer can become exceedingly dependent on the support of others.

Moon in Scorpio

The Moon in Scorpio is in the sign of its fall; additionally, the Moon is peregrine through the entire sign of Scorpio. Why is Scorpio such a difficult energy for the Moon to express itself in? Scorpio experiences emotions perhaps with the greatest intensity of all the signs, something that the Moon should be able to enjoy; but Scorpio also has the greatest difficulty expressing itself, and this is where the Moon encounters the challenges. Planets in fall tend to operate on the physical plane, and individuals with the Moon in Scorpio are highly aware of this. If they are not able to express their feelings, the emotional blocks will manifest in their physical bodies, and they will get physically ill—most frequently in the form of stomach discomfort (the Moon rules the stomach). The peregrine aspect of the Moon in Scorpio exists both because the Moon in Scorpio must search for other ways to express itself, and because Scorpio energy is primarily focused on one-to-one relationships. Individuals with the Moon in Scorpio often find that their built-up emotional energy tends to get focused and expressed (often with tremendous intensity) in their relationships, but not in other areas of their life. As the Moon wanders in Scorpio, these individuals search for ways that they can express their Moons in a more even, moderated manner, and experience emotional connections in all areas of their lives, not only in relationships.

Moon in Pisces

Moon in Pisces is peregrine, although not nearly as challenged as the Moon in Scorpio. Actually, the Moon in Pisces has quite the opposite challenge from what it has in Scorpio. Expression of emotions is not a problem for Pisces energy; focus, however, is. The Moon in Pisces becomes so hypersensitive that individuals with the Moon in Pisces become receptors for all the emotions around them—and since Pisces energy is about transmuting negativity, the Moon in Pisces often becomes an unconscious magnet for other people's negativity. The Moon in Pisces is comfortable expressing compassion, love, and understanding, and will absorb and transmute the pain and emotional discomfort of others almost instinctively. Because the Moon in Pisces radiates compassion and acceptance, individuals with the Moon in Pisces naturally attract other individuals who need someone who will really listen to their problems. What this means is that individuals with the Moon in Pisces *must* learn how to take care of their personal energy fields, and to clear and release the negativity that they have picked up during the day. As the Moon in Pisces wanders and evolves, it must learn how to stay focused and to discriminate between its own emotions and those that it has absorbed from others.

The Moon in Earth Signs

The Moon is the nocturnal triplicity ruler of the element of earth. In a night chart, the energy of the earth signs provides a necessary and welcome source of structure and grounding, helping to focus and balance the Moon's fundamentally changeable and emotional nature. In a day chart, however, the overly practical nature of the earth signs takes precedence, and the Moon can find it difficult to express itself at all.

Moon in Taurus

The Moon is exalted in the sign of Taurus, and also dignified by triplicity at night. Taurus is the most sensual and stable of all the earth Signs, and provides a container to hold and support the Moon's energy without restricting the Moon's ability to express itself. The Moon in Taurus is Meryl Streep working with an excellent director: she's not allowed to turn every scene into an emotional rollercoaster; rather, the emphasis is on subtlety and subtext, and on gradually building toward an Oscar-winning climax. It's not necessarily what the Moon (or Meryl, for that matter) wants, but the choices are being made in the Moon's best interest, and the results are usually excellent. In a night chart, when the Moon is also dignified by triplicity, it can really start to sink its teeth into the performance, discovering how to experience and express emotions through the physical plane. The Moon in Taurus finds comfort and security in the physical and the material plane. The Moon in Taurus can, however, sometimes overidentify with the physical and the sensual, using pleasure and material possessions as a way to avoid unpleasant emotions.

Moon in Virgo

As with the water signs, the Moon is not nearly as well supported in the other earth signs as it is in Taurus. The Moon in Virgo is peregrine in a day chart, but has dignity by triplicity by night. In a day chart, Virgo's focus on details and on what is logical and practical can make the Moon quite uncomfortable expressing emotions. Virgo acts methodically, while the Moon wants to operate on an instinctive level. The Moon in Virgo, in a day chart, wanders until it can find the point where it can understand the logical and rational reasons for instinctive reactions. Peregrine or not, the Moon in Virgo will always be concerned with learning and improving its ability to express emotions; but while the Moon in Virgo is the most comfortable and secure when things are well organized, precise, neat, and logical, these concepts rarely describe our lives for any length of time, and almost never apply to our emotions. The Moon in Virgo may tend to worry too much about understanding and analyzing emotions. Up to a point, this detached and analytical approach provides a welcome balance and structure to the Moon's emotional nature; but when the Moon in Virgo becomes too concerned with analyzing its feelings, it finds it increasingly difficult to express them in the first place.

Moon in Capricorn

The Moon in Capricorn is in the sign of its detriment, and also peregrine during the day. In a night chart, the Moon in Capricorn is both dignified (triplicity) and debilitated (detriment) at the same time. Planets in detriment are operating on the mental and emotional plane; and individuals with the Moon in Capricorn tend to worry about how appropriate their emotional responses are. Planets in detriment are still very strong—but they get themselves into difficult situations because of their strength, and must learn how to use their strength in a less familiar and comfortable manner in order to get out of trouble. The Moon in Capricorn is like a gifted actress who, after being savaged by the critics because she has a tendency to overact, becomes afraid to show any emotional range at all. The Moon in Capricorn is often afraid to express emotions, but what the Moon in Capricorn is learning is how to express emotions in an appropriate and acceptable manner. In a day chart, this lesson can be more challenging because the Moon is peregrine and wandering, and does not have anyone to guide it. In a night chart, however, when the Moon is dignified by triplicity, the Moon finds some positive reinforcement very quickly, and is quick to find situations where it can express itself, albeit in a more structured and restrained manner.

The Moon in Fire Signs

The Moon is peregrine in all fire signs except from 11° to 20° of Sagittarius, where it has dignity only by face. Fire signs are too one-pointed in nature, and too focused on only a limited range of emotions, to allow the Moon the free-dom to experience its entire emotional repertoire.

Moon in Aries

Impulse control is always an issue for planets in Aries, and the Moon in Aries is no exception. In Aries, the Moon has a tendency to overreact, and to do so very quickly—most frequently with either anger or joy. The Moon in Aries is only concerned with expressing itself freely, and does not find it easy to consider how appropriate a given reaction may be at the time. In Aries, the Moon wanders primarily because it is so intent on taking action that it never occurs to the Moon to stop and ask for directions. The Moon in Aries wants to express emotions immediately and then move on. The Moon in Aries does not hold a grudge; once it is able to express itself, the Moon in Aries is able to move on. The biggest challenge for individuals with the Moon in Aries is that when they are not able to express their feelings immediately, anger and frustration quickly enter the picture.

Moon in Leo

The Moon in Leo can become very self-centered. Leo energy is warm and generous, and the Moon in Leo enjoys giving and sharing, nurturing and protecting others; but Leo energy must be acknowledged and appreciated for its gifts. The Moon in Leo is only truly comfortable when it is the center of attention, and it is not above acting out emotionally in order to keep it that way. The Moon in Leo wanders because it is too focused on its individual self-worth and too concerned with receiving emotional validation from others. In Leo, the Moon has to learn how to connect with the group consciousness and rediscover its eternal connection to the source.

Moon in Sagittarius

In Sagittarius, the Moon is following a quest for truth and understanding. Individuals with the Moon in Sagittarius look for comfort and security through higher knowledge and an appreciation for how they as individuals fit into the greater, universal plan. Sagittarius energy is famous for its inadvertent lack of tact, and the Moon in Sagittarius can often seem to express more "tough love" than in other signs. Emotions and feelings are only a path to discover the ultimate truth, and the Moon in Sagittarius does not tend to dwell on the past, or on emotional trespasses. For most of Sagittarius, the Moon is peregrine, wandering largely because it must learn how to truly express its emotional and nurturing nature as a part of its quest for truth. The Moon has dignity by face from 11° to 20° of Sagittarius, where it at least understands that compassion is an important key to its journey, although truly expressing and experiencing compassion is still a difficult task.

The Moon in Air Signs

As with the fire signs, the Moon is not very comfortable in air signs, and is peregrine in air signs except from 1° to 10° of Libra and 21° to 30° of Aquarius, where it has dignity only by face.

Moon in Gemini

The changeable and social energy of Gemini is difficult for the Moon, because Gemini doesn't stay in one place long enough to form any kind of emotional connection. Gemini is always in motion, always exploring new possibilities and experiences, but only touching on them briefly before moving on. The Moon in Gemini will wander until it discovers enough common themes and connections between the various expressions of duality in the world to be able to encompass and experience the essence of the opposites all at once. Only then will it be able to focus long enough to put down roots and explore what lies beneath the surface. The Moon in Gemini is the most comfortable and secure when being presented with new ideas and information. Emotions are expressed with a light touch, and no emotion is ever sustained for very long.

Moon in Libra

The Moon in Libra is most comfortable when the world is beautiful, balanced, and harmonious. Emotions and feelings have a tendency to throw things out of balance, and the Moon in Libra is always very careful to avoid expressing anything that could disturb the peace (or more often, the surface appearance of peace). For the first 10° of Libra, the Moon has dignity by face, and here, at least, it understands that true balance can only be achieved in relationships when both individuals are expressing their true selves fully—and this includes expressing and sharing their emotional natures as well. The Moon understands this for the first 10° of Libra, but is nonetheless scared to express itself.

For the last 20° of Libra, the Moon is completely peregrine, and it must wander while it tries to discover that true balance and harmony extend far below the surface, and in order to experience true balance, we must be willing to express our true feelings and emotions.

Moon in Aquarius

The Moon in Aquarius has a tremendous amount of compassion on an abstract, removed plane. It finds the idea of nurturing, protecting, and supporting humanity extremely appealing; but when the Moon in Aquarius has to actually interact with individual humans, it is at a serious disadvantage. Interacting with and nurturing individuals requires recognizing the importance of individuals, something that Aquarius energy finds very challenging. The Moon in Aquarius can nurture the group, support the cause, and give of itself in abstract ways (donating money to charity, for example); but for the first 20° of Aquarius, the Moon in Aquarius is peregrine, and must go in search of the true meaning of compassion—that which comes as much from the heart as it does from the head. For the last 10° of Aquarius, the Moon does have dignity by face. Here, at least, it understands that a more personal level of involvement is called for, which gives it a certain amount of focus and direction; but with dignity only by face, the Moon still struggles—the Moon in Aquarius is aware that it must give of itself, but it is still frightened and completely unfamiliar with how to do so.

Mercury

Rulership: Gemini and Virgo

Exaltation: Virgo

Triplicity: Air (night)

Detriment: Sagittarius and Pisces

Fall: Pisces

Peregrine: Aries (1° to 14°, 21° to 30°), Taurus (15° to 30°), Cancer (1° to 10°, 21° to 30°), Leo (1° to 6°, 13° to 30°), Libra (by day, 1° to 19°, 24° to 30°), Scorpio (1° to 20°, 27° to 30°), Sagittarius (11° to 14°, 19° to 30°), Capricorn (1° to 6°, 12° to 30°), Aquarius (by day, 1° to 6°, 21° to 30°), Pisces (1° to 14°, 24° to 30°)

Mercury is the only completely neutral body in astrology. Mercury is equally diurnal and nocturnal, masculine and feminine, and represents our ability to reason, think, and communicate. Because Mercury is so inherently flexible and able to embody and encompass the widest range of energies and expressions, Mercury has at least some dignity in every sign, even signs where it is also debilitated. Mercury wants to make connections, to gather information, and to explore, and functions at its best in signs that support Mercury's speed and flexibility.

Mercury in Air Signs

We tend to associate Mercury with the mental and social element of air, and indeed, Mercury is the nighttime triplicity ruler of air, as well as the ruler of Gemini, the first air sign. Mercury doesn't do nearly as well in the later air signs, though, where the focus on perspective can limit Mercury's natural flexibility and speed.

Mercury in Gemini

Mercury in Gemini enhances Mercury's dual nature, and in Gemini, Mercury is at its most curious. Mercury in Gemini is able to operate at top speed, exploring the world and making new discoveries and connections. Mercury calls all the shots in Gemini, and it can be dazzling to behold (think Robin Williams on amphetamines); but as is always the case with a planet in rulership, Mercury in Gemini is apt to make some interesting choices. Because Mercury is the essence of duality, and Gemini is the sign that expresses duality most clearly, Mercury in Gemini can have a great deal of difficulty focusing on any one thing for any length of time. Moreover, let us not forget that one of the faces of Mercury is the trickster—Mercury in Gemini is far more likely to pull the "evil twin" act than it is in other signs. Mercury in Gemini can delight in playing tricks, in stirring things up—a barbed comment here, a bit of well-placed gossip there, and just watch how interesting things can get. In a night chart, when Mercury is also dignified by triplicity, Mercury in Gemini will tend to be far more lucky, and to get into less trouble with its pranks.

Mercury in Libra

Mercury in Libra is quite a different story. While Libra is an air sign, and operates on the mental and emotional plane where Mercury is quite comfortable,

Libra is also very focused on one particular aspect of the mental and emotional plane: one-to-one relationships. Libra is concerned with the question of balance, and with the question of responsibility for our actions. Mercury in Libra finds it difficult to explore any single idea without devoting equal time and energy to the opposite point of view. These concepts aren't necessarily too comfortable for Mercury to work with. In a nocturnal chart, Mercury has dignity by triplicity, and is able to balance Libra's need for harmony with Mercury's inherent appreciation for duality. Mercury isn't able to explore things quite as freely as it might like, but Mercury is still able to find enough material to work with in the interpersonal relationship arena that Mercury in Libra can turn in a very convincing performance. In a day chart, however, Mercury in Libra is peregrine, except for being in terms from 19° to 24° of Libra. In a day chart, when Saturn is the triplicity ruler of air, Mercury can feel limited by the need to consider the consequences of its actions; and having to worry about saying the wrong thing at the wrong time means that Mercury isn't able to move as quickly as it likes, or with as much objectivity. When Mercury is dignified by terms, it makes a valiant effort to communicate—it's no longer wandering, and it understands the context and structures that it's been given, but it still struggles to find the freedom to communicate and express itself fully while maintaining the balance and harmony that Libra requires.

Mercury in Aquarius

Mercury in Aquarius fares a little better than it does in Libra. Aquarius is also Saturn-ruled and concerned with structures and responsibilities; but Aquarius takes a much broader and more abstract point of view—our place in society as opposed to our role in relationships—and this gives Mercury a bit more to work with. Mercury in Aquarius is free to express a much broader range of ideas, although overall it will tend to be attracted to issues relating to personal freedom and social dynamics. As with Libra, in a night chart Mercury is able to function quite well—it is able to latch onto the objective (if somewhat idealistic) energy of Aquarius, and express itself quite comfortably. In a day chart, however, Mercury has more difficulty. The rules and structures of Aquarius make independent thought (or at least thoughts and ideas that don't support the ideals of the group) very difficult. Mercury has dignity by term from 6° to 12° of Aquarius, and by face from 11° to 20° of Aquarius (and from 11° to 12°

of Aquarius, Mercury gathers up enough "points" by being both in terms and face to actually become quite effective). For the rest of Aquarius, though, in a day chart, Mercury is peregrine, wandering while it tries to discover how to explore and express its own ideas within the context of the group environment.

Mercury in Earth Signs

Mercury has a love-hate relationship with the element of earth. On one hand, earth is just the thing to ground, focus, and stabilize Mercury's overly active and changeable nature, and enable Mercury to put some of its ideas to more practical use. On the other hand, earth is by nature so slow and plodding that Mercury can get too bogged down to function well at all.

Mercury in Taurus

Mercury is peregrine for the second half of Taurus, but not for the first half. Granted, Mercury isn't very strong in the first half of Taurus—it has dignity by face for the first 10°, and dignity by term from 8° to 15°. For the first 8° of Taurus, Mercury is worried: it can't act quickly at all (Taurus is the slowest of the signs), and although it understands that forethought and focus are important qualities, it hasn't quite mastered them. Between 8° to 10° of Taurus, when Mercury is dignified by both term and face, Mercury finds the point of balance where even though it can't act as quickly as it wants to, when it does act, it does so with precision and efficiency. From 11° to 15° of Taurus, Mercury begins to lose its edge, and for the last half of Taurus, Mercury is peregrine, wandering, and trying to capture that point of balance where it can express itself with efficiency and subtlety. Mercury in Taurus isn't going to waste a lot of time with small talk; and for that reason, when Mercury in Taurus does speak up, it usually has something very important and well-considered to say. Individuals with Mercury in Taurus will communicate as much through the physical as they will with words. They frequently tend to be rather kinesthetic in their approach to the world, and are primarily concerned with how something *feels* to them.

Mercury in Virgo

Not only does Mercury rule Virgo, Mercury is also exalted in Virgo. It's very difficult for a planet to be more strongly dignified than Mercury is in Virgo. Virgo brings out the precise, detail-oriented, analytical side of Mercury. Mercury in

Gemini is merely curious, while Mercury in Virgo is curious with a purpose: to learn how things work in order to make them better. Mercury in Virgo calls the shots because it's in a sign that it rules; but since Mercury is also exalted in Virgo, it has an entourage of sorts. Mercury gets to set its own agenda, but it also has some well-respected advisors and assistants who work very hard to make sure that Mercury stays focused and on track. Mercury in Virgo is, then, an "A-list" star with an "A-list" manager and press agent who make sure that Mercury in Virgo is always seen in the best possible light. Still, Mercury in Virgo can become overly critical and so focused on the details that it can't even conceive of the larger scheme of things. It's not that Mercury's observations aren't accurate—they usually are. It's just that they're not always appreciated, no matter how well intended they are.

Mercury in Capricorn

Mercury in Capricorn has the most difficulty of all the earth signs. Peregrine, except for having dignity by term from 6° to 12°, Mercury in Capricorn becomes so focused on the practical and tangible applications of its ideas that it has great difficulty exploring new possibilities. Because Capricorn is a cardinal sign and is fundamentally concerned with the question of identity, Mercury in Capricorn takes its ideas and perceptions very personally, and must be careful to avoid becoming ego-involved and argumentative. Capricorn energy is about maintaining the status quo, and being efficient and responsible. Capricorn is not big on imagination or flights of fancy. When Mercury is in terms in Capricorn, Mercury can try to channel its imagination toward more practical uses, with limited effectiveness; but for the rest of Capricorn, Mercury wanders, trying to discover how to think and explore outside of the box, while still being limited by the box itself.

Mercury in Fire Signs

Mercury doesn't have any particular affinity with fire signs. When all is said and done, fire tends to be too focused and one-pointed for Mercury's taste, and at the same time, tends to encourage Mercury to act more impulsively and aggressively—two qualities that Mercury does not need reinforced.

Mercury in Aries

Aries energy is too focused on expressing individual identity to even think about exploring anything else. Mercury in Aries becomes very limited by this energy: as fascinating a subject as each of us is, we're not really the center of the universe! Mercury needs more freedom to explore, and with more objectivity than Aries allows it. For most of Aries, Mercury is peregrine, wandering, and searching for an approach to understanding the universe that both reinforces its individual identity and at the same time accepts that the universe has more to offer and understand than the self. From 14° to 21° of Aries, Mercury has dignity by term, and is able to gain a certain amount of perspective; but terms isn't much of a dignity, and Mercury in Aries can operate along the lines of, "Well, that's enough talk about me. Let's talk about you. What do you think of me?" The biggest challenge for Mercury in Aries is the tendency to start talking before engaging the brain. Mercury in Aries communicates with a very direct and forthright approach that is often perceived as a challenge or invitation to debate the issue—and in typical Aries fashion, Mercury can often find that it has asserted itself into a corner and wound up in an argument that it can neither win nor concede without losing face.

Mercury in Leo

Mercury in Leo is much the same as Mercury in Aries, except that in Leo, Mercury is *really* concerned that you appreciate Mercury for how wonderful it is. Leo is one of the more dramatic signs, and Mercury in Leo can be a very dynamic, powerful, and charismatic communicator—but also one that loves the sound of its own voice (and wants you to love it, too). Mercury has dignity by term from 6° to 13° of Leo, and for these 7°, at least, Mercury is able to connect with the open and generous heart energy of Leo, and express and communicate this genuine warmth and generosity. For the rest of Leo, Mercury is peregrine, and will tend to wander until it learns not to rely on the support and approval of others for its perceptions, thoughts, and ideas. Leo energy is extremely creative, and Mercury in Leo often will express itself through writing, public speaking, or acting.

Mercury in Sagittarius

Mercury in Sagittarius fares the worst of all the fire signs. Mercury is only peregrine for half of Sagittarius, true, but Sagittarius is the sign of Mercury's detriment, and Mercury is always uncomfortable there. Sagittarius is one of Jupiter's signs, concerned with the quest for truth, freedom, and uncovering the big picture. Mercury, of course, is concerned with the little details and is so fascinated with the subtle nuances and infinite variety of experiences in life, that it's not even aware that there *is* a big picture in the first place. Planets in detriment are still very strong—but they've gotten themselves into a difficult spot because of their strength. Mercury in Sagittarius is convinced that the way to discover the big picture is by *really* focusing on the details, and that since the big picture is so big, then every little detail must be equally important. For half of Sagittarius, this approach isn't quite as disastrous as we might think. Mercury has dignity by face in the first 10° of Sagittarius, and by term from 14° to 19° of Sagittarius, and at least has some focus and direction. For the rest of Sagittarius, though, Mercury is both peregrine and in detriment, believing that each new idea, each new piece of information is the key to the truth—and often trying to convince others of this as well.

Mercury in Water Signs

Mercury isn't terribly happy in water signs. Water signs are too emotional and subjective for Mercury. Words are often poor tools for conveying feelings, and Mercury in water signs can have difficulty communicating clearly.

Mercury in Cancer

Mercury is peregrine in Cancer except from 11° to 20°, where it has dignity by face; and from 13° to 20°, Mercury also has dignity by term. In these degrees of Cancer, Mercury is able to communicate with a surprising level of focus, compassion, and love. For the rest of Cancer, however, Mercury is peregrine, struggling to pull words and concepts out of the emotional bath of Cancer. Even when Mercury has some dignity in Cancer, it still finds it difficult to be objective and detached. All communication is about emotional connections as far as Mercury in Cancer is concerned. Being a cardinal sign, Cancer is expressive and active, and Mercury in Cancer will reach out to others and try to bond with them. Mercury in Cancer has the greatest difficulty communicating with individuals who do not easily express emotions, because Mercury in Cancer listens more to *how* something is said than it does to what is actually said. Without a strong emotional undercurrent, Mercury in Cancer finds it very difficult to communicate.

Mercury in Scorpio

Mercury has an even more difficult time in Scorpio because Scorpio operates on the deepest, most intense emotional level of all the signs. Mercury in Scorpio has dignity by term from 21° to 27°, and here the intense and focused energy of Scorpio finally allows Mercury the ability to begin to convey the depths of its feelings. For the rest of Scorpio, Mercury is peregrine, and searches for ways to find the words that will carry forward the emotional, healing, and transformational energy of Scorpio. The biggest challenge for Mercury in Scorpio is learning how to translate the powerful emotional energy of Scorpio into words. Something is always lost in the translation, and Mercury in Scorpio finds this exceptionally frustrating. Mercury in Scorpio is fascinated by the darker, hidden motivations both of the self and of others. By sharing these emotions and feelings, Mercury in Scorpio hopes to create an emotional and spiritual connection with another individual. Mercury in Scorpio is far more comfortable plumbing the depths of the soul than it is carrying on polite conversation.

Mercury in Pisces

Mercury in Pisces is both in detriment *and* in fall, as well as being peregrine for all of Pisces except from 14° to 20°. Pisces is the least focused, least discriminating energy. In many ways, it is the antithesis of Mercury. Like Sagittarius, the other sign ruled by Jupiter, Pisces is focused on the big picture; Pisces is the energy that motivates us to return to the source, to remember that all separation is illusion, that we are truly one with everything in the universe. In Pisces, Mercury is operating both on the mental/emotional plane and on the physical plane, and Mercury's frustration in Pisces will manifest on both these levels. Mercury's primary function is to communicate, and the most important aspect of communication is how we describe the world to ourselves. Individuals with Mercury in Pisces have a *very* different understanding of the universe from most other people. Other people notice differences between things, but people with Mercury in Pisces see the fundamental connections between everything. Communicating this to individuals who don't have Mercury in Pisces, however, is a very big challenge—one that basically requires that these individuals learn how to see the world from an entirely different perspective, and then try to translate between the two. When Mercury has dignity by term in Pisces, it has more focus and perhaps an easier time bridging the gap between the different experiences of reality; but when Mercury is peregrine in Pisces, the journey can be long and winding. Pisces energy is extremely intuitive, something that Mercury doesn't particularly trust. Mercury wants to reason, think, and analyze, not to operate based on instinct and spiritual guidance; but in order for Mercury in Pisces to discover its true path, it must learn to listen to and follow its intuition.

Venus

Rulership: Taurus and Libra

Exaltation: Pisces

Triplicity: Earth (day)

Detriment: Aries and Scorpio

Fall: Virgo

Peregrine: Aries (1° to 6°, 14° to 20°), Gemini (1° to 14°, 21° to 30°), Cancer (11° to 20°, 27° to 30°), Leo (1° to 13°, 19° to 30°), Virgo (by night, 1° to 7°, 21° to 30°), Scorpio (1° to 14°), Sagittarius (1° to 8°, 14° to 30°), Capricorn (by night, 6° to 30°), Aquarius (11° to 12°, 20° to 30°)

Venus is nocturnal, yin, receptive, and responsive. Venus forms bonds and connections based on affinity and love, and Venus forms relationships in order to connect with something bigger than the individual self. Venus is receptive and emotional by nature, and does best in water and earth signs, much like the Moon (Venus shares rulership of the earth triplicity with the Moon). Venus' focus on relationships, beauty, and balance, though, is supported best not by earth or water, but by Libra, an air sign. Because Venus was one of the "benefic" planets, Venus has frequent dignity by term, and spends relatively little time peregrine.

Venus in Earth Signs

Venus rules the earth triplicity by day. In a day chart, the element of earth grounds Venus, providing support and structure, giving it form—not to mention the fact that the element of earth relates to physical comfort and sensory (and sensual) stimulation, areas where Venus is the happiest. In a night chart, however, the earth signs can become too practical and heavy for Venus. Venus needs to be able to dream, to create, and to aspire. In a nocturnal chart, instead of anchoring and supporting Venus' dreams, earth can weigh them down completely.

Venus in Taurus

The weight of the earth energy isn't an issue for Venus in Taurus, because Venus in Taurus is in rulership. Taurus brings out the sensual, hands-on, creative side of Venus. Venus in Taurus wants to experience the world—first-class, of course. Taurus is a very hard-working and practical energy, and so even though Venus in Taurus has very expensive tastes, it also understands the value of things and that sometimes we have to work hard in order to be able to afford the best that life has to offer. In a day chart, Venus in Taurus is also dignified by triplicity, and tends to be more focused—and generally more fortunate. Venus may be willing to work hard, but in a day chart, it tends to be in the right place at the right time, usually when someone else is willing to pick up the tab. In a night chart, Venus in Taurus has more of a tendency to focus on immediate gratification rather than on long-term comfort. Venus in Taurus values stability, loyalty, creativity, and practicality, and will tend to relate to others in a grounded, methodical, and rational manner.

Venus in Virgo

Venus in Virgo is in the sign of its fall. Planets in fall are in a difficult situation, but unlike planets in detriment, it's not one they created for themselves. It's not that they don't have any strength, it's just that the situation they're in doesn't call for any of their particular gifts. Planets in fall operate on the physical plane—a condition that Virgo, an earth sign concerned with perfecting the material and physical world, resonates with very strongly. Venus in Virgo can become so focused on the details, on the ways that things can be improved, that it finds it difficult to appreciate things the way they are. Needless to say, this can make forming relationships a bit of a challenge, because Venus in Virgo is always focused on perfection, and this can result in both finding fault with potential romantic partners, and in feeling that we are not perfect enough, and therefore don't deserve a worthy partner. In a day chart, Venus has dignity by triplicity, and its constructive criticism is far more likely to be met with the approval of others. From 10° to 13° of Virgo, when Venus is also dignified by both term and face, Venus actually comes out ahead of the game and is able to find a balance between appreciating things as they are and striving to improve them even more. In a night chart, however, Venus is peregrine and in fall for much of Virgo (except for 7° to 20°, where it has dignity by term and/or face). When Venus is peregrine in Virgo, Venus wanders, always seeking perfection, until it finally realizes that perfection is a process, not an end result. Venus in Virgo must learn to actually appreciate the beauty of the roses, even as it pulls out the weeds from the flower bed.

Venus in Capricorn

Venus is peregrine in a night chart for all but the first 6° of Capricorn. When Venus is peregrine in Capricorn, Venus tends to focus on the acquisition of material wealth in all forms. In and of itself, this isn't a bad thing, but Venus in Capricorn can sometimes choose relating to objects over relating to individuals. In interpersonal relationships, this can sometimes manifest as always keeping score, for example. Venus in Capricorn in a night chart tends to wander until it learns how to value intangible and impractical things (like feelings and emotions) at least as much as it values tangible and physical ones. In a day chart, however, when Venus is dignified by triplicity, Capricorn's energy grounds and focuses Venus. Venus can still be focused on the tangible aspects of pleasure (and of relationships), but when dignified by triplicity, Venus in Capricorn is much more open to sharing the wealth with others. Since Capricorn is concerned with creating a tangible expression of our identity, Venus in Capricorn will tend to value and appreciate the various status symbols that are often associated with an individual's success in the world. This can become an issue in relationships when Venus is in Capricorn—we can become too concerned with how much our partner can be of use to us.

Venus in Water Signs

While Venus certainly has a natural affinity with the emotional nature of the water signs, Venus also needs to be able to maintain perspective and balance in relationships, something at which the irrational and emotional water signs don't usually excel.

Venus in Cancer

Venus is peregrine from 11° to 20° and 27° to 30° of Cancer, and even when it's not peregrine, it only has dignity either by term or by face. Venus in Cancer becomes very concerned about meeting emotional and security needs through relationships. Certainly, relationships do provide emotional support and nurturing, protection, and spiritual connections; but not all relationships operate on this level. Venus in Cancer leads with the heart in *every* relationship. When dignified by term or face, Venus in Cancer at least has some appreciation that relationships are about balance, and that it must also be able to function on more levels than the purely emotional level (although term and face are not strong enough dignities for Venus to maintain this understanding without a struggle). When Venus is peregrine in Cancer, it will tend to wander, forming predominantly emotional connections in relationships, until it discovers that one's emotional needs can be met without the help and participation of a partner—and that people in relationships can form strong connections on different levels.

Venus in Scorpio

Venus in Scorpio is in detriment, and peregrine for the first 14°. Like Venus in Cancer, Venus in Scorpio is focused on the deep, emotional, and spiritual connections that can be experienced through relationships, and this single-minded focus is ultimately limiting to Venus. In Scorpio, however, Venus has power, and Venus is determined to pursue the most intense, transformational, and emotional relationships possible. (Scorpio's energy is so deep and inwardly focused that Venus in Scorpio finds it very difficult to be social.) Venus in Scorpio generally prefers group therapy to cocktail parties. Venus in Scorpio can certainly experience powerful and healing relationships, but sometimes it seems that those are the *only* types of relationships that Venus in Scorpio can have. When Venus has dignity by term or face in Scorpio, it becomes even more focused—but at least Venus knows that it's ultimately looking for a spiritual connection through the relationships. When Venus is peregrine in Scorpio, it can become ego-involved quite easily, and more than that, has difficulty understanding that not everyone is willing to experience such deep emotional bonds. These are lessons that Venus in Scorpio can learn, over time.

Venus in Pisces

Venus in Pisces, however, finally finds the perfect balance between the emotional/spiritual nature of the element of water, and Venus' drive to relate to all things beautiful and harmonious. Venus is exalted in Pisces, and operates on the level of the higher self. Pisces energy is about dissolving the boundaries between us, letting go of the illusions of separation, and reconnecting with the true source of the universe. Venus in Pisces ultimately understands that when we relate to other individuals, and to things of beauty and balance, we're really relating to the universe, and trying to rediscover our connection to the perfection of all creation. Venus in Pisces finds letting go of outdated structures and conventions in relationships very easy and natural. Pisces still operates on the emotional and spiritual plane, but the emotional connections that Venus makes in Pisces are far more gentle than those it creates in Cancer and Scorpio.

Venus in Air Signs

As with the water signs, while Venus benefits from the social energy of air, it has to be in the right balance to suit Venus well.

Venus in Gemini

Venus is peregrine from 1° to 14° and 21° to 30° of Gemini, although, truth be told, Venus probably doesn't notice. Gemini brings out the social butterfly in Venus—it becomes charming and beautiful, but it also tends to keep moving. Gemini energy is not conducive to the focus, routine, and constancy that relationships require. This is *not* to say that individuals with Venus in Gemini are incapable of having committed relationships! But individuals with Venus in Gemini *do* tend to need constant social activity. Venus in Gemini approaches Venus' need to be connected to the universe by trying to relate to and connect with the entire world.

Venus in Libra

Libra's energy, on the other hand, is a perfect fit for Venus, and Venus rules the sign of Libra. Unlike Gemini, Libra focuses on one relationship at a time, something that Venus appreciates. Libra energy is about balance and harmony, and when Venus is in Libra, it is able to express its more refined artistic abilities. Venus in Taurus is about working with crafts, with gardening, and with creating things using the body as an instrument (such as singing). Venus in Libra works with tools and instruments to create more refined expressions of beauty and balance. Venus in Libra is the painter, musician, sculptor, composer, and mathematician, as well as the diplomat and peacemaker. Venus in Libra, however, can often place the ideals of balance and harmony (or at least the appearance of balance and harmony—Libra is, after all, an air sign) above all else. Venus' charm can be used to manipulate, to cajole, and to entreat—anything at all, in fact, to avoid any disruption of the peace. Venus in Libra must learn the most important lesson for Libra energy: that balance is a process—things go back and forth because the two individuals in the relationship are just that: individuals. In order to find true balance in the relationship, each one has to be himself or herself fully, while taking the other person into consideration as well.

Venus in Aquarius

Aquarius energy is the most structured and stable of the air signs. It's not nearly as nice a fit for Venus as Libra is, but it's also much more comfortable overall for Venus than Gemini. Venus in Aquarius tends to be the least emotionally oriented Venus of all. Aquarius energy is not concerned with the individual, but rather with the needs of the group. Venus in Aquarius is far more comfortable relating to groups and ideals than to individuals. Aquarius is concerned with justice and freedom, and is very compassionate, if on a more abstract level. Venus in Aquarius is more likely to be attracted to a partner based on his or her ideals and beliefs, and Venus in Aquarius has difficulty maintaining harmony and balance with those who hold different beliefs and affiliations. Venus has dignity by term and face through part of Aquarius, and in these degrees Venus is at least aware that it must work from the more universal compassion of Aquarius energy in order to be able to translate that to more specific compassion (and emotional connections, too) with individuals rather than with groups. When Venus is peregrine in Aquarius, Venus doesn't carry this awareness, and will tend to wander, relating to groups and ideals, until it discovers that the people who form and support the ideals are at least as important as the ideals themselves.

Venus in Fire Signs

Venus is particularly uncomfortable in fire signs because the element of fire is so one-pointed and focused only on individual expression and action. Fire does not naturally take others into consideration, so Venus in fire signs tends to lose some of its natural ability to relate to others and to maintain harmony and balance.

Venus in Aries

Aries, in particular, is an uncomfortable placement for Venus, because Venus is in detriment in Aries. Again, Venus is very strong in Aries—it's just that Venus in Aries directs that strength in an atypical manner. Remember that one of the lessons Venus must learn, particularly when it is in a more relationship-oriented sign, is that in order to truly maintain balance in a relationship, all individuals must express themselves fully—they must fill up their half of the relationship completely. In relationship-oriented signs, Venus sometimes wants to compromise too much, to hold back and give in to the partner's wishes in the name of harmony and balance. Well, Venus in Aries doesn't have this problem. Venus in Aries, in fact, is very capable of going after the things it wants—and since Aries energy tends to be very impulsive, Venus in Aries tends to want what it wants, when it wants it. The difficulty for Venus in Aries is that Aries energy is the *least* aware of other individuals, and Venus in Aries can be so busy making sure it's happy, that it tends not to notice how its actions are impacting others. When Venus is peregrine in Aries, it has to learn the lessons about relationships and good boundaries the hard way—by crossing boundaries and having to experience and hopefully learn from the consequences. Venus has dignity by term from 6° to 14° of Aries, and by face for the last 10°, and here at least Venus understands that it has to learn to take other individuals into consideration; but term and face are not strong enough dignities to make much difference—Aries energy is so impulsive that Venus will still tend to act first, and without thinking. The only difference when Venus has some dignity is that it is more quickly aware of having crossed a boundary in a relationship than when it is peregrine.

Venus in Leo

All things considered, Venus in Leo is in much better shape than Venus in Aries. Venus is peregrine through most of Leo, but it's no longer in detriment. Unlike Aries, Leo energy is aware of others, and is able to relate to them on some level; but like Aries, Leo energy is quite self-centered, and when it relates to others, it basically wants others to appreciate and acknowledge Leo for being so wonderful and generous. Venus in Leo can be warm, giving, fun, charismatic, and charming. Leo energy is inherently creative, and combined with Venus' flair for the artistic, this can be a very productive role for Venus—as long as the critics love Venus, of course! An unkind remark, or even worse, no remark at all, can inspire truly dramatic tantrums and outbursts. If Venus in Leo can't be appreciated, then at the very least it needs to be noticed (preferably as the center of attention). Venus in Leo has to learn about the more spiritual, selfless aspects of relationships and the creative process. Ultimately, Venus in Leo has to learn to value its own opinions above anyone else's.

Venus in Sagittarius

Venus is also peregrine through most of Sagittarius. Like Leo, Sagittarius energy has an element of relationships to it—but the relationship in Sagittarius is the relationship between an individual and the cosmos. Sagittarius is ruled by Jupiter, the planet of expansion and freedom, and Venus in Sagittarius values freedom above all else. As is the case with Venus in Gemini, this is *not* meant to imply that Venus in Sagittarius is not able to maintain committed relationships; however, Venus in Sagittarius *is* very sensitive to boundaries and restrictions, particularly those that might limit Venus' quest for truth. Venus in Sagittarius expects a great deal of faith and trust in relationships—and if that trust is violated or the faith is misplaced, Venus will not stay in the relationship. Sagittarius is so focused and one-pointed that in Sagittarius, Venus tends to lose some of its natural diplomatic abilities. When Venus is peregrine in Sagittarius, it searches for the truth about our relationships to the universe. As it wanders, Venus can ultimately discover that when we truly connect with another individual on a spiritual level, we *are* connecting with the universe.

Mars

Rulership: Aries and Scorpio

Exaltation: Capricorn

Triplicity: Water (day and night)

Detriment: Taurus and Libra

Fall: Cancer

Peregrine: Taurus (1° to 26°), Gemini (1° to 10°, 21° to 25°), Leo (1° to 20°), Virgo (1° to 20°, 24° to 30°), Libra (1° to 20°, 24° to 30°), Sagittarius (1° to 20°, 25° to 30°), Aquarius (1° to 25°)

Mars is one-pointed, masculine, yang, expressive, and completely focused and single-minded in expression. Mars was also considered to be one of the "malefic" planets—one whose nature was better neutralized than emphasized. This is the reason that Mars was designated as nocturnal rather than diurnal in nature. Mars is fundamentally hot and dry, and the ancients believed that being in a cold and wet place would greatly diminish the more unfortunate and aggressive expressions of Mars. This is also how Mars became the triplicity ruler for the element of water, in both day and night charts. (Later systems assign Mars as only the nocturnal triplicity ruler of water, and designate Venus as the diurnal ruler, but we're going to stick with Ptolemy here.)

Mars in Fire Signs

The element of fire is hot and dry by nature—the same as Mars. When Mars is in a fire sign, these qualities are emphasized, something that tends to make Mars even more susceptible to ego-control, which is where Mars causes trouble. A case in point is Mars in Aries.

Mars in Aries

Mars rules Aries, and is extremely powerful there. Aries brings out the active, expressive, aggressive, and impulsive side of Mars. Mars in Aries is the warrior, a finely tuned, well-trained, extremely powerful soldier. Like any soldier, Mars in Aries can be extremely effective, productive, and supportive when well guided—and can be equally destructive when not kept under close supervision. The problem here, of course, is that when Mars is in Aries, Mars is its own boss—the top of the chain of command, as it were. More than anything, Mars wants to take action; combine that with Aries energy, the most impulsive and action-oriented sign, and we've got a pretty impressive combination. Mastering Mars in Aries energy requires discipline and training. Individuals with Mars in Aries *must* be able to express their energy consistently. If they are not able to take action, the bottled-up energy becomes frustration and then anger, and when it finally does manifest (and it *always* does), it will be unpredictable and explosive. The best way to keep Mars happy is through physical activity. Individuals with Mars in Aries enjoy all forms of competition and physical challenges—the only thing they have to remember is that the healthy challenges are the ones that we make to ourselves. When we start to focus on how well we compete with others, our egos can get involved and cause trouble.

Mars in Leo

Mars is peregrine for the first 20° of Leo, and then only has dignity by term and/or face. Mars in Leo is less of a challenge than Mars in Aries in that it is far less impulsive, and (more importantly) it's only a soldier, it's not in command of the whole army. Mars in Leo takes orders from the Sun, and the standing orders are to take any action that will encourage others to appreciate, support, and acknowledge us. Now anything that makes Mars think before acting can't be all bad; but Mars in Leo does lose some of its autonomy. Mars is the part of ourselves that defends who we truly are, but in Leo, Mars has a potential conflict of interest. It's as important that people *like* us for who we are as it is for us to actually *be* and express who we are. When Mars is peregrine in Leo, Mars wanders, gradually discovering that our self-image is enhanced the most not by the acknowledgment of others, but when we truly express ourselves, regardless of how others may react. When Mars has dignity by face, Mars has an awareness of this lesson, but will still struggle with Leo's overwhelming need for the support and attention of others.

Mars in Sagittarius

Mars is peregrine for all but the last 5° of Sagittarius. Sagittarius is the least focused of the fire signs, and has the greatest amount of perspective. In general, Mars isn't too comfortable with perspective—Mars just wants to take action, not to think about it first. Mars in Sagittarius is motivated to discover the truth, although since Mars operates more on the physical level than on the mental level, anytime Mars in Sagittarius comes across a new idea or philosophy, Mars wants to do something with it. The result is sometimes akin to a search and destroy mission to find the truth—Mars will simply attempt to obliterate all obstacles along the way. Mars in Sagittarius will actively defend its ideas and ideals—and this can manifest as zealotry and religious crusading. Mars in Sagittarius can have extremely strong convictions that its beliefs are *right* and everyone else's are *wrong* (an ego issue, of course). As Mars wanders in Sagittarius, it must learn how to operate from a more personal level rather than a universal one. Ultimately, Mars in Sagittarius must learn how to act based on its beliefs and philosophies, and let others do the same without feeling the need to convert them.

Mars in Water Signs

Mars is the triplicity ruler of water in both day and night charts, which means that Mars is inherently lucky in water signs, and less likely to get into trouble. Water both cools off the fiery nature of Mars, and slows and focuses Mars' expression. Water is very deep, and it can contain the force and energy of Mars quite well. The emotional and spiritual aspects of water also make Mars more aware of the consequences of its actions.

Mars in Cancer

Mars in Cancer is in fall, as well as dignified by triplicity. The two don't cancel each other out, however, and Mars in Cancer still can have a difficult time. Being a cardinal sign, Cancer is very impulsive and expressive, and has the least amount of perspective of the water signs. Mars in Cancer then tends to act impulsively, motivated by the need for emotional connections and support. Planets in fall are in an uncomfortable situation, through no fault of their own. Mars is our defender and protector. When Mars is in Cancer, Mars is motivated to defend and protect every time it experiences any kind of emotional slight. Since our emotions are often vague and unfocused, Mars doesn't always have a clear course of action—the need to act is there, the energy is building up, but there's not always an obvious target, and so Mars is rather impotent. This is, of course, not necessarily a bad thing, and one of the benefits of the dignity by triplicity. Mars in Cancer may not be able to act when it wants to, but since Mars in Cancer has a natural tendency to overreact from the emotional motivations, not being able to take action can save it a great deal of trouble. Mars still needs to be able to express itself, however, and being in fall, when Mars energy is kept bottled up for too long, it will manifest in the physical body as pain and discomfort, most often in the stomach and solar plexus area (third chakra).

Mars in Scorpio

Mars in Scorpio, on the other hand, is in excellent shape, being dignified both by rulership and by triplicity (and, for the first 6° of Scorpio, also by term and face!). Scorpio is the slowest-moving of the water signs (it is, after all, a fixed sign), and so Mars in Scorpio will tend to take longer to act. When Mars in Scorpio does act, it acts with a tremendous degree of precision and focus. Mars in Scorpio wants to explore the unconscious, to plumb the depths of our emotional and soul nature, to face down our demons, and ultimately to return to the source. The combination of it being its own boss and of being very lucky makes Mars in Scorpio a successful and courageous warrior, one that usually picks its battles with care, and that also realizes that some of the most challenging and dangerous battles are fought within our psyches. Mars in Scorpio is, however, still susceptible to bouts of ego, and can be very manipulative at times. Although Scorpio is not specifically a sexual energy, one way that Mars in Scorpio energy can express itself is through sexuality. This can, of course, be very healthy, but it's important that sex does not become the primary outlet for this energy. Mars in Scorpio, in its higher manifestations, is about healing and transformation.

Mars in Pisces

Mars in Pisces, again, tends to be well placed because of luck rather than because of strength. Pisces energy is so unfocused and diffuse that Mars in Pisces has trouble gathering up enough anger to make any real trouble. As with Mars in Cancer, Mars in Pisces is very sensitive to emotional and spiritual issues, and ultimately wants to defend itself against boundary violations and suffering. Since Pisces doesn't really recognize the separation between individuals, Mars in Pisces can become a crusader for other people's causes, reasoning that if it can help to alleviate and avenge the suffering of other people, then somewhere along the line, its own suffering will also be eliminated. Mars becomes more focused in the later degrees of Pisces, where it gains dignity by both term and face (perhaps in preparation for moving into Aries). In any event,

Mars in Pisces tends to be more moody and oversensitive than overtly aggressive. The main ego trap that Mars in Pisces succumbs to is the martyr/savior archetype. Mars in Pisces sometimes crusades for those who really neither want nor need Mars' help.

Mars in Earth Signs

Much like water, earth is an element that tends to lessen Mars' ability to act—and this can often be a blessing. For the most part, though, earth tends to simply slow Mars down and make it work harder.

Mars in Taurus

Taurus is a particularly uncomfortable sign for Mars: Mars is in detriment, as well as being peregrine for all but the last 4°. Mars in Taurus is strong, but tends to direct its focus in an inappropriate and less than productive manner. Taurus energy makes Mars very slow and plodding, but also very determined; and it also makes Mars extremely stubborn. The result is a Mars that pursues a course of action the way it wants to, against all odds, and usually ignores the evidence and suggestions of others that there may be considerably easier ways to accomplish its goals. Other than the tendency to get ego-involved and defend its course of action, the upside of Mars in Taurus is that it's consistent—we're always pretty sure of where it is and what it's up to. The downside is that Mars in Taurus tends to waste a great deal of energy doing things the hard way. This is both an effect of Mars being in detriment, and an effect of Mars being mostly peregrine in Taurus. What Mars needs to learn is how to be more flexible, and to be open to change; but true to form, Mars in Taurus will tend to learn this lesson the hard way.

Mars in Virgo

Mars in Virgo is peregrine for all but the last 6°. Virgo's practical nature helps to ground Mars, but Virgo's obsession with the little details has a tendency to keep Mars occupied with the small stuff rather than with the big picture. Of course, Mars in Virgo will actively defend its position that it's the details that are really important. Think of Mars in Virgo as Dustin Hoffman in the movie *Tootsie:* Hoffman plays an actor so obsessed with the little details (such as whether or not a tomato can sit down in a commercial!), that no one wants to work with him. Mars in Virgo is happiest when it is able to be of use—then the energy and drive of Mars is focused on being helpful, and on trying to make the physical world a better place.

Mars in Capricorn

Mars in Capricorn is very well placed—in fact, Mars is exalted in Capricorn. Capricorn is an earth sign that combines the practical, structured, grounded energy that Mars needs, with the initiating, active drive of the cardinal signs. In Capricorn, Mars gets to take action (which makes Mars very happy), but Mars is not the one calling the shots. Mars has an agenda laid out for it—and considering that Saturn, the planet of structure, boundaries, and hard work, rules Capricorn, it's a busy agenda indeed! This is just fine with Mars, though, because Mars doesn't care what it's doing or why, only that it's able to do *something*. Remember, Mars is like the engine of a car: as long as it's moving, it doesn't really care who's doing the driving. Mars in Capricorn channels Mars' aggression into more tangible, constructive pursuits. If you cross Mars in Capricorn, it won't punch you out, it will work for twenty years building up an empire, acquire the company that you work for in a hostile takeover, and then fire you. Needless to say, Mars in Capricorn is susceptible to the pitfalls of the ego—Mars in Capricorn can be very competitive (even for Mars), and is driven by a need to be recognized for its accomplishments.

Mars in Air Signs

Mars, like the Sun, is single-minded and focused in its nature and expression, and therefore does not do very well in the air signs, which are all double signs and fundamentally dual-natured. Mars needs to be able to take action, not to be presented with choices, options, and consequences.

Mars in Gemini

Mars doesn't fare nearly as poorly in Gemini as it does in the rest of the air signs, mainly because Gemini's nature is so quick that Mars simply has to do double-duty, acting on both options in turn. Ultimately, Mars in Gemini is extremely curious, but also very unfocused. Gemini is so changeable in nature that Mars in Gemini often finds it difficult to complete any task before jumping into another. Mars is peregrine for half of Gemini, and here, while Mars most needs to learn how to focus, Mars is also the least aware of this problem, being kept largely off-balance by Gemini's dazzlingly fast energy. Mars has dignity by term in the last 5° of Gemini, and by face from 10° to 20° of Gemini. Here, Mars is aware that it needs to focus, to cut through the distractions presented by Gemini; but term and face are very weak dignities, and Mars in Gemini does not have the natural strength and resources to keep Gemini's energy in check. The lesson Gemini needs to learn is how to blend opposites and discover the truth that exists as the connection between them. Mars is well suited to cutting through distractions and illusions, and given time, Mars in Gemini can become very effective.

Mars in Libra

Mars in Libra, on the other hand, is pretty miserable. Libra is the sign of Mars' detriment, and on top of that, Mars is peregrine for all but the last 6° of Libra. Mars needs to be able to act freely and directly. Libra is, of course, concerned with relationships, and with maintaining balance and harmony. Mars in Libra is motivated to take action in order to maintain balance, harmony, and relationships, but at the same time, Mars in Libra *also* knows that by taking action, it will upset that balance. It's not that Mars in Libra isn't strong, it's just that it has trouble learning how to make use of that strength. Mars in Libra often feels like it's "damned if you do and damned if you don't." Libra's lesson that balance and harmony is about give and take, about taking action and also taking responsibility for those actions, is particularly difficult for Mars. Mars is perfectly capable of acting and expressing itself fully; it just has difficulty taking others into account when it does express itself, because Mars is so self-centered and one-pointed in nature. As planets in detriment operate on the mental/emotional plane, individuals with Mars in Libra often find that they spend a great deal of energy worrying about what actions to take, and worrying about the consequences of their actions. Mars in Libra approaches relationships from the outside in (an excellent description of what it means to be peregrine), and has no real frame of reference. Ultimately, Mars in Libra has to learn to take a stand and act—and then act again to accept the repercussions of its actions and try to restore balance.

Mars in Aquarius

Mars in Aquarius is peregrine for all but the last 5°. Aquarius is a group-oriented energy, and Mars, of course, is happiest when it can act on an individual level. Mars in Aquarius is motivated to take action to support the integrity, freedom, equality, and ideals of the group. This can set up a conflict of interest for Mars, since Mars' primary function is to assert and defend its individuality—and often this can be at cross-purposes with the interests of the group. Mars in Aquarius is the most comfortable when it is taking action to help the group. Mars in Aquarius has a different type of ego struggle: to actually maintain an individual identity that is separate from the group identity. One of the functions of Aquarius is to evaluate the structure and rules of society and then determine if they continue to support the best interest of the group. If they have become outdated, Aquarius will disrupt and dismantle them, and replace them with new structures that are more supportive of the group. Mars in Aquarius is happiest when it is campaigning for change and transformation; but Aquarius isn't all action, and it's not about constant revolution and change. Once the new rules are in place, Aquarius seeks to maintain them, and this is where Mars can become frustrated. Mars peregrine in Aquarius searches for a cause to fight for, a group ideal to defend. Ultimately, Mars in Aquarius must discover that it's okay to act as an individual, rather than as a representative of society.

Jupiter

Rulership: Sagittarius and Pisces

Exaltation: Cancer

Triplicity: Fire (night)

Detriment: Gemini and Virgo

Fall: Capricorn

Peregrine: Aries (by day, 6° to 30°), Taurus (1° to 15°, 22° to 30°), Gemini (14° to 30°), Leo (by day, 1° to 10°, 26° to 30°), Virgo (1° to 13°, 18° to 30°), Libra (1° to 11°, 19° to 20°), Scorpio (1° to 6°, 14° to 30°), Capricorn (12°, 19° to 30°), Aquarius (1° to 20°, 25° to 30°)

Jupiter is diurnal, expressive, and expansive by nature. Jupiter is the nocturnal triplicity ruler of fire, and does well in fire because Jupiter is able to expand and express joy and optimism in fire signs. Jupiter also has a very spiritual nature, and therefore also does rather well in the spiritually oriented water signs. Jupiter is the least comfortable in earth signs (which by nature are restrictive, something Jupiter doesn't enjoy), and in the air signs.

Jupiter in Fire Signs

Jupiter's affinity with the fire signs is mostly one of luck and circumstance; hence the fact that Jupiter is the nocturnal triplicity ruler of fire. Fire signs tend to be too focused and one-pointed for Jupiter (which *really* needs to be able to see the big picture). However, fire signs are very comfortable with expressions of joy and excitement, which resonates strongly with Jupiter's "fun" reputation.

Jupiter in Aries

Jupiter has the most difficulty with the exceptionally impulsive, quick, and self-centered energy of Aries. In a day chart, Jupiter is peregrine for all but the first 6° of Aries, although in a night chart, of course, Jupiter is dignified by triplicity. When you combine the impulsive energy of Aries with the expansive and optimistic energy of Jupiter, you frequently end up with someone who acts too quickly, and without thinking things through, leading to mistakes and general bouts of (otherwise avoidable) trouble. When Jupiter is dignified by triplicity, Jupiter tends to be lucky—Jupiter is still impulsive and careless, but it seems to make fewer costly mistakes. Jupiter has so much essential difficulty with Aries because Jupiter is a social planet, one that specifically has to do with our relationship to society and to the universe; Aries energy, on the other hand, is entirely and completely concerned with the individual.

Jupiter in Leo

Jupiter in Leo fares a bit better than it does in Aries because in a day chart, Jupiter is only peregrine from 1° to 10° and 26° to 30° of Leo. Leo is a far more social sign than Aries in that it recognizes the presence of the group consciousness, but Leo is fundamentally motivated to gain the approval and attention of the group. Jupiter in Leo gets to express its generous, charismatic nature, which is, truth be told, a pretty good fit for Jupiter. Jupiter in Leo likes to "hold court," entertaining friends (and even strangers) with stories and anecdotes. In general, Jupiter in Leo can be counted on to be the life of the party; but as is usually the case with planets in Leo, the ego has a tendency to get in the way. Jupiter in Leo can come to *depend* on the attention, focus, and approval of others for validation. When Jupiter is dignified by triplicity, Jupiter is lucky, and generally is in situations where people are more than happy to appreciate it. When Jupiter is peregrine, however, the search for the approval of others can get confused with Jupiter's primary urge to discover its spiritual nature. As is always the case, dignity by either term or face is enough to give a planet some focus and understanding of its lessons, but not necessarily enough strength to help the planet actually *learn* those lessons. For much of Leo, in a day chart, Jupiter is aware that it must discover its spirituality within, and not look for it through the attention and approval of others—it's just difficult for Jupiter in Leo to break out of this pattern.

Jupiter in Sagittarius

Jupiter in Sagittarius, however, is a different story. Jupiter rules the sign of Sagittarius, and the mutable energy of Sagittarius gives Jupiter more than enough room to explore. Sagittarius is also concerned with philosophy, higher education, and basically anything that will help us better understand our place in the universe. In Sagittarius, Jupiter tends to pursue spirituality in a more structured, focused manner. Organized religion is something that Jupiter in Sagittarius finds very appealing (while Jupiter in Pisces, on the other hand, tends to take a more holistic approach to spirituality). Jupiter in Sagittarius is motivated by universal law, and by the quest for truth. Sagittarius energy is still fire, however, and no matter how mutable and flexible it may be, Sagittarius maintains its fundamentally one-pointed nature; and one of the best-known side effects of this one-pointed nature is a tendency to operate in absolutes (not to mention a tendency to be more than a little tactless). "Truth above all else" is Jupiter in Sagittarius' motto, and this can often result in bruised feelings (and heated debates). When Jupiter is dignified by triplicity (in a night chart), again, Jupiter is far more lucky, and while it's still as susceptible to ego traps, it has a knack for avoiding the bigger ones.

Jupiter in Water Signs

Jupiter does well in two out of three water signs (Scorpio is too structured and limiting to allow Jupiter to express itself freely). Water signs tend to have difficulty with boundaries—a perfect match for the planet that rules all forms of expansion. In water signs, Jupiter is able to express its more spiritual nature, and Jupiter in water signs tends to express a strong connection to the source.

Jupiter in Cancer

Jupiter is exalted in Cancer, and further dignified by term from 6° to 13°. Cancer energy is about discovering, expressing, and hopefully meeting our emotional and spiritual needs. Ultimately, Cancer represents our longing to reconnect with the source, to remember the time when we were able to experience our connection to all creation, and since we were part of all creation, we could not ever experience lack of any kind: all our needs were met. Planets in Cancer often operate out of fear that our needs in this lifetime will *not* be met, and they seek to either nurture others, or to be nurtured, looking to others to help us survive. Jupiter is the only planet that can truly expand to meet all of Cancer's needs. When Jupiter is in Cancer, Jupiter can experience and express that our emotional needs will truly be met because there is more than enough love in the universe to go around. Jupiter in Cancer certainly can be open, loving, and nurturing to others (and to itself!), but Jupiter is always teaching as well. Jupiter in Cancer wants to teach others how to realize that we *are* truly loved and protected, that we are more than enough because we are all the universe.

Jupiter in Scorpio

Jupiter in Scorpio is not very comfortable because Jupiter is a very expressive, outgoing planet, and Scorpio energy is perhaps the least outwardly expressive, and certainly one of the most introverted and inwardly focused of all the signs. It's not just Scorpio's fault, of course, because Jupiter isn't particularly comfortable in *any* of the fixed signs. Jupiter in Scorpio is peregrine for all but 6° to 14°, where it has dignity by term. Jupiter's spiritual quest takes a very personal and private route in Scorpio. Transformational, emotional experiences are quite welcome, because they also represent opportunities for growth and allow us to move closer to our true spiritual connections. Jupiter always carries issues of overdoing things, though, and with Jupiter in Scorpio, we can sometimes take the process of personal discovery, healing, and transformation a bit too far. One of the traps of Jupiter in Scorpio is to always seek out crisis and change. On a spiritual level, Scorpio energy is related to all things hidden and mysterious, and Jupiter in Scorpio may tend to explore its faith and spirituality through the occult, or by delving into the more obscure, esoteric aspects of religion. As Jupiter wanders, peregrine in Scorpio, it must ultimately learn that growth can happen on the surface, and at a steady and enjoyable pace—it doesn't always have to involve psychological trauma.

Jupiter in Pisces

Jupiter rules the sign of Pisces, the mutable water sign; additionally, Jupiter has dignity by term from 8° to 14° of Pisces, and by face from 10° to 20° of Pisces. Pisces is the least structured, most flowing energy of the zodiac, so naturally, Jupiter is very strong and happy there. Boundaries? What boundaries? Pisces energy is a fog: it moves over, under, around, and through any obstacles, without even noticing them. Jupiter in Pisces sees the truth that all boundaries, all separation and distinctions are simply illusions: we are all connected, we are all part of the source, of the universe. Jupiter in Pisces exudes compassion for all creation, and is very sensitive to the pain and discomfort of others. Jupiter in Pisces is likely to take a direct and personal approach to spirituality—the rituals of organized religion in and of themselves don't hold any attraction; it's the spirit, the intention, that matters, and ultimately, we don't need organized religion to experience a connection to the creator and all creation. The biggest challenge for Jupiter in Pisces is, of course, the question of boundaries. Jupiter in Pisces always means well, but has a tendency to get mixed up in other people's business, trying to help them in some way; and no matter how good its intentions may be, Jupiter's help may still not be welcome.

Jupiter in Air Signs

Jupiter is fundamentally one-pointed in nature (even though it can take a broad focus), and finds the dual-natured energy of the air signs rather uncomfortable.

Jupiter in Gemini

Jupiter in Gemini is in its detriment, although Jupiter does have dignity by term and/or face in the first 14° of Gemini. Gemini is the sign concerned with exploring all the possibilities, while Jupiter is the planet that strives to discover and express the ultimate unifying truth. Once again, we have a situation where the planet is strong, but very misguided in its focus. Jupiter goes after everything in a big way, and is really only able to handle one idea or concept at a time. Gemini energy is working toward the idea of a unified truth, but operates at the far end of the spectrum, exploring opposites to discover how they are related. Gemini deals with small concepts, but Jupiter makes everything bigger. Jupiter in Gemini, especially when peregrine, tends to latch onto each new idea as if it were the answer, and then change and latch onto the opposite idea with the same amount of conviction and fervor. When Jupiter is dignified by face and term, it at least understands that this approach doesn't work, and that a more integrated approach is needed. Ultimately, Jupiter in Gemini has to learn how to focus on the space between the two opposing concepts, not on the concepts themselves: this is where the path to the truth lies.

Jupiter in Libra

Jupiter in Libra is as comfortable as Jupiter gets in an air sign (it has at least weak dignity from 11° to 19° and 21° to 30°, and so is only peregrine for 12°). Libra is the most focused of the air signs, specializing as it does in one-to-one relationships; and since it's a cardinal sign, Jupiter at least gets to be active and initiating in Libra, which counts for something. Ultimately, though, the confines of one-to-one relationships are too limiting and structured for the freedom-loving, independent, and expansive Jupiter. Libra is much less frantic than Gemini, although equally concerned with duality. Jupiter is able to make use of Libra's connection with fairness and justice, particularly as it relates to universal laws; and, of course, Jupiter in Libra simply makes being in a relationship a lot of fun. When Jupiter has dignity by term or face in Libra, it has a sense of purpose: to learn, grow, and experience truth through relationships, balance, and harmony. When Jupiter is peregrine in Libra, it has to search for this direction. In any case, Jupiter works best alone; always having to take a partner into consideration, and to be aware of how its actions are impacting others, is a challenge for Jupiter.

Jupiter in Aquarius

Jupiter in Aquarius has to deal with the group rather than with individuals, and even though Aquarius has a reputation for supporting freedom and individuality, Jupiter is still peregrine in Aquarius from 1° to 20° and 25° to 30°. When Jupiter is peregrine in Aquarius, it may not even know that it's wandering and searching for its true purpose. Aquarius tends to be very idealistic and social, two qualities that Jupiter also embodies, and Aquarius operates on a mental/theoretical level that resonates quite well with Jupiter's philosophical approach. So why is Jupiter peregrine in Aquarius? Because the truth and freedom that Aquarius supports are not universal truths: they only apply to the members of the group. Jupiter can certainly roam freely within the boundaries and confines of Aquarius and be quite happy there, until Jupiter hits on an idea or notion that doesn't fit in with the ideals of the group. Aquarius, remember, is ruled by Saturn—when you cross a boundary or violate the rules, you are held responsible. Once Jupiter discovers that Aquarius actually *does* have boundaries, Jupiter is no longer happy and will try to break free. When Jupiter has dignity by term in Aquarius (20° to 25°), Jupiter is aware of the boundaries, and tries to work within them, and also to find ways to expand them. Jupiter peregrine in Aquarius is oblivious to the true nature of its situation, and is completely surprised when it encounters resistance.

Jupiter in Earth Signs

Jupiter is the least comfortable in the earth signs. Earth energy brings Jupiter down—well, down to Earth. This both limits and confines Jupiter, and also presents a significant challenge for Jupiter's fundamentally spiritual nature. Earth signs are practical, material, and tangible, and don't have any patience or understanding for the higher planes of existence.

Jupiter in Taurus

Jupiter is peregrine in Taurus from 1° to 15° and 22° to 30°, only having dignity by term from 15° to 22°. As is the case with Jupiter in Aquarius, Jupiter may not be too unhappy in Taurus. But Jupiter in Taurus has a tendency to focus on issues of material abundance. Taurus is one of the most sensual and tactile signs, and Jupiter in Taurus can become very attached to the "good life," and has a tendency to overindulge in all things physical. Ultimately, of course, the physical plane isn't ever going to satisfy Jupiter, which has a fundamental need to connect with the universe on all levels, not only the physical. When Jupiter is peregrine in Taurus, Jupiter will tend to wander, exploring and enjoying the physical, but also knowing that something very important is missing. When Jupiter has dignity by term, Jupiter understands that it's searching for the spiritual truth; however, Taurus energy primarily confines Jupiter to searching for spirit in the material world. It can be found there, of course, but it's a longer, more winding road.

Jupiter in Virgo

Jupiter in Virgo is in detriment, and peregrine from 1° to 13° and 18° to 30°, to boot. Put simply, Jupiter in Virgo is the planet that needs faith, in the sign that demands proof. Since planets in detriment also operate on the mental/emotional plane, individuals with Jupiter in Virgo tend to struggle with spiritual connections—faith does not come easily to them. These individuals are always searching for some tangible evidence that their faith is well-placed. Jupiter in Virgo is motivated to perfect and improve the physical plane, in a big way. On the positive side, Virgo energy makes Jupiter much more precise and careful; and Virgo's analytical, practical, and detail-oriented approach to life helps Jupiter actually build something tangible out of its huge dreams and ideas. But Jupiter in Virgo can easily get frustrated by the gap between the ideal and the finished product. Jupiter in Virgo seeks a connection to the universe, to spirit and the creator, by creating perfection on the physical plane. Again, it's possible to discover and connect with our spirituality on the material plane, rather than on the spiritual plane; it's simply a more challenging path to take. Jupiter in Virgo struggles with the inherently flawed nature of the physical plane, as it searches for the spark of life and divine inspiration that is nonetheless always present.

Jupiter in Capricorn

Jupiter in Capricorn is in fall, although only peregrine at 12° and from 19° to 30° (again, the cardinal nature of Capricorn helps). While Jupiter in Cancer (in exaltation) is able to experience and express endless abundance and security, Jupiter in Capricorn tends to struggle with issues of lack. Jupiter in Capricorn has great skill at manifesting things in the physical plane, and is very driven to succeed. This can, of course, be a very positive influence; the challenge is that

Jupiter in Capricorn is driven to succeed in order to ensure that it will always have enough security. Achievement, accomplishments, money, prestige—these can seem to come quite easily to Jupiter in Capricorn, but they're never quite enough. Because Capricorn energy operates on the physical plane, rather than on the spiritual plane, Capricorn has difficulty addressing emotional and soul needs. Jupiter in Capricorn tries to fill the spiritual void through structuring, organizing, conquering, and taking responsibility for the physical world, attempting to meet the physical needs not only of itself, but also of others. Like Cancer, Capricorn is motivated to protect and ultimately to help others become self-sufficient; but Capricorn can become ego-involved and lose sight of this goal. When Jupiter is peregrine in Capricorn, Jupiter has the most difficulty discovering the true lessons of Capricorn (which include the lesson that meeting our physical needs and taking responsibility for the physical is only half the battle—our spiritual needs must also be addressed). When Jupiter is in terms or face, Jupiter is highly aware that it is missing something, but it doesn't always know what it's missing, or how to fill that need.

Saturn

Rulership: Capricorn and Aquarius

Exaltation: Libra

Triplicity: Air (day)

Detriment: Cancer and Leo

Fall: Aries

Peregrine: Aries (1° to 26°), Taurus (1° to 20°), Gemini (by night, 1° to 20°, 25° to 30°), Cancer (1° to 27°), Leo (11° to 30°), Virgo (1° to 18°, 24° to 30°), Scorpio (1° to 27°), Sagittarius (1° to 19°), Pisces (11° to 26°)

Saturn is diurnal, restrictive, limiting, and focused, and represents responsibility in all forms, as well as all structures. Saturn is the triplicity ruler of air by day and, additionally, rules one air sign (Aquarius) and is exalted in another (Libra). Air's inherently objective and fair approach is the most supportive energy for Saturn, which can become very heavy-handed in other signs. Saturn likes the earth signs because Saturn makes everything tangible. Fire and water signs, however, are far less comfortable for Saturn. In fire signs, Saturn can become aggressive and lose much of its ability to be fair; and Saturn simply doesn't like the emotional nature of the water signs.

Saturn in Air Signs

Saturn is the diurnal triplicity ruler of the element of air. Air is inherently objective and has the greatest amount of perspective (and the least amount of emotional involvement) of any of the elements. These are qualities that make for a good judge (impartial, objective), and in a day chart, Saturn benefits from them. Dignity by triplicity doesn't indicate any particular skill, of course, only that the planet tends to be very lucky. Saturn in air signs is still Saturn, and it's still going to make its rulings and judgments as it sees fit; but in diurnal charts, Saturn's decisions tend to be much more fair and just.

Saturn in Gemini

That Saturn's decisions tend to be more fair and just in a day chart is quite important to Saturn in Gemini, because other than dignity by term from 21° to 25°, luck is all that Saturn has in Gemini. Because of Gemini's dual nature, Saturn in Gemini can manifest as a double standard of behavior, particularly when peregrine. Rather than always accepting the rules as they are, Saturn in Gemini sometimes tries to find an alternate interpretation of the rules that will allow it to rationalize its desires and actions. Gemini is the most inconsistent sign, fluctuating rapidly between polar opposites, making snap judgments and evaluations, and never exploring anything beyond the most surface appearances. Saturn in Gemini can often seem to set arbitrary rules and limitations—an eccentric judge whose rulings can never be anticipated or predicted. In a day chart, these rulings also happen to work (surprisingly enough). In a night chart, however, when Saturn is peregrine in Gemini, the rules and boundaries tend to be much less defensible. Saturn peregrine in Gemini wanders in search of the structures and boundaries that can ultimately embrace and support both ends of the spectrum, rather than validating one aspect of duality and penalizing the other.

Saturn in Libra

Saturn is extremely strong in Libra. Not only is Saturn exalted in Libra, but Saturn has dignity by term for the first 6°, and by face for the middle 10°; and of course, in a day chart, Saturn is also the triplicity ruler. In a day chart, in fact, Saturn has more dignity in Libra than does Venus, the ruler of Libra. Saturn in Libra is like the chief justice of the Supreme Court: he doesn't get to make his own rules (exalted planets don't set their own agendas), but he's very well supported and informed, and in a position to make fair, balanced, just, and impartial rulings on the issues that he is given to address. Saturn in Libra understands the true nature of relationships and the true lessons of personal responsibility. We must fulfill our half of the relationship completely, and we must be responsible for our actions, intentions, and their direct consequences. At the same time, we must also understand when and where our responsibility ends—we are not, for example, responsible for other people's feelings (but we are responsible for our own). Being in a cardinal sign, Saturn in Libra is also concerned with the question of identity, and defines who we are as individuals through exclusion and relationships: "This is where you begin, so it must therefore be where I end." In a day chart, Saturn's boundaries, decisions, and understanding of responsibility tend to be far more on-the-mark than in a night chart; but even when Saturn isn't lucky in Libra, it's always ready to accept responsibility for its actions and choices, even the ones that ultimately weren't as successful as it might have hoped.

Saturn in Aquarius

Saturn is also very strong in Aquarius, although this time, Saturn calls the shots—it makes the rules and also enforces and interprets them. Saturn in Aquarius is very concerned that the rules and structures that are in place do their job and support the integrity and safety of the group, while allowing for the greatest level of personal and individual freedom within those constructs. If the rules start to outgrow their usefulness, Saturn will immediately tear down the old and create new, more supportive rules in their place. Of course, Aquarius is famous for its very, shall we say, flexible approach to what constitutes a group. Saturn in Aquarius does not respect just any old authority figures, but only those authority figures that are associated with its group of choice. When Saturn is dignified by triplicity in a day chart, it tends to be a bit more conventional in its recognition of and respect for authority; in a night chart, however, Saturn in Aquarius can feel entirely justified in violating the rules, structures, and laws of society that it feels don't support the general good. Saturn in Aquarius can appear to be a rebel and even an outlaw; however, Saturn always adheres to an internal code of ethics and follows a very strict set of rules and guidelines for its behavior and actions. It's just that these guidelines aren't always obvious to others, or widely accepted.

Saturn in Earth Signs

Saturn is not quite as well-off in earth signs as in air signs. While the grounded, practical, tangible energy of the earth signs is certainly consistent with Saturn's mode of operation, in order to be truly just, Saturn also needs perspective, something that earth signs have in rather short supply.

Saturn in Taurus

Saturn in Taurus is peregrine for the first 20°, and like most planets in Taurus, Saturn becomes very oriented toward the physical and the sensual here. Saturn's work ethic tends to dampen the enthusiasm in any situation, and Saturn in Taurus can sometimes take all the fun out of pleasure. While Saturn in Taurus certainly appreciates the value of the finer things in life, it believes that they must be earned through hard work and perseverance. Even once the work has been done, Saturn in Taurus can often make us feel guilty for taking a vacation to enjoy the rewards we earned from all our hard work. When Saturn has dignity in Taurus (and from 22° to 26° of Taurus, Saturn has dignity by both term and face, so it's not doing too badly), Saturn has at least some awareness that we have to take some time and actually enjoy ourselves because we deserve it. Saturn peregrine in Taurus, however, tends to wander, until it ultimately learns the old lesson about "all work and no play."

Saturn in Virgo

Saturn in Virgo is peregrine from 1° to 18° and 24° to 30°. Combine Saturn's obsession with rules, structure, authority, responsibility, and chain of command with Virgo's obsession with details, and the result can range from a finely tuned legal mind to the typical employee at the local Department of Motor Vehicles. Virgo energy has perhaps the greatest difficulty with perspective. Saturn in Virgo can become so focused on the importance of the little details that it's never able to accomplish the larger, more important tasks at hand. The details are important, of course, but Saturn in Virgo can tend to weigh each little detail with equal importance (resulting in the literal-minded bureaucrat at the DMV who informs you—after you've waited in line for a hour, no less—that you've filled out the wrong form in the wrong color ink, and that you must wait in another line for another hour to get the correct form, and then come back and wait in line again for them to be able to renew your license). With Saturn in Virgo, the end *never* justifies the means. Saturn in Virgo isn't necessarily difficult or disruptive; it's just in unfamiliar territory, and, particularly when peregrine, it will tend to wander until it can learn that sometimes it's more important that things just get done than it is that they get done according to the prescribed procedure.

Saturn in Capricorn

Saturn in Capricorn, on the other hand, is in a sign that it rules, and so is very strong. Capricorn energy is about creating structures and rules in order to protect and enhance the integrity of the group. Capricorn energy is also about taking personal responsibility for our actions, and about being useful and practical with our lives: about accomplishing things and creating tangible and lasting expressions of our individual identities. Saturn is very happy in Capricorn, and able to operate with complete autonomy. Whereas Saturn in Aquarius can also be dignified by triplicity, and have the attendant extra luck supporting its decisions, Saturn in Capricorn doesn't have that help. Capricorn energy is grounded, practical, and very traditional. Saturn in Capricorn does not have the perspective that Saturn has in Aquarius, and will tend to uphold tradition above all else. Saturn in Capricorn doesn't question the rules, and ultimately doesn't care if the rules are helping people or not. All Saturn in Capricorn cares about is that the rules are upheld, and that we're all accountable for our actions. Saturn in Capricorn is the judge that always rules based on precedent—this is the way things have always been done, and this is the way we're going to continue to do them. Saturn is, of course, very happy with this arrangement, but it's not always the most beneficial situation for us.

Saturn in Fire Signs

Saturn in Aries

Saturn is not well supported by the impulsive, aggressive, focused energy of fire. Take Saturn in Aries, for example. Saturn is in fall in Aries, and peregrine to boot, for all but the last 4° of Aries. While Saturn in Libra is the fair and impartial judge, Saturn in Aries is a judge with a personal vendetta. The ultimate lessons of Saturn in Aries have to do with taking responsibility for our actions and our impulses—particularly for our physical actions, since Saturn in Aries (in fall) is operating with special attention to the physical plane. As astrologer J. Lee Lehman puts it, "Saturn in Aries is *ticked-off!*" (Actually, she didn't phrase it *exactly* like that, but you get the general idea.) On a more personal level, Saturn in Aries is driven to express its individual identity (Aries), but at the same time, to be responsible for the repercussions of its actions. Aries, remember, is the *least* aware of the presence of anyone or anything else in the universe—it's entirely focused on breaking away from the collective as an individual. Individuals with Saturn in Aries may expect authority figures to tend to be impulsive, arbitrary, and aggressive, and may form their patterns for interacting with authority and for taking positions of authority around that model (one, I might add, that lacks a certain amount of diplomacy and people skills). Ultimately, Saturn in Aries must learn about self-limitation and maintaining strong personal boundaries in order to respect other people.

Saturn in Leo

Saturn in Leo is in detriment, and operates largely on the mental/emotional plane, and is peregrine for the last 20°. Planets in detriment are strong, but tend to use their strength in inappropriate ways. Saturn in Leo can become entirely self-centered and adopt a "looking out for Number One" approach to the world (as opposed to Saturn in Aquarius, which takes a broader focus and looks out for the good of the group, not of the individual). Saturn's practical, structured, limiting approach to all things is particularly ill-suited to the open, warm, generous energy of Leo. When Saturn is in Leo, it becomes much more stingy with the warmth and generosity, and much more focused on the Leo need for acknowledgment and attention. Individuals with Saturn in Leo have difficulty giving freely and expressing and sharing their unique individual gifts with others. ("Make 'em buy a ticket," thinks Saturn in Leo.) The mental/emotional level comes into play because Leo energy focuses on its self-image, and Saturn is, of course, the ultimate taskmaster. The result is that individuals with Saturn in Leo may worry quite a bit about their self-worth and value as individuals. For the first 6° of Leo, Saturn is dignified by both term and face, and is able to function reasonably well, if only because Saturn's dedication to hard work can actually help us realize more of our full potential as individuals (although this isn't enough to counteract the debility of being in detriment, and Saturn will still struggle with its fundamentally self-centered approach to things). When Saturn is peregrine in Leo, however, Saturn tends to wander, and we struggle with fears about our worth as individuals, keeping much of our true gifts hidden. Ultimately, when Saturn is in Leo, we can learn to connect with something bigger than ourselves, something that requires that we give 100%, finally revealing (and realizing) our full potential as individuals.

Saturn in Sagittarius

Saturn in Sagittarius is as happy as Saturn gets in a fire sign. Saturn is free from any essential debility in Sagittarius, and has dignity in the last 11° of Sagittarius by term and/or face. Where Saturn and Sagittarius share common ground is on the subject of universal law. Sagittarius focuses on the search for truth and on discovering our relationship to all creation and to the creator. Sagittarius tends to be too abstract for Saturn's taste, but Saturn can certainly appreciate the structure of Sagittarius' religious and philosophical ideals. Sagittarius, however, is a fundamentally freedom-loving energy, while Saturn sets boundaries and limitations; and, of course, as a fire sign (and a mutable one at that), Sagittarius wants to be impulsive, energy that generally doesn't support the skillful applications of Saturn. Saturn in Sagittarius tends to adopt a philosophy and attempt to apply it to the more tangible, practical arenas of life. Sometimes this works; sometimes it doesn't. The gap between theory and application can be very wide, and, along the way, the theory usually has to be adjusted to accommodate reality. Saturn in Sagittarius isn't happy about that—pure, original ideals are sacred. Not only can Saturn in Sagittarius try to force its philosophy on itself, but it also has a tendency to look for converts, since anyone who lives by a different set of beliefs is obviously wrong. As Saturn wanders in Sagittarius, looking for tangible representations of universal truth, it must learn to be more flexible and accept that, ultimately, universal truth is far more subjective than it is objective, and what is truth for one person may not be truth for another.

Saturn in Water Signs

As a rule, Saturn isn't particularly comfortable in water signs. Water signs operate in the realm of emotions, and while it's not a bad idea for us to have some structure and boundaries when it comes to our emotional expression, Saturn in water signs can become too restrictive.

Saturn in Cancer

Saturn has the greatest difficulty in Cancer, where it is in detriment and peregrine for all but the last 3°. Cancer energy is about creating, initiating, and expressing an emotional and soul identity. Cancer energy is about nurturing and protecting, but also about meeting emotional needs, both our own and those of our families. Emotions and feelings are fundamentally irrational, intangible, and impractical—but Saturn in Cancer tries to make them structured, practical, and organized. Saturn in Cancer tries to find tangible ways for us to meet our intangible emotional needs, and of course, is very concerned that we take full responsibility for our needs and our feelings. Saturn's self-reliant nature isn't a bad thing for Cancer, which ultimately needs to learn some independence; but Cancer energy needs to be able to receive nurturing from others as well as to give it, and this is where Saturn has difficulty. The mental/emotional component of Saturn in Cancer tends to manifest as worrying about other people's feelings, and a tendency to want to take personal responsibility for other people's reactions and responses to our actions. Individuals with Saturn in Cancer must learn where to draw the line and distinguish between their own feelings, emotions, and reactions (where they are personally responsible) and the feelings, emotions, and reactions of others (where they are not personally responsible).

Saturn in Scorpio

All things considered, Saturn in Scorpio is an improvement over Saturn in Cancer. In Scorpio, Saturn is only peregrine (from 1° to 27°), and also not in detriment, so Saturn in Scorpio is simply in unfamiliar territory. Scorpio energy experiences emotions with the greatest depth and intensity of all the signs, and also has the most difficulty expressing itself on the surface. On the surface, the reserved, limited, structured, and controlled energy of Saturn seems to be a good match with Scorpio. The challenge with Saturn in Scorpio is that Scorpio energy *does* need to be able to express itself eventually, and when it does express itself, it's often very transformational and even destructive. Saturn in Scorpio tends to latch onto these qualities of Scorpio and try to assert itself through manipulation, control, and hidden methods. Ultimately, individuals with Saturn in Scorpio must learn how to structure and take responsibility for their deepest emotional and soul needs, which includes the need to connect with others on an all-encompassing level. In the meantime, though, Saturn in Scorpio may try to orchestrate these connections through less subtle and more heavy-handed tactics.

Saturn in Pisces

Saturn in Pisces is only peregrine from 11° to 26°, and although it's not saying much, Saturn is somewhat less fundamentally uncomfortable in Pisces than it is in Cancer and Scorpio. In Pisces, Saturn is tempered by universal compassion, which is certainly not a bad quality for Saturn to have; but Pisces energy, with its natural abhorrence of boundaries and structures, is difficult for Saturn to operate in effectively. Saturn needs to teach responsibility, but Pisces makes it difficult to discriminate and determine exactly who is responsible for what, because we're all a fundamental part of all creation. Saturn in Pisces tends to struggle with its boundaries, searching for a point of balance where the structures are sturdy enough to protect and support, but at the same time flexible enough to allow for compassion and mercy. It's not an easy task for Saturn, as you can probably imagine. Pisces operates on an energetic, spiritual level, while Saturn needs tangible results. It's no wonder that by the time Saturn makes it into Aries, it's ticked-off and frustrated.

The Outer Planets Through the Signs

The outer planets, which include Chiron, Uranus, Neptune, and Pluto, don't operate on an individual level the way the inner planets do, and they don't fit into the system of essential dignities. Uranus, Neptune, and Pluto spend so much time in each sign that they define the characteristics of entire generations, not of individuals. Chiron moves a bit more quickly through the shorter Virgo/Libra end of its orbit—about one year in each sign; but it spends about eight years each in Pisces and Aries. However, Chiron still relates to group issues rather than personal ones.

We experience the outer planets on a personal level when one or more of our personal planets aspects an outer planet. (We'll cover aspects in detail in chapter 8.) Otherwise, the outer planets in our charts operate in the background, defining our cultural and generational identity and values.

Chiron Through the Signs

Chiron represents our core wound: the spiritual issues that we have the opportunity to explore and heal in this lifetime. Chiron represents both how we are wounded, and also how we may tend to wound others (as a result of our own woundedness).

Chiron in Aries

Individuals with Chiron in Aries have a wounded sense of identity and leadership. Aries seeks only to be able to express the self freely, impulsively, and without limits. Individuals with Chiron in Aries often find this type of self-expression difficult, and frequently have painful emotional and spiritual connections to it. Even while impulsive and uncensored self-expression may be difficult, individuals with Chiron in Aries also tend to experience a deep and fundamental identity crisis, on a spiritual level. They have a deep and abiding need to discover who they truly are, and at the same time, may experience an unconscious fear of self-expression. When the pain of the identity crisis outweighs the fears, the healing journey begins for these individuals, and they begin to seek out their true selves. Through this process, they discover, either consciously or unconsciously, their gifts of leadership, because their efforts to explore who they are and to discover and reclaim their true spiritual identities set examples and blaze trails for others who are following their own quests. By dedicating themselves to finding their own answers and healing their own identities, individuals with Chiron in Aries light the way for others to find and heal their own wounds.

Chiron in Taurus

Chiron in Taurus energy relates to a wounded sense of our physical worth. People with Chiron in Taurus have core issues with the worth, value, and endurance of the material plane, and by extension, with their own bodies, personal worth, and self-image. Chiron in Taurus can also indicate pain associated with enjoying the pleasures of the physical body and the senses. Working with and healing this wound will enable these individuals to discover the true spiritual elements of the physical plane, and overcome their concern about the limited, finite, and changing nature of the physical.

Chiron in Gemini

Chiron in Gemini can indicate a wounded sense of duality, a wounded sense of curiosity and fascination. Chiron in Gemini can also indicate a wound associated with the ability to make choices. The idea that there is only one option, only one true path, is entirely alien to Gemini. An underlying fear may be that if we allowed ourselves to acknowledge that there is always another option, we would run the risk of having made the "wrong" choice. Working with Chiron in Gemini can mean learning how to play again, learning how to explore. The fear, the wound of Chiron in Gemini may ultimately relate to an individual's fundamental perceptions of the world and how it works. By being willing to open themselves to other possibilities, to other perceptions, and to other choices, these individuals can begin to heal their Chiron wound, and ultimately discover a much stronger and more enriching spiritual connection.

Chiron in Cancer

Chiron in Cancer indicates a wound related to our ability to nurture and to be nurtured, and often involves a fundamental fear that our survival needs will not be met. Although Cancer is strongly associated with women in general and with mothers in particular, Chiron in Cancer does not necessarily indicate issues with one's mother. Chiron in Cancer may have a tendency to be overly needy, continually demanding the support and attention of others. No matter how much love and support is offered, however, it will never be sufficient, because until the Chiron wound is healed, Chiron in Cancer is not capable of truly accepting this love and support, or of feeling safe and secure. This energy can also manifest through being a constant caregiver and caretaker and never allowing others to give back (for fear that if we stop giving, others will not give back in return). Working with the Chiron in Cancer wound requires exploring and confronting our fundamental survival fears, and realizing that they are illusions. Because we are one with the universe, our needs will always be met. Chiron in Cancer, then, offers the chance to learn the true spiritual laws of abundance.

Chiron in Leo

Chiron in Leo indicates a wounded sense of specialness and of self-worth. Leo is where we express our creativity, where we give of ourselves and ask that others recognize us for our unique abilities. Chiron in Leo can represent the fear that others will not appreciate us for who we are. This can result in difficulty or pain associated with being creative, or with giving too much of ourselves. By working with this energy, by making the conscious effort to open their hearts and to share their true sense of self with others, individuals with Chiron in Leo can begin to discover where their creativity and uniqueness lie. Often the fear and hesitation encountered with Chiron in Leo is linked to trust issues. If we are able to work through our fears and be the first to open our hearts, and to trust that others will be there for us and will accept and honor us for our courage, we can simultaneously show others how to open their hearts to trust and to love.

Chiron in Virgo

Chiron in Virgo relates to a wounded sense of discrimination and service. Virgo is concerned with the perfection and completion of the physical plane, and with being of use and of service to others. Virgo's first function is to be able to discriminate—to analyze and evaluate, and to be able to separate, as it were, the wheat from the chaff. Individuals with Chiron in Virgo may find this process difficult and uncomfortable, perhaps fearing that if they begin to judge and evaluate the worth of the world, that the world will in turn evaluate and judge their worth—and find them wanting. Chiron in Virgo often manifests as physical challenges and health issues, often chronic ones. These individuals are then forced to pay attention to the physical in a very personal way because they must learn how to heal and perfect their own physical bodies. Being of service, in the true sense, can also be a challenge at first with Chiron in Virgo, as these individuals may initially approach service as a penance and suffering, playing into the martyr and self-sacrifice aspects of Virgo. By exploring their core wound, individuals with Chiron in Virgo can discover the true meaning and purpose of being of service to others: because we are all one, and all separation is illusion, when we give of ourselves to others, we are in fact giving to ourselves.

Chiron in Libra

Individuals with Chiron in Libra have a wounded sense of relationships. The core issue with Chiron in Libra is one of individual identity, although the context of this issue is in one-to-one relationships, and interpersonal boundaries in particular. Maintaining true balance and harmony in relationships is particularly challenging for these individuals, because until they explore and transcend their Chiron-in-Libra wound, they will only feel safe in unsafe and imbalanced relationships. These individuals may find that they attract partners who violate their boundaries and make them deny their individual desires and identities in order to comply and conform to the wishes of their partners. They may also express their Chiron wound by being the dominant partner in the relationships themselves. Only through exploring their Chiron wound and having the courage to acknowledge the patterns of imbalance and violations in their relationships can these individuals move through their fear and pain and discover how to create and maintain truly healthy, supportive, and balanced relationships.

Chiron in Scorpio

Individuals with Chiron in Scorpio have a wound that is related to deep and transformational emotional issues, and that ultimately relates to their sense of emotional self-worth. Because of this wound, these individuals may find that they have a tendency to avoid probing too deeply into their own psyches. Scorpio works deep beneath the surface, and by focusing on more pleasant, stable experiences, individuals with Chiron in Scorpio may be able to avoid triggering their wounds. The key to their healing and to their spirituality, however, lies deep inside on a primal level. Once they choose to begin exploring their deepest emotions and the depths of their unconscious, they will be able to heal and release some exceptionally powerful patterns and wounds both from this life and from past lives. The resulting transformation will leave them open to experiencing true emotional connections with others, as well as the regenerative effects of reconnecting with their true spirituality.

Chiron in Sagittarius

Individuals with Chiron in Sagittarius have a wounded sense of identity and a fundamental struggle with understanding and accepting their place in the universe. Sagittarius is about the quest for truth and usually manifests through the realms of higher education, religion, and philosophy. Sagittarius is also very much oriented toward associating itself with lessons, religions, and beliefs that support and enhance personal freedom. Chiron in Sagittarius can indicate a fundamentally wounded belief system, and can manifest as an individual constantly in search of a cause to follow, but who is never able to commit truly to the ideals and course of action required. It can also indicate individuals who at once feel a desperate need to explore their spirituality and place in the universe, as well as a crushing fear that what they would discover if they were to do so, is that they are insignificant and unworthy as individuals. Working through the wound of Chiron in Sagittarius requires faith, both in our value and worth as individuals, and in the ultimate truth that we are truly integral and essential parts of creation.

Chiron in Capricorn

Individuals with Chiron in Capricorn have a wounded sense of responsibility. By no means does this mean that these individuals are irresponsible; rather, Chiron in Capricorn indicates that learning the true meaning of responsibility is a key lesson. The biggest challenge with responsibility is learning to distinguish between where we are truly responsible, and where we are not. We must learn to be responsible for ourselves, for the choices that we make, for our actions, and for the consequences of those actions. While we must certainly learn to accept responsibility for how our actions affect and impact other individuals, we must also recognize that there is a point where our responsibility ends, and where we must let go. Individuals with Chiron in Capricorn may feel that they carry the burden of responsibility for other people in their lives, and may have difficulty in establishing and maintaining good boundaries in these areas. Most often, however, these individuals become involved in helping others as a way to avoid looking at their own lives and accepting responsibility for them. The healing begins for these individuals when they find the courage to accept responsibility for their own lives, and to give others the opportunity to do the same for theirs.

Chiron in Aquarius

Individuals with Chiron in Aquarius have a wounded sense of group identity. This could be experienced as a need to conform to the accepted standards of society, a struggle with expressing personal freedom, or a hesitation in expressing their own uniqueness while in the presence of others. Essentially, Chiron in Aquarius indicates a generation of individuals with a wounded sense of social worth. The key to healing this wound is through group activities, especially humanitarian pursuits. Engaging in activities that require individual egos to be set aside in the name of something greater can be an outstanding way of healing the self. Chiron in Aquarius indicates that the path to healing and spiritual connection for these individuals is through social interaction. As they learn to take their rightful place as equal members of the groups they choose to join, they can learn how to connect with the group consciousness, and to free themselves from the limitations of the ego.

Chiron in Pisces

Individuals with Chiron in Pisces encounter their woundedness through their spirituality and their compassion. Pisces is concerned with absorbing and transmuting negative emotions. As a mutable water sign, and as the last sign of the zodiac, the mission of Pisces is to complete the last stage of our healing, which occurs on the emotional and soul level, and to reconnect each of us to the knowledge that we are all part of the collective, that there are truly no boundaries and no separation from the ultimate source of love and life. Pisces can often manifest in a martyred quality, and individuals with Chiron in Pisces may be highly aware of this side of Pisces. Although they may be filled with compassion and drawn to help and heal others, they may experience great personal discomfort in order to accomplish this healing. Chiron was one of the greatest healers in mythology, and yet was ultimately unable to heal himself, and in fact was only able to escape his pain through self-sacrifice, giving up his immortality. Eventually, he was elevated to the stars, and therefore was able to transcend his own pain. Individuals with Chiron in Pisces must learn how to heal themselves by learning how to elevate, transmute, and transcend their own woundedness in the same way that they are naturally able to heal others.

Uranus Through the Signs

Uranus represents the new ideas and innovations that are getting ready to break through into the conscious and material realms. Uranus spends approximately seven years in each sign, and during its residency in a given sign, Uranus is responsible for significant changes and advancements in the arenas ruled by that sign. These may not necessarily lead to permanent change. They do, however, always signify the introduction of a new and unexpected point of view that will be the vanguard of the eventual, inevitable changes brought about by Neptune and Pluto.

Uranus in Aries (1927–1935)

The last time Uranus was in Aries, the United States fell into the Great Depression with the stock market crash in 1929. The total collapse of the economy necessitated new and innovative approaches to expressing individual identity, an energy that was carried by Uranus in Aries. The Great Depression was a period of tremendous opportunity for individuals who were able to harness this new and revolutionary approach to the world. Many fortunes were made during this time period by entrepreneurs who were willing to do whatever was necessary to build their businesses—individuals who refused to let their individual drive and purpose be bound by the circumstances and restrictions of others. Uranus in Aries saw the reintroduction of the pioneering spirit into the United States. As the country began to rebuild itself, this new paradigm gained acceptance by the masses. Along with this new, pioneering spirit also came a far more ruthless approach to business, and to the world in general—an "every man for himself" kind of attitude that was a direct result of the unpredictable influence of Uranus.

Uranus in Taurus (1935–1942)

The last generation with Uranus in Taurus was born at a time when the world was focused on putting down roots and building a new, safe, and stable society. Much of America was still feeling the effects of the Depression, and hard work seemed to be the best antidote to the excess and frivolity of the 1920s. Uranus, however, is a very quick energy, and is not comfortable in the slow, steady, plodding sign of Taurus. The generation born with Uranus in Taurus seek both to build new, stable structures in their lives, and at the same time feel compelled to rebel against those structures.

Uranus in Gemini (1942–1950)

The last generation with Uranus in Gemini was born at a time when new information and new technology was of great national concern. Gemini is a double sign, and is always aware of the dual nature of the universe. During the time that Uranus last moved through Gemini, the world saw both the good that the new technologies and discoveries could do, and also the devastating destruction that it could bring with the threat of nuclear war. Those born with Uranus in Gemini carried forth innovations in communication and electronics, and have a special connection with (and perhaps also a special sensitivity to) new technology.

Uranus in Cancer (1950–1955)

The last generation with Uranus in Cancer was born at a time when the role of women in society, and particularly the role of mothers, was beginning to change. During the war, women took jobs and joined the work force, enjoying a sense of independence and power that they had never before experienced. For many of these women, settling back down into their previous roles as housewives and mothers no longer seemed to be as satisfying. Although working mothers didn't become commonplace until many years later, the changes began during this time period. Individuals born with Uranus in Cancer then experienced a different kind of nurturing from the generation before. This generation was the first to experience the breakup of the nuclear family, and as they came of age, this was the first generation to ultimately challenge and change the roles of women in society.

Uranus in Leo (1955–1962)

The last generation with Uranus in Leo embodies new ideas about self-expression and individuality. This generation began to come of age in the 1970s and early 1980s when the "Me" decade was in full swing. Leo energy is not about being self-centered, however; it is about learning how to open up our hearts and share our individual gifts with love and generosity. Individuals with Uranus in Leo help pave the way for others to learn how to express their true and loving selves.

Uranus in Virgo (1962–1968)

The last generation with Uranus in Virgo is the vehicle for radical changes in health care, and in the workplace in general. The purpose of Virgo is to perfect, work, analyze, and discriminate in order to improve the quality of life for everyone. The Uranus in Virgo generation is finding different ways of being of service both to other individuals, and to the planet. This most recent generation born with Uranus in Virgo is actually a subset of the Pluto in Virgo generation, and, in fact, most of these individuals have a Uranus/Pluto conjunction that intensifies the Uranus in Virgo energy and adds a more destructive and transformational element to the picture. In order for the Uranus in Virgo generation to truly make a difference, it's going to have to pull up the existing structures by their roots and completely replace them with new and different paradigms.

Uranus in Libra (1968–1975)

The current generation born with Uranus in Libra is coping with the disruption of the traditional ideas of relationships and partnerships. This is the generation whose parents were getting divorced, and one of the issues that this generation will cope with is maintaining stable relationships that allow for personal freedom. One of the key issues that was introduced during Uranus in Libra was that of personal responsibility in relationships. Just as Uranus in Aries changed how we expressed ourselves as individuals, Uranus in Libra disrupted the idea that relationships must maintain harmony at all cost, and replaced it with the concept that we must be able to explore and express our individuality within the relationship—and that we do not need to stay in a relationship that does not serve our highest good. Marriage as an institution was the hardest hit by Uranus in Libra, as divorce rapidly changed from something that was not discussed in polite society, to a part of our everyday lives. Add to this the energy of the sexual revolution in the late 1960s and early 1970s, and Uranus in Libra truly disrupted and changed our ideas about relationships.

Uranus in Scorpio (1975–1982)

The current generation born with Uranus in Scorpio is coping with the aftermath and repercussions of the Sexual Revolution. Uranus in Scorpio disrupted how we connected on a romantic and sexual level with others. The ideals of "free love" from the 1960s evolved into the singles bar and the "one night stand" in the 1970s. The "Me" generation became so focused on personal gratification both on a sexual and on a material level, that they rapidly began to lose touch with their ability to form deeper, powerful emotional connections with other individuals. Uranus in Scorpio forced us to take a deeper look at ourselves, and saw tremendous growth in all forms of therapy. Psychiatry and psychology were the tools on the cutting edge of transforming and uncovering the darker aspects of our psyche, and as Uranus traveled through Scorpio, seeing an analyst went from being a private matter to being a status symbol. Uranus in Scorpio also changed how we looked at our natural resources, thanks to the energy crisis, and prompted innovations in recycling and conservation.

Uranus in Sagittarius (1982–1988)

Uranus in Sagittarius looks for insights into the ultimate truth, and the impetus here is to latch onto an ideal and pursue it. In the United States, Ronald Reagan took hold of this energy by stirring up a sense of national pride and creating an enemy in Russia (the "Evil Empire"). As Sagittarius operates on the level of ideals and philosophies, the Cold War was really about the difference between our truth (capitalism) and their truth (communism); communist beliefs, in the typically focused and single-minded manner of Sagittarius, must by definition be wrong since they differ from our beliefs, which are by definition right. Uranus in Sagittarius also saw innovations and advancements in higher education, most notably thanks to the growing popularity and availability of computers.

Uranus in Capricorn (1988–1996)

When Uranus transits through Capricorn, the major institutions of society, which include not only government but also business and industry, are disrupted and society begins to look at them in a very different light. Uranus in Capricorn doesn't necessarily cause major changes and restructuring in these institutions, but it does represent the first crack in their foundations; and what Uranus starts, Neptune and Pluto will most certainly finish. The last time Uranus was in Capricorn, Neptune was also in Capricorn, preparing to move into Aquarius, and the two planets spent many years in close proximity to each other, working in tandem. The disruptive energy of Uranus helped to speed up the disillusionment process of Neptune, and the world began to become acutely aware that the foundation and structure of society was in need of significant change. In the United States, Uranus in Capricorn heralded the first backlash against the massive consumerism and materialism of the Reagan administration. Iran-Contra and other deceptions disrupted the country's faith in its leaders, and more individuals began to protest and speak out against the policies and laws that were only in the best interest of the rich and powerful.

Uranus in Aquarius (1913–1920, 1996–2003)

Uranus in Aquarius has a tendency to create worldwide upheaval on a social and humanistic level. The last time Uranus was in Aquarius, we saw fundamental disruptions and changes in society thanks to World War I, a war fought, at least in principle, in the name of freedom and equality. Human rights and freedom are once again a primary concern as Uranus has returned to Aquarius, and the world has returned to an effective state of war, attempting to protect the freedom and the lives of the persecuted in Bosnia and Yugoslavia. Aquarius relates to our concept of a perfect society, where everyone is equal and personal freedom is protected at all cost, so long as it does not pose a threat to the overall integrity and structure of society. Uranus in Aquarius is making us aware, once again, of where society's rules and structures have failed and where we must become agents of change. During the current passage of Uranus through Aquarius, we have seen the creation of an entirely new community through computers and the Internet.

Uranus in Pisces (1920–1927, 2003–2010)

The last time Uranus was in Pisces, we saw a major resurgence of interest in astrology, thanks largely to the introduction of Sun sign horoscope columns into many newspapers and magazines. This type of activity is typical of the energy of Uranus in Pisces, which encourages us to discover new and different ways of approaching our spirituality. As is often the case in the wake of a great tragedy (in this case, World War I), we look to our spiritual leaders for guidance as to how to cope with the loss. With Uranus in Pisces, we experienced a disruption of that support—traditional spiritual practices began to feel too limiting and restrictive, and many people began to look elsewhere for guidance and support. We can expect much the same types of changes when Uranus moves into Pisces again in the year 2003. Already the world is feeling disillusioned and confused by the transition from the twentieth to the twenty-first century. The "New Age" movement, which has been growing in popularity and public acceptance for over twenty years now, will be greatly affected by this energy, since once again Uranus will introduce new and disruptive elements that will force us to reexamine the structure and foundation of our belief systems.

Neptune Through the Signs

Neptune represents the collective dream, the ideals and wishes of the collective unconscious. Neptune relates to our fantasies and desires, as well as to our hopes and aspirations as a society. In many ways, Neptune's position by sign relates directly to the *Zeitgeist* or spirit of a given time, and when Neptune changes signs, the dreams of the world undergo fundamental and significant changes. Because Neptune moves so slowly, we're only going to look at Neptune's sign positions in the twentieth century.

Neptune in Cancer (1901–1914)

The dreams and ideals associated with Neptune in Cancer had to do with being nurtured and ensuring that our needs, both emotional and physical, were met. Cancer always relates to the role of women in society, and with Neptune in Cancer, the dream involved women living a life of leisure as housewives and mothers. For the first time, the men were going off during the day to work at jobs rather than at trades, and the women were left largely to their own devices. Food was quite important during this time period, as being well nourished also means that our needs have been met. Taking this dream to a rather extreme level, Neptune in Cancer saw the election of 300-pound William Taft to the office of the president, as well as the introduction and passage of both the Meat Inspection Act and the Pure Food and Drug Act.

Neptune in Leo (1914–1929)

Neptune's passage through Leo saw the focus of society's dreams turn to the individual. Leo energy wants to share itself, to be generous and loving, and above all, to be acknowledged and appreciated for this in return. While Neptune was in Leo, we dreamed of being recognized and appreciated, of being placed in the spotlight—even if only for our fifteen minutes of fame. The country was enjoying a period of unprecedented prosperity and leisure thanks to the wartime economy and the United States getting involved in World War I. This was the era of speakeasies and bathtub gin, flappers, fashions, and glamour—all of which (except, perhaps for the flappers) are very much related to Neptune. Not surprisingly, the movie industry made its most significant and rapid advancements during this period of time. (Neptune, of course, rules all forms of film and photography, glamour and illusion.) Movie stars were born, and became the kings and queens of our country, in typical Leo fashion. Neptune in Leo, of course, dreams of royalty, and through the movie industry, it created, worshipped, and eventually destroyed many a star.

Neptune in Virgo (1929–1943)

The energy of Virgo has to do with service, with giving of oneself in order to make the world a better place for everyone. The last time Neptune was in Virgo, we saw great advancements in labor relations when the labor unions won the right to collective bargaining; but the dream of a perfect society built on service to the greater good was also responsible for Hitler's rise to power in Germany and the resulting Holocaust. The generation born with Neptune in Virgo carries forth the dream of creating a perfect world, a place where each individual selflessly contributes to the greater good, and a place where the contributions of each individual truly make a difference. Many of these individuals became very active in the 1960s with the various civil rights movements, joining together with others of their generation to try to change the world for the better.

Neptune in Libra (1943–1957)

The generation born with Neptune in Libra dreams of balance, of harmony, and of relationships. Because Neptune dissolves all structures that separate, and encourages a merging with the universal force, individuals with Neptune in Libra share a generational need to learn how to structure and maintain appropriate personal boundaries, particularly in relationships. The Neptune influence can encourage the belief that a relationship should involve a loss of self, a complete merging with another individual, but this is not what Libra energy is about. Libra energy is about forming and maintaining one-to-one relationships that involve balancing our individual identity with another individual. Libra is not limited to personal relationships, however; Libra relationships are about finding harmony between ourselves and the world, and can be expressed through art, music, and spirituality. On the highest level, Libra is motivated to find a balance and harmony, a one-to-one relationship between our individual sense of self, and the creative force of the universe. The generation born with Neptune in Libra taps into this spiritual urge to reconnect with the universe.

Neptune in Scorpio (1957–1971)

During Neptune's transit through Scorpio, the limitations and boundaries that governed our expression of sexuality and our exploration of our unconscious and subconscious natures began to dissolve. The energy of Scorpio relates to our desire and ability to connect with another individual in a deeply emotional and transformational way, to unite so that, at least for a brief moment, we lose all sense of separation, all sense of individuality and ego. While Neptune relates to the ideal, it also relates to disillusionment, and the generation born with Neptune in Scorpio has certainly experienced disillusionment with respect to their ability to express themselves sexually. This generation is the first to use sex as an escape, as a drug, and also the first to be truly impacted by the hidden consequences of this form of escape which manifested when Pluto entered Scorpio in the 1980s with the advent of the AIDS virus. Scorpio is not simply about sex, however; Scorpio is about learning how to probe deeply into the unconscious, learning how to allow ourselves to be completely transformed by emotions. On the highest level, the generation with Neptune in Scorpio is learning to look deep within themselves to find their personal spiritual connection.

Neptune in Sagittarius (1971–1984)

The generation born with Neptune in Sagittarius is learning about and experiencing the dissolving of the structures of organized religion. Finding a spiritual connection through established structures is especially difficult for this generation. This generation is more concerned with finding creative ways of expressing and understanding their relationship to the universe. Neptune in Sagittarius dissolves faith in structures, in doctrine, and in the teachings of others with respect to spirituality. While Sagittarius encourages planets to seek the truth, Neptune already is the truth. Neptune in Sagittarius will find the truth by dissolving the illusions of ego and separation that hide the truth from us. The energy of Neptune in Sagittarius was also responsible for the creation of many false prophets and self-proclaimed spiritual leaders. Anyone who proclaimed that they had found the truth loudly enough would find him or herself mobbed by people seeking "The Answer™," people willing to follow any and all instructions from their guru in their quest for enlightenment. Individuals born with Neptune in Sagittarius still carry this energy, and while they search for the truth, they must also learn to be very discriminating in their choice of guides and teachers.

Neptune in Capricorn (1984–1998)

The collective dream of Neptune in Capricorn involved maintaining the status quo while at the same time being ruthlessly ambitious and accumulating as much material wealth and social status as humanly possible. This time period was exemplified by the Ronald Reagan/George Bush leadership of the United States. The country bought into Reagan's dream of wealth and economic growth when Neptune was in the last part of Sagittarius, and pledged to follow him wherever he led. Reagan led much of the country to a dream of wealth and prosperity; however, this dream was one where the rich got richer and the rest of the country received little or no help from Reagan's fictional theory of "trickle-down economics." Capricorn energy wants to maintain the rules and structures of society based on tradition, and conservative politicians saw a tremendous gain in power and control both in the United States and abroad. In the United States, a Republican Congress strongly influenced by the so-called "Religious Right" made tremendous headway with legislation that restricted the rights of many while lining the pockets of the wealthy. Controversial issues such as abortion and gay rights rose to the forefront of debates again, and took severe beatings in many cases, as Congress took advantage of the Neptune in Capricorn dream of security, structure, and protection at all costs by playing on the fears of the country.

Neptune in Aquarius (1998–2011)

Now that Neptune has moved into Aquarius, however, the collective dreams of society have changed, and the conservatives currently in power are already feeling the repercussions. The dream is now about protecting the rights and freedom of each individual. Neptune in Aquarius dreams of a utopian society where all people are indeed created equal and where our fundamental right to choose how we live our lives is held as sacred. In the United States, the backlash against the conservative Republicans for the Clinton impeachment proceedings is only the first sign of significant change. Already the Republicans are trying to distance themselves from the right-wing conservatives and take on a more moderate platform, one that allows for greater personal freedom and choice. As Neptune continues to move through Aquarius, we will see fundamental changes in human rights worldwide, as the energy of Aquarius examines the existing laws and policies and tears down those that no longer support the greater good of society.

Pluto Through the Signs

Pluto is the final frontier, as it were. Pluto is the ultimate destroyer, tearing down all structures that no longer serve us, ultimately destroying all our illusions and leaving only the truth that we are eternal beings at one with all creation. Pluto's position by sign shows the particular arenas that will be undergoing powerful, transformational, and irrevocable change in society. Since Pluto moves so slowly through the signs, we're only going to look at Pluto's travels through the twentieth century.

Pluto in Gemini (1885–1913)

The last time Pluto was in Gemini, we saw drastic and fundamental changes in how we travel and communicate. It's one thing to dream about a new technology or idea, but quite another to experience the irrevocable changes that occur once that new idea has been implemented. During this time period, the first subways were built in London, the first telephone switchboard was created, Marconi invented the radio, and Zeppelin invented his airship. While we take these changes for granted today because they are so much a part of our lives, they represented major upheavals and fundamental paradigm shifts when they first appeared. Pluto in Gemini forever changed how we looked at and experienced communication and travel.

Pluto in Cancer (1913–1939)

Cancer energy is related to how we nurture and protect ourselves, and to the role in society of women in general and mothers in particular. When Pluto was last in Cancer, the United States saw the most drastic changes in how its needs were being met. The economy soared with the U.S. involvement in World War I, and the country enjoyed an unprecedented time of luxury and comfort. This was, of course, followed by a typically Plutonian reversal when the stock market crashed in October of 1929, and the country was plunged overnight into the worst economic period in history. People went from caviar to the breadline in the blink of an eye. Suddenly, the country's needs weren't being met anymore, and this experience left an indelible impression on the country that is felt even today—we are taught not to take our abundance for granted, because in an instant, our needs could no longer be met. This is certainly not a healthy or supportive approach to life, but it is one of the lasting remnants and fears that resulted from Pluto in Cancer.

Pluto in Leo (1939–1958)

Leo energy is about opening our hearts to express and receive unconditional love. Pluto's time in Leo put a great deal of emphasis on our hearts, often necessitating a Plutonian death and rebirth of the heart. For the first time in history, heart disease became a serious health issue, brought on as much by poor diet and exercise habits (which, of course, underwent significant changes when Pluto was in Cancer), as by a growing tendency for individuals, particularly for men, to hold in their feelings and emotions. In true Leo fashion, a man during this time period was supposed to be the "king of his castle." He had to provide for his family and maintain his daily responsibilities, and he had to be prepared to leave his family in order to defend his country during times of war. Openly expressing emotions was simply not acceptable behavior for a so-called real man. The generation born with Pluto in Leo carries this energy with them, and are working both individually and collectively, both men and women, on learning how to open their hearts.

Pluto in Virgo (1958–1971)

With Pluto in Virgo, a mutable earth sign, the societal transformations involved changes and power struggles concerning the health of the planet and the conservation of our natural resources. During the Pluto in Virgo period, we saw the formation of ecological groups, and a rise in awareness of how we have been poisoning and polluting our planet. The Pluto in Virgo generation is also currently involved in making changes in health care, as well as changes in how each of us serves and supports the community.

Pluto in Libra (1971–1984)

Libra is concerned with one-to-one relationships, and with the boundaries, responsibilities, and need for balance and harmony in these relationships. When Pluto transited through Libra, it was the final blow to our old models and concepts of interpersonal relationships. The generation born with Pluto in Libra must learn to build a new way of relating to others. This generation came into a world of chaos in terms of relationships. Uranus in Libra sparked a rash of divorces and a desire for personal freedom. The Neptune in Libra generation created the ideas of codependence and the need for good personal boundaries. Pluto in Libra obliterated the last remnants of the old and outdated relationship models.

Pluto in Scorpio (1984–1996)

Pluto in Scorpio forever changed the way we view sex. Pluto in Scorpio brought the AIDS virus to the world, and no one can dispute that AIDS has resulted in fundamental and often traumatic changes in our sexuality. Gone are the promiscuity and "free love" ideals that first surfaced in the 1960s. Monogamy is popular again, if only as a health precaution. Both Pluto and Scorpio are related to the processes of death and rebirth, and both involve making us face our personal demons and fears, to confront them, and to be transformed by this process. AIDS is the great plague of the twentieth century, and while it has brought out the most noble qualities in many, it has also been responsible for revealing some of our greatest atrocities. Pluto in Scorpio has stripped us down to our core emotional natures, and only now are we beginning to be able to pick up the pieces and build again.

Pluto in Sagittarius (1996–2009)

After the devastation we experienced during Pluto's transit through Scorpio, many individuals have looked to a higher power for help in coping with this destruction. We look to the church, to schools, and to our doctors and philosophers for guidance; and now that Pluto is in Sagittarius, we're discovering that the advice they have to offer us is often considerably lacking. The last time Pluto was in Sagittarius was from 1749 to 1762, a period of time known as the Enlightenment. Newspapers and the availability of education to common people fueled this period of extremely rapid change and transformation in thought. This was the "Age of Reason," when science gained its first foothold in the long climb to fight religion and superstition for the seat at the top of the mountain. Today, organized religion is falling on hard times as more and more individuals are seeking more personal spiritual paths. Education is once again a top priority. The last time Pluto was in Sagittarius, newspapers helped to educate common people. Today, anyone with a computer and an Internet connection has access to an almost infinite store of knowledge. Once again, Pluto in Sagittarius is tearing down old beliefs and philosophies, and encouraging us to learn to think for ourselves.

6

The Angles, the Houses, and the Part of Fortune

We have already met the actors and become familiar with their roles and costumes, and we've even looked at how well each actor seems to play each role. Now it's time to take a look at where the actors play out their scenes—the houses of the chart. But before we get into defining the qualities of each individual house (and we will, I promise), we're going to take a short digression and look at the mathematics and history of houses in astrology.

A Brief Overview of House Systems

Although there are a number of different house systems in use today, they all fall into one of four different categories: Equal, Time, Space, or Quadrant. Most of these systems use at least one of the angles, either the Ascendant or the Midheaven, as a reference point and house cusp. The most significant differences between the different house systems are the locations and sizes of the intermediate houses (houses 2, 3, 5, 6, 8, 9, 11, and 12). To address the question of which house system is "best," the thing to remember is that *all* house systems work. Some seem to work more effectively with certain types of astrology, but ultimately, it doesn't matter what house system you use. I personally use Koch houses in my natal charts, Regiomontanus houses for my horary and electional work, and Campanus houses for my return charts.

Equal House Systems

By far the oldest group of house systems are the Equal house systems. As you can probably guess from the name, in Equal house systems, all the houses are of equal size: they are each 30°, and there can be no intercepted houses. The oldest house system, used by the ancient Greeks, was an Equal house system of whole-sign houses. In this system, the angles are not necessarily house cusps (mainly because at the time this system was used, the tools for measuring time, distance, and angles were not advanced enough to give accurate readings). Whatever sign was rising became the first house, and the rest of the houses followed in sequence, each comprising an entire sign. One curious feature of this house system is that it is possible, if a very late degree is rising, for most of the first house to be *above* the horizon where we would expect to see the twelfth house. This system is used today by astrologers who work with some of the newly recovered classical techniques.

The two most common Equal house variations in use today are based on the angles. The most popular system starts with the Ascendant as the cusp of the first house, and each subsequent house cusp follows at 30° intervals. The Midheaven is not necessarily a house cusp in this system. The alternative is a Midheaven-based Equal house system, where the Midheaven is the point of origin, defining the cusp of the tenth house, and all subsequent houses follow at 30° intervals from this point. In this variation, the Ascendant is not necessarily a house cusp.

Equal house systems today are the most popular when calculating charts for extreme latitudes. The farther away from the equator you get, the more distorted the results from the other house systems become, until you can end up with charts where some houses are only a few degrees wide, while others cover up to three signs at a time.

WARNING! The next few sections will describe how the different house systems are calculated. These sections will include numerous references to spherical geometry, astronomy, and trigonometry terms that I'm not even going to attempt to define here. These explanations can be found in the NCGR Level II Study Guide. They are provided here in the interest of being thorough. If you are particularly math-phobic, you can safely skip over the next few sections. I'll let you know when it's time to start paying attention again.

Quadrant Systems

Quadrant systems basically divide the chart into four quadrants using the Ascendant and Midheaven axis, and then use different methods of calculating the intermediate cusps.

Campanus

The Prime Vertical is divided into twelve equal arcs by lunes (sections of the sphere), whose poles are the north and south points of the horizon. Where the lunes cut the ecliptic are the house cusps.

Regiomontanus

The Celestial Equator is divided into twelve equal segments, beginning at the East Point. The house cusps are formed by the intersections of the house semicircles with the ecliptic. Since the equator is not perpendicular to the North Point-South Point axis of the horizon, the houses are not equal.

Porphyry

The cusps of the intermediate houses are determined by trisecting the arc of longitude in each quadrant. The arc between the Midheaven and Ascendant is trisected, giving the cusps of the eleventh and twelfth houses. The same is done for the other quadrants.

Alcabitius

Divisions in the arc are described by the movement of the degree of the Ascendant. Equal division of the diurnal cycle created by the degree of the Ascendant is determined by hour circles from the poles. This system is the first of the modern house systems.

Time Systems

Time systems take the semi-arc of some major mundane sensitive point and trisect it; that trisection becomes the basis for the house divisions.

Placidus

The house cusp curves are formed by points, each of which trisects its own diurnal or nocturnal semi-arc. Where these complex curves cross the ecliptic determines the ecliptic cusps given in the Placidian Table of Houses.

Koch

The diurnal semi-arc of the Midheaven is trisected. Calling the trisections of the semi-arc "x," the Midheaven is then rotated backwards through the diurnal semi-arc. At this point, the Midheaven comes to the horizon. Then the Midheaven is rotated x degrees off the horizon. The new Ascendant is the eleventh-house cusp. Rotating the Midheaven another x degrees brings the twelfth-house cusp to the Ascendant; another x degrees brings the first-house cusp (the final Ascendant) to the Ascendant; another x degrees brings the second-house cusp to the Ascendant; and finally, another x degrees brings the third-house cusp to the Ascendant.

Space Systems

Meridian (Equatorial Houses)

The Celestial Equator is divided into twelve equal arcs by lunes from the poles of the Celestial Equator. The intersections of lunes with the ecliptic are considered the house cusps. Each house is exactly two sidereal hours long. The Midheaven is the cusp of the tenth house, and the Equatorial Ascendant (the Ascendant if the chart were calculated at the Equator) is the cusp of the first house. The chart Ascendant is not a house cusp.

O.K., we're finished with the complicated, scary stuff. You can come back now.

Quadrants and Hemispheres

We're going to work our way into the individual houses gradually, taking in the big picture first, and then looking at the individual components. Much as the signs have elements and modalities, the houses have hemispheres and quadrants, as seen in figure 8.

The first thing you're likely to notice about the houses and quadrants is that the cardinal directions aren't where you would expect to see them. The top hemisphere of the chart is the *Southern* Hemisphere, while the bottom hemisphere is the *Northern* Hemisphere. Likewise, the left hemisphere of the chart is the *Eastern* Hemisphere while the right hemisphere is the *Western* Hemisphere.

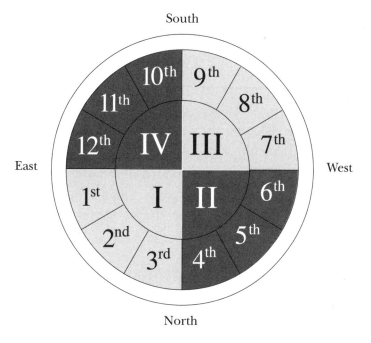

Figure 8. Quadrants and Hemispheres

The Southern Hemisphere

The Southern Hemisphere of the chart includes houses 7 through 12. These houses are above the horizon; planets in these houses can be seen in the sky (assuming, of course, that the Sun isn't also in these houses!). Planets in the Southern Hemisphere then tend to be more visible, and more extroverted in their expression. The houses in the Southern Hemisphere are meant to be seen by other people, and planets in these houses tend to express themselves more openly.

The Northern Hemisphere

The Northern Hemisphere of the chart, which includes houses 1 through 6, is below the horizon, and can't be seen. Planets in the Northern Hemisphere of the chart are hidden from view, and they tend to be more introverted and private in their expression. These houses are more personal, and aren't meant to be shared with everybody.

The Eastern Hemisphere

The Eastern Hemisphere of the chart includes houses 1, 2, 3, 10, 11, and 12. These houses surround the Ascendant, the point in the chart where we are the most focused on our individual expression. Planets in the Eastern houses tend to be more self-reliant, self-initiating, and active.

The Western Hemisphere

The Western Hemisphere of the chart includes houses 4, 5, 6, 7, 8, and 9. These houses surround the Descendant, the point in the chart where we are the most focused on relating to other individuals. Planets in the Western houses tend to be more receptive and focused on taking others into consideration.

The Quadrants

Each quadrant combines the qualities of two hemispheres. Quadrant I (houses 1, 2, and 3) is both introverted (Northern) and self-reliant (Eastern). Quadrant II (houses 4, 5, and 6) is introverted (Northern) and reactive (Western). Quadrant III (houses 7, 8, and 9) is extroverted (Southern) and reactive (Western). Quadrant IV (houses 10, 11, and 12) is extroverted (Southern) and self-reliant (Eastern).

Understanding the Houses

In natal astrology, it sometimes helps to think of the houses not as actual houses, but rather as "rooms" that are inside each of us. Each room has a special purpose and is reserved for certain types of experiences. Think of it this way: when we're hungry and want something to eat, we go to the kitchen, not the bedroom or the study; and we usually don't sleep in the bathroom or the dining room. It's the same way with the houses in the birth chart. The sixth house is our office—it's where we go to work. When we want to go out and have fun, on the other hand, we go to our fifth house. We meet up with our friends in the eleventh house, and our family in the fourth.

The signs on the cusps of the houses show how each room is decorated. We all have all twelve signs in our charts, although the signs are associated with different "rooms" of our chart. We all have a "Gemini room" where we find our books, toys, games, and distractions, and we all have a "Capricorn room" which is usually done over in mahogany and hardwood with very practical, business-like furnishings. What's different for each of us is *which* room is the "Gemini room" and *which* room is the "Capricorn room." Those of us with the seventh house of relationships being our "Gemini room" are going to approach relationships with a very different style from those who have their relationship room decorated in "Capricorn."

So who decorated the rooms? The planets that rule the sign did—and they decorated the rooms in the style of the role that they're currently playing. The "Capricorn room" is going to have a much lighter, more open feel when Saturn is in Gemini than it will when Saturn is in Scorpio (in which case the decoration of the room probably leans heavily toward black leather). The "Cancer room" is going to be much more plush and comfortable when the Moon is in Taurus than when the Moon is in Sagittarius. The rulers of the houses keep close tabs on their rooms; when the planet that rules a house is in a different house, the affairs of the two houses are linked. For example, if we have Aries (which Mars rules) on the second-house cusp, and Mars is in the ninth house, our finances (second house) will be connected to the affairs of the ninth house (travel, higher education, religion, etc.).

When we have planets in a house, then we will tend to experience and express the energy of those planets whenever we go into that house—and every time we go into that house, we're going to have to deal with the planet (or planets) there. If we have Saturn in the seventh house, we're going to encounter Saturn's energy through our relationships. Mars in the ninth house could lend a more competitive edge to our higher education and religious studies. Houses without planets are just empty rooms: we can go there and be (reasonably) alone; when we're in an empty house, we're still influenced by the energy of the house ruler, but not nearly as strongly as we are by a planet in the house itself.

Occasionally, you will come across a chart where a house contains an entire sign: for example, a chart with 28° of Gemini on the second-house cusp and 4° of Leo on the third-house cusp has the entire sign of Cancer intercepted in the second house. The astrologer Kim Rogers-Gallagher describes intercepted signs as rooms with antechambers, or rooms within rooms. Gemini is still the ruler of the second house in this example, and Mercury still did the decorating; but the Moon (and Cancer) is also involved in the process, and, in fact, the furnishings and structure of the room are all the Moon's—Mercury and Gemini just picked out the wallpaper, the colors, and the fabrics. It may *look* like Mercury and Gemini, but once you settle into the room, it will really *feel* like the Moon and Cancer.

Understanding the Angles

The angles are extremely important points in the chart—they are usually also house cusps, but not always (it depends on the house system used). The angles represent the façade that we show to the world—they are how other people perceive us. More importantly, the angles are the primary "doors" in our chart that open to the outside world. The Ascendant is our Front Door: it's where we go when we set out into the world to interact with other people. The Descendant is the Back Door, where we receive visits from the people who know us. The Midheaven (or MC) is the door to the roof—the most visible place in our home, and it's where we want to impress the world in general. The *Imum Coeli* (or IC) is the most hidden, secret door, the Private Entrance used only by close friends and family.

The Three Types of Houses: Angular, Succedent, and Cadent

Houses can also be either angular, succedent, or cadent. The angular houses (1, 4, 7, and 10) are the houses that, not surprisingly, are usually connected to the angles. Because the angular houses are the closest to the main "doors" to the outside world (the Ascendant, Midheaven, Descendant, and *Imum Coeli*), planets in angular houses are considered to be "strong" and tend to express themselves in more external and obvious ways. Angular houses are very action-oriented and are similar in quality to cardinal signs. A planet in an angular house is usually considered to be accidentally dignified. Succedent houses (2, 5, 8, and 11) follow (or succeed) the angular houses, and are relatively neutral in quality. Planets in succedent houses aren't in the foreground of the chart, but they're not in the background, either. Succedent houses are concerned with security and stability, so the succedent houses are similar to the fixed signs in this respect. The cadent houses (3, 6, 9, and 12) follow the succedent houses, and are the least expressive points in the chart. Planets in cadent houses, particularly the third and sixth houses, are sometimes considered to be accidentally debilitated because they have much greater difficulty making themselves noticed. Cadent houses are concerned with learning and with adaptation, and are similar to the mutable signs. The last few degrees of the cadent houses, however (usually the 4 to 6° before the angles), are extremely strong. Planets in a cadent house within 6° of an angle are considered to be angular and accidentally dignified.

A Tour of the Houses and Angles

Now that we have a general understanding of what the houses are, let's look at what each of these "rooms" contain, and when and why we spend time in each of them. For review, another illustration of the houses and angles is presented in figure 9.

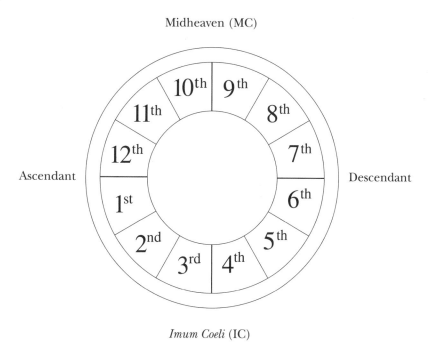

Figure 9. The Houses and Angles

The Ascendant

In the majority of house systems, the Ascendant is used as the cusp of the first house. The Ascendant, which is also known as the "rising sign," is the degree of the zodiac that was on the Eastern Horizon (in other words, the degree that was rising) at the moment of birth, as "seen" from the location of birth. The Ascendant is one of the most important points in the chart: it's not only the "door" to the first house, it's also our "front door." The Ascendant is the door we use when we go out into the world—it's the first thing people see about us, and first impressions are very important.

In fact, the Ascendant represents our first impressions of the world. The sign on the Ascendant shows how we expect to encounter and experience the world. Individuals with Gemini rising have a core belief that the world is a fascinating place that is meant to be explored. People with Cancer rising, on the other hand, take a very different view, and approach the world as a place that can be a bit scary and lonely, where their needs may not be met, so they need to connect with other people on an emotional level for protection. The Ascendant has often been described as the "mask that we wear" when we relate to other people. The thing about this mask, though, is that it also colors the way we see the world.

The First House

The Ascendant is also the "door" to the first house, which is where we keep all the things that make us who we are as unique individuals. The first house is the "this is who I am" room. It relates to our appearance (and is usually decorated with pictures of ourselves), as well as to all the things that make up the essence of our unique personality. The first house represents our physical body and our overall health and vitality.

The Second House

The second house is where we keep all our "stuff." The first house is what is "me," and the second house is what is "mine." Not only do we store our physical and material possessions in our second house, but we also store our gifts, talents, and skills there as well. The second house is one of the "money" houses (along with the sixth and tenth houses), and can indicate *how* we make money. The second house also relates to our physical senses, to the things we value, and the ways in which we experience the physical world.

The Third House

The third house is the mail and telephone room—the communication hub of our chart. When we want to keep tabs on our environment, siblings, and neighbors, this is where we go. The third house also relates to short journeys, letters, writing, and our early education. Being a cadent house, the third house is, of course, about learning, and about how we interact with our environment in particular. The third house also relates to religion and spirituality, although it seems to have more to do with religions that are not widely accepted at the time. (In classical astrology, the third house was the house of heresy.)

The *Imum Coeli*

The *Imum Coeli*, or IC, as it is usually known, is the most private and hidden point in the chart. It is still a "door" to the outside world, but it's more of a secret, hidden entrance, one that is only ever used by our close friends and family, because it leads to the most private, protected, and personal facets of our lives. Even though the IC is the most hidden point in the chart, it is also the one where we experience the greatest connection to the universe—through the IC we can connect with our past, our heritage, and ultimately with the memory of what it was like to be a part of all creation. The IC is the point that relates to all beginnings and endings in the chart, and is the point through which the soul enters our bodies.

The Fourth House

The fourth house is the family room—it's hidden and somewhat closed off from the rest of the chart, so most people won't ever see it or know it's there. This house is reserved for our private, personal time, and it's a space that we share with our families (of choice and of origin) and intimate friends. Although we can go here when we want to be alone, we generally go to the fourth house when we want to feel a sense of connection and community to those we love— and, of course, the fourth house is in the Western Hemisphere of the chart, and so here we are more focused on relationships and interacting with other individuals than we are on being alone and self-sufficient. The fourth house relates to real estate and property, and rules the father in the chart (even though modern astrology associates the mother with the fourth house). Even though the fourth house is an angular house and therefore action-oriented, because it is the most hidden, least-visible point in the chart, planets in the fourth house do not tend to express themselves in very public ways.

The Fifth House

The fifth house is the party room—it's where we go here when it's time to let our hair down and have fun. All forms of creativity, self-expression, games, speculation, and gambling are found in the fifth house. Oh, and sex is in the fifth house, too (and so are children). The fifth house relates to love affairs—any romantic relationship that does not involve a contractual commitment or where the individuals don't live under the same roof. (Once two people either get married or move in together, it becomes a seventh-house relationship.) So what do all these things have in common? Well, the fifth house is essentially where we go when we want to feel special and unique. Everything we experience in the fifth house makes us feel *good*—both in general, and about ourselves as individuals in particular.

The Sixth House

The sixth house is our office—it's where we go to take care of business on a daily basis, and in the sixth house, we find all the routines and activities that we have to do on a daily basis in order to maintain an existence on the physical plane. The sixth house is a cadent house, and here we are concerned with learning about the material world. The sixth house relates to our job (but not necessarily to our career or life's work), and to our coworkers and working environment. It also relates to our physical body and health, in that the sixth house is the house of illness (at least in classical astrology). Having planets in the sixth house doesn't indicate that we're going to have health problems, but six-house planets do tend to describe the types of things that we will have to do in order to *prevent* health problems.

The Descendant

The Descendant is the back door to our chart—it's where we attract and interact with other individuals. Just as the Ascendant can operate as a kind of a mask that changes both how others see us and how we view the world, the Descendant shows what we look for in partners (primarily romantic partners, of course, but not exclusively). The Descendant is exactly opposite the Ascendant, and it makes sense that the qualities we are the most attracted to in others are the qualities that we feel we ourselves are missing, because we don't see or express them through our Ascendants. Whenever the Descendant is involved, we're relating to other individuals on a one-to-one basis.

The Seventh House

The seventh house is the guest room—we generally reserve the seventh house for activities that involve other people, so much so, in fact, that we have a tendency to forget that the seventh house is still a part of us. The seventh house is opposite the first house. While the first house is everything that is "me," the seventh house is everything that is "not me." We experience our seventh house through relationships, particularly through one-to-one, contractual relationships. The seventh house is the house of marriage as well as the house of open enemies. Because we're always dealing with other people in the seventh house, we have a tendency to give away planets in the seventh house *to* other people. We often feel that we lack the qualities and planets in our seventh house, and until we learn to accept that they are, in fact, a part of us, we will experience them externally, through relationships.

The Eighth House

The eighth house is where our guests store their things, to extend the analogy. Being directly opposite the second house of what is "mine," the eighth house contains everything that is "not mine," and is generally associated with other people's money and resources. The eighth house relates to more than money, though—the eighth house is the house of death, taxes, and inheritance. Being a succedent house, the eighth house is concerned with security—in this case, with emotional and soul security. The eighth house is visible, being above the horizon in the Southern Hemisphere, and it involves other people because it's in the Western half of the chart. Nevertheless, the eighth house is a very private room—it's where we keep many of our secrets as well as our fears. The eighth house relates to the occult, and to buried and hidden things, and so psychology and psychotherapy can be found here. Thanks to Freud and modern psychology, however, the eighth house has gradually become associated with sex (probably because of the Freudian connection between sex and death).

Ancient astrologers would never have understood this—they knew that sex was supposed to be *fun,* and therefore it belonged in the fifth house.

The Ninth House

The ninth house is our combination research library and travel agency. Opposite the third house of early education and short journeys, the ninth house relates to higher education and long journeys—both in duration and in distance. The ninth house is where we explore the world and experience and encounter new and unfamiliar cultures, ideas, and people. The ninth house is also related to organized religion and the clergy. We go to the ninth house when we dream and fantasize. What we study and learn in the ninth house is for our own personal growth and enlightenment; anything we learn to help us on a career or professional level is found in the tenth house next door.

The Midheaven

The last (but by no means the least important) angle is the Midheaven. The Midheaven is the door to the roof of our building—it's where we stand out, where we're the most visible to the outside world. The Midheaven relates to our career and life path in the sense that this is how we want to be recognized by society as individuals. While the Midheaven is the most public and prominent point in the chart, it is also the most isolated and lonely. The roof is only big enough for one person at a time, and it's a long, narrow climb to get there. The Midheaven is opposite the IC, where we are the least visible, but the most connected to our roots and our source. The Midheaven is our crowning achievement as individuals, our most public face, and the way we take responsibility for our role in society.

The Tenth House

The tenth house is the corporate office—this is where all public appearances are scheduled, and where we plan and receive recognition for our individual accomplishments in life. The tenth house relates to our life path, which, if we're lucky, is also related to our chosen career. The tenth house is related to authority figures and policy makers and, traditionally, to that ultimate authority figure and policy maker, Mom. Even though modern astrology has decided that the father should be represented by the tenth house and the mother by the fourth house, in classical astrology, Dad is behind the scenes at the foundation, while Mom is the one who takes the more prominent role in shaping our lives and how we appear in public.

The Eleventh House

The eleventh house is the clubhouse—the place where we go to hang out with friends and colleagues, and to do things in groups. The eleventh house is opposite the fifth-house game room, and the two do have much in common (they're both pretty fun places to be). The main difference is that when we're in the eleventh house, we're spending time with groups of people; in the fifth house, we're either alone, or in more intimate circumstances that usually don't call for more than one other person. The eleventh house then relates to friendship and friends, and it also has to do with our hopes and wishes (as opposed to our dreams, which, you remember, are found in the ninth house).

The Twelfth House

The twelfth house is the meditation room (although it's been called far worse than that). The twelfth house is opposite the sixth house, which contains the things we have to do in order to maintain a physical body. Well, the twelfth house contains the things we have to do in order to maintain a soul and spiritual essence. The twelfth house is associated with prisons—and from the point of view of our eternal souls, being housed in a physical body is very much like being in a prison. We go to the twelfth house when we need time alone, when we need to take a break from the demands and stresses of daily life. The thing about the twelfth house, though, is that it is *above* the horizon, and that means that even though *we* think that it's nice, hidden, and private, it's completely visible to everyone else in the world. We are always the last to know about what's in our twelfth house (which is one of the reasons that the twelfth house is also associated with hidden enemies). Think of the twelfth house as our shadow: we can't always see it ourselves, but everyone else can. The twelfth house relates to the unseen, the psychic, and the spiritual. We are not always consciously aware of the influences in our twelfth house; they tend to operate behind the scenes.

The Part of Fortune (and the Part of Spirit)

The Part of Fortune, also known as Fortuna, is a mathematically calculated point. It is one of many Arabic "Parts" (or Greek "Lots") that are calculated by comparing the arc distance between three points in the chart. The Part of Fortune is a point that synthesizes the Sun, Moon, and Ascendant, and therefore, we can assume that it's pretty important. Of course, very little information exists in modern astrological literature on what it actually represents. We're going to get to that shortly, but first we need to understand exactly how it's calculated.

The Part of Fortune is calculated differently depending on whether the chart is diurnal (day chart, i.e., the Sun above the horizon in houses 7 through 12), or nocturnal (night chart, i.e., the Sun below the horizon in houses 1 through 6).

Diurnal chart: Ascendant + Moon − Sun

Nocturnal chart: Ascendant + Sun − Moon

So what the heck does this mean? Well, it helps if you work backward in the formulas. Taking the diurnal chart formula, it means that the distance between the Sun and the Moon (in degrees) is the same as the distance between the Ascendant and the Part of Fortune. The degrees are always measured through the signs (counter-clockwise around the chart).

Interpreting the Part of Fortune is pretty easy: it's a point of increase and good fortune for the individual. This makes a certain amount of sense, of course, because the Part of Fortune synthesizes the three most important points in the natal chart: the Sun, Moon, and Ascendant. When all three of these can work together, we're naturally going to be pretty happy and successful in our endeavors.

Looking at the sign and house location of the Part of Fortune will show how we're motivated to be successful, and the types of activities that will tend to bring us good fortune (sign), and where we're likely to find these activities in our lives (house). As with any other point in the chart, we can go one level deeper and look at the ruler of the Part of Fortune and its dignity or debility, position in the chart, and overall relationship to the rest of the chart, to learn how and where we're likely to pursue and encounter success.

Since I've brought it up, I'll also mention that the Part of Spirit is similar to the Part of Fortune, except that the Part of Spirit represents how we will expe-

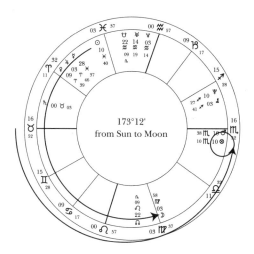
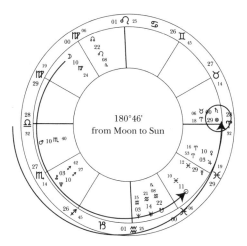

173°12' from Ascendant to Part of Fortune

Calculating the Part of Fortune
in a Diurnal Chart:

Ascendant + Moon – Sun

180°46' from Ascendant to Part of Fortune

Calculating the Part of Fortune in a
Nocturnal Chart:

Ascendant + Sun – Moon

Figure 10. Calculating the Part of Fortune

rience our spiritual connections and our spirituality. It's an interesting point to consider from time to time, but frankly, most people are more concerned with the more tangible elements of their lives, and the Part of Fortune is significantly more important in traditional astrology than the Part of Spirit.

7

Basic Interpretation

Now that we've covered the basics—planets, signs, and houses—we can see how they fit together in astrological interpretation. Even though we have a lot more to cover before we can begin to come up with a synthesized interpretation, we can find a great deal of information in a chart simply by working with the planets and their essential dignities, the houses, and the house rulers.

Interpretation Example 1: Sylvester Stallone

Since we poked fun at him in chapter 5, let's start out by looking at Sylvester Stallone's chart (which is pictured on the next page.) Stallone's birth information comes from his mother, and is considered to be very accurate.

Stallone was born in Hells Kitchen, New York, the elder of two sons. His father was a hairstylist, and his mother, Jacqueline Stallone, was a former chorus girl and future astrologer. Stallone had a difficult childhood: he was boarded with a woman in Queens until the age of five, and only saw his parents on weekends. He and his parents moved to Maryland; then his parents divorced when he was eleven, and he went to live in Philadelphia with his mother and her new husband. By the age of fifteen, he had been expelled from no less than fourteen schools because of his aggression and scholastic difficulties. Finally, he discovered sports as a channel for his aggression. When he graduated, he went to beauty school for a while—needless to say, it didn't work out! He earned a scholarship to the American College in Switzerland to study drama, and the applause and acclaim that came from his performance on stage made him decide to become an actor.

When Stallone returned to the United States and enrolled at the University of Miami, he had a somewhat less positive experience (his teachers weren't too encouraging), and he ultimately dropped out just before he completed his degree, and moved to New York to become an actor. Stallone's mother (who by this time was an accomplished astrologer) predicted that he would struggle for seven years before making it as a writer, so Stallone supported himself by writing screenplays, taking any odd job he could find (including cleaning the lion cage at the zoo), and winning small parts in films. Ultimately, he decided to leave New York and try his luck in Hollywood, where he saw a fight between Muhammad Ali and Chuck Wepner, which inspired him to write the screenplay for the movie *Rocky.*

Stallone struggled to find a backer to produce *Rocky* because no one wanted to let him star in it. (Evidently, the studios wanted Ryan O'Neil.) Ultimately, Stallone found a backer, made the film, and the rest, as they say, is history. The role of Rocky Balboa launched Sylvester Stallone's career as both a writer and an actor, and later roles (such as John Rambo) built Stallone's reputation as one of Hollywood's premier action heroes.

So now that we know a bit about Sylvester Stallone, let's see how much of this we can see from his chart. For this and all the interpretations that we will cover in this book, we will follow the steps in the Natal Chart Interpretation Worksheet, which can be found in appendix A.

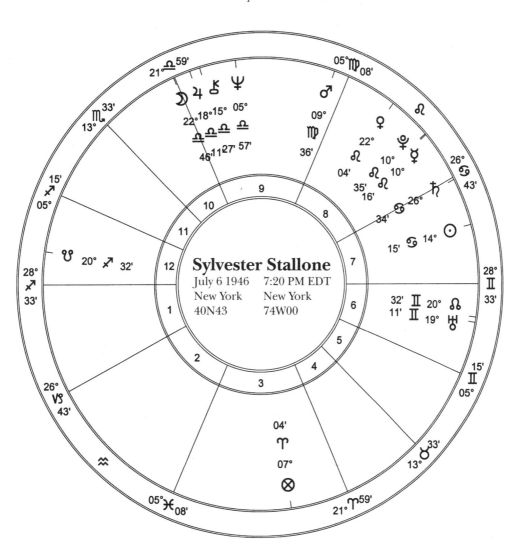

Figure 11. Sylvester Stallone's Natal Chart

Part 1: Elements and Modalities

Element/Modality	Personal Planets	Personal Points (Angles)	Outer Planets
FIRE	☿♀	AS ⊗☋	♇
EARTH	♂		
AIR	☽♃	MC ☊	♅♆♇
WATER	☉♄		
CARDINAL	☉☽♃♄	⊗MC	♇♆
FIXED	☿♀		♇
MUTABLE	♂	AS ☊☋	♅

Part 2: Temperament

Hemisphere	Planets	Quadrant	Planets
Northern (Houses 1–6)	♅	1st Quadrant (Houses 1–3)	
Southern (Houses 7–12)	☉☽☿♀♂♃♄♇♆	2nd Quadrant (Houses 4–6)	♅
Eastern (Houses 10–12, 1–3)	☽	3rd Quadrant (Houses 7–9)	☉☿♀♂♃♄♇♆
Western (Houses 4–9)	☉☿♀♂♃♄♇♆	4th Quadrant (Houses 10–12)	☽

Comments: Summarize Temperament and Fundamental (Elemental) Personality

The first thing to notice about Stallone's chart is that almost all his planets are found in Quadrant III, in houses 7, 8, and 9. We can certainly see right away that Stallone has some very extroverted tendencies, and that he is very relationship-oriented. He is very expressive, but he depends on the support and input of other people in his life. We'll have to see if this tendency seems to be repeated in other areas of the chart, but for now, let's make note of it as something that is possibly quite significant.

On an elemental level, Stallone has the strongest influence in fire and air, particularly when we include the angles and the outer planets. Fire and air tend to be the most expressive and outgoing energies, and this would seem to support Stallone's more extroverted approach to the world. Stallone also has a very strong emphasis in cardinal energy in his chart, which, more than anything else, would be responsible for his active, self-motivated, pioneering, and driven qualities. Individuals with a strong cardinal signature in their charts, remember, are fundamentally concerned with discovering, exploring, and expressing their individual identities.

The only earth element in Stallone's chart is his Mars in Virgo—and as earth signs go, Virgo tends to be the least grounded, and to have the most mental and air-like qualities. Stallone has the temperament of a dreamer thanks to the cardinal, fire, and air emphasis in his chart. Stallone fits the mold of someone who comes up with new ideas and immediately acts on them—someone, it must also be said, who may tend to overlook many of the more practical considerations that are usually required to make their dreams into reality. Stallone will have to look for his earth energy on a conscious level, and teach himself to ground and anchor himself, to build a sturdy foundation for his dreams.

Part 3: Essential Dignities

Planet	Ruler	Exalt.	Trip.	Term	Face	Detri.	Fall	Score
☉ (in ♋)	☽	♃	♂	☿	☿	♄	♂	–5 p
☽ (in ♎)		♄	♄	☿	♃	♂	☉	–5 p
☿ (in ♌)	☉	—	☉	☿+	♃	♄	—	+2
♀ (in ♌)	☉	—	☉	♃	♃	♄	—	–5 p
♂ (in ♍)	☿	☿	♀	♀	☉	♃	♀	–5 p
♃ (in ♎)	♀	♄	♄	♃+	♄	♂	☉	+2
♄ (in ♋)	☽	♃	♂	♀	☽	♄–	♂	–10 p
AS (in ♐)	♃	☋	☉	♂	♄	—	—	—
MC (in ♎)	♀	♄	♄	☿	♃	—	—	—
⊗ (in ♈)	♂	☉	☉	♀	♂	—	—	—

Part 4: Dispositor Tree Diagram

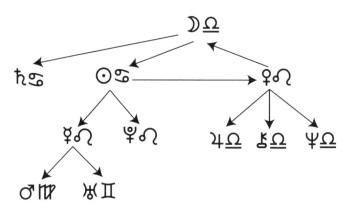

Stallone's chart is a perfect example of how the essential dignities do not have anything to do with our ultimate success or happiness in life. I think we can all agree that Stallone has led a very successful life, and yet most of his planets are peregrine, and the only two planets with any essential dignity at all (Mercury and Jupiter) only have dignity by term. From Stallone's biography, we can see the wandering quality of the peregrine planets reflected in his life, but they certainly haven't prevented him from achieving success.

From looking at his dispositor tree, we can see that Stallone has an interesting relationship going on between his Sun, Moon, and Venus, and that this trio of planets (perhaps as a committee of some sort) is in charge of the rest of his chart—we can see that every planet in his chart ultimately must answer to these three planets. It might also be safe to say that Stallone is ruled by his need for individual self-expression (Sun), his security and emotional needs (Moon), and his desire to relate to other individuals (Venus). Because of the very strong connection between these three planets in the dispositor tree, Stallone may have a difficult time distinguishing between these three different aspects of his identity. They won't act as a unit because they are in different signs; however, any time Stallone wants to express one of these three planets, the other two are going to have a very strong say in how the third gets to express itself.

Let's take a moment, then, and explore the theme of relationships in Stallone's chart. When interpreting a chart, the key is to look for common themes, concepts that are repeated in many different ways in different areas of the chart. The more often a theme is repeated, the more obvious and important it will be to the individual. Stallone absolutely *must* be able to relate to other people—this is an extremely important foundation in his chart.

We first got a hint of how important relationships might be to Stallone when we observed that he has nine planets in Quadrant III of his chart—the extroverted, relationship-oriented houses. Among these planets in the relationship houses are two of the three key planets in Stallone's chart, namely the Sun and Venus. The Moon and Venus are also both heavily involved in interpersonal relationships, as is, of course, the sign of Libra (in which Stallone has four planets—the Moon, Jupiter, Chiron, and Neptune). This fits in very nicely with our earlier observation that with such a strong Quadrant III emphasis in his chart, Stallone is going to be very relationship-oriented. Stallone also has his Sun in Cancer in the seventh house of relationships. The Sun in the seventh house often indicates a person who defines his or her sense of self in terms of other people. Factor in the influence of Cancer, which is motivated to form emotional connections, and we have another strong indicator in support of our theory. Leo energy, which involves Stallone's Mercury, Venus, and Pluto, is also very oriented toward relationships in that it is focused on gaining the attention and approval of others. Finally, Stallone's Moon in Libra is conjunct his Midheaven—the most prominent and public point in the chart. Stallone will have no difficulties making his needs known to the world at large. With the Moon in Libra, Stallone's security needs revolve around harmony, balance, and artistic expression, and, of course, one-to-one relationships. Taking all these elements into account, we could safely say that Stallone absolutely depends on the support, feedback, and approval of other people.

Now, by no means does this mean that Stallone is needy and codependent! He has simply taken this energy, an approach to the world that is one of the foundations of his entire personality, and applied it in an arena where he can express and share many of the higher qualities of Libra, Leo, and Cancer. He strives to be an artist as an actor, is able to convey and share emotional connections and catharsis with millions of moviegoers across the world, and in turn, he receives the adoration, attention, and acceptance of his fans.

Now let's try to integrate and synthesize Stallone's Sun, Moon, Ascendant, and Part of Fortune to get an idea of his core identity and approach to the world. Stallone has Sagittarius rising, so his chart is therefore ruled by Jupiter in Libra conjunct the Midheaven, which means that his Jupiter is effectively a tenth-house planet (even though technically it is in his ninth house). Sagittarius is a mutable fire sign, one of the few mutable points in his chart. We can perhaps take this to indicate that he may appear far more flexible than he really is! Of course, anyone with a strong emphasis in Libra, particularly in such a public arena as the Midheaven and tenth house, is naturally going to have some very advanced negotiating skills, something that can help Stallone appear to be accommodating and flexible, when he's really simply clearing the way so that he can proceed with his original ideas. Sagittarius energy has an expansive, exploring feel to it; Sagittarius is always on a mission to find the ultimate truth. Being half-man and half-horse (not to mention a fire sign), Sagittarius energy can be very physically active. With his ruling planet (Jupiter) in Libra, Stallone may tend to be very concerned with his appearance—Libra energy always wants to look its most attractive, after all; and having the ruler of the Ascendant conjunct the Midheaven is a pretty good indication that this is an individual who is going to be noticed by others in a broader, more public arena. One last thing that we can look at is the terms of the Ascendant. William Lilly often used the terms of the Ascendant to add to the overall physical description of an individual. Stallone's Ascendant is in the term of Mars, which seems quite appropriate for a man who is best known for his portrayal of fighters, warriors, and action heroes!

So Stallone is a person who expresses his identity through emotional connections (Sun in Cancer), and who at the same time is not comfortable with deep emotions, and feels safe and secure when things are balanced and harmonious and everyone gets along with each other (Moon in Libra). Thanks to his Sagittarius rising, his approach to the world is very direct and focused, and carries with it an absolute conviction that he will find the truth and that his beliefs and convictions are correct. He will tend to appear to be larger than life thanks to the influence of Jupiter, and also perhaps to be unaware, at times, of the somewhat conflicting nature of his Sun and Moon.

The Part of Fortune is the point in the chart that combines the energy of the Sun, Moon, and Ascendant. This point shows where and how an individual will be the most integrated and focused, and therefore will be able to experience the greatest amount of success and prosperity in his or her life. Stallone's Part of Fortune is in Aries in the third house, ruled by his Mars in Virgo. Stallone, of course, is best known for his portrayals of warriors ranging from Rocky Balboa to Rambo—in other words, his success and fortune has most certainly come from Mars-related activities! Stallone's Mars is in Virgo, influenced most strongly by Mercury (rulership and exaltation), and then by Venus (triplicity and terms). Mercury and Venus, then, would greatly influence his success. Stallone's first big break was as a writer (he was the author of *Rocky*), and writing, of course, is ruled by Mercury. The third house, too, relates to all forms of writing and communication. By working with his third house, Stallone was able to define and integrate his public identity. Both Mercury and Venus are in Leo, and Stallone's fortune very much comes from his need to be appreciated by other people for his gifts and talents.

Look at how much information we've been able to delineate using just these few basic techniques. We haven't even started to look deeper into the chart (we'll take another look at Stallone's chart in chapter 10), but what we have is a very strong, solid foundation and understanding of Stallone's temperament and personality. Everything else we interpret is going to fit somewhere into this framework. Keeping this foundation in mind will help guide us to make more accurate interpretations of how Stallone is likely to experience and express the energies in his chart.

Interpretation Example 2: Meryl Streep

Next, let's take a quick look at Meryl Streep's chart (because we poked fun at her, too). Streep is perhaps the premier film actress alive today. She is renowned for her acting technique (which she learned and honed at Vassar College, the Yale School of Drama, and New York's Public Theater). Streep earned an Academy Award nomination for the film *The Deer Hunter*, and that same year won an Emmy Award for her role in the *Holocaust* miniseries. While she was enjoying all this professional acclaim, she was experiencing personal tragedy, as her lover, John Cazale, slowly lost his battle with bone cancer.

After losing her lover, Streep channeled her energy into her work, winning two Oscars and seven Oscar nominations in the process. Streep also found time to get married and have four children along the way. Streep has proven that an actress' career doesn't have to end at age forty. Her persistence, as well as her tremendous acting ability, have allowed her to continue to turn out noteworthy performances to this day.

While Streep has demonstrated a tremendous range in her film career, she has frequently been criticized by those who feel her exceptional technique tends to put a damper on her ability to appear natural and spontaneous. She is also infamous for wanting to come up with new accents for each of her characters, whether it seems appropriate to the film or not.

Comments: Summarize Temperament and Fundamental (Elemental) Personality

The first thing we notice about Streep's chart is that she has no personal planets in fire—they are all balanced between earth, air, and water; so although her North Node and Midheaven (her public persona) are both in Aries, Streep isn't going to be a particularly active, fiery, passionate type. She may perceive this as an imbalance, and may tend to compensate by actively pursuing fire activities, which usually include all types of physical exertion, competitive and otherwise. Streep has a very good balance of modalities, with no marked emphasis on cardinal, fixed, or mutable signs.

Streep's planets are also quite balanced between the Northern and Southern Hemispheres, indicating that she will tend to be equally introverted and extroverted. The very strong emphasis on the Eastern hemisphere of her chart indicates that she is extremely self-motivated and self-reliant and does not depend on the input and support of others; however, since all of Streep's inner planets can be found in Quadrant IV, she may tend to appear to be more of a self-reliant extrovert.

While this information is certainly relevant, we don't yet have a "hook" to work with. No key themes jump out at us, so we'll move on to the next phase of interpretation and look at Streep's essential dignities and dispositor trees.

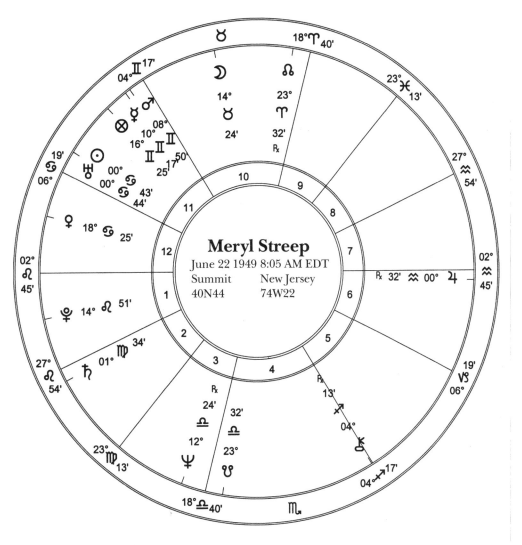

Figure 12. Meryl Streep's Natal Chart

Part 1: Elements and Modalities

Element/Modality	Personal Planets	Personal Points (Angles)	Outer Planets
FIRE		AS MC ☊	⚷ ♇
EARTH	☽ ♄		
AIR	☿ ♂ ♃	☋ ⊗	♆
WATER	☉ ♀		♅
CARDINAL	☉ ♀	MC ☊ ☋	♅ ♆
FIXED	☽ ♃	AS	♇
MUTABLE	☿ ♂ ♄	⊗	⚷

Part 2: Temperament

Hemisphere	Planets	Quadrant	Planets
Northern (Houses 1–6)	♃ ♄ ⚷ ♆ ♇	1st Quadrant (Houses 1–3)	♄ ♆ ♇
Southern (Houses 7–12)	☉ ☽ ☿ ♀ ♂ ♅	2nd Quadrant (Houses 4–6)	♃ ⚷
Eastern (Houses 10–12, 1–3)	☉ ☽ ☿ ♀ ♂ ♃ ♄ ♅ ♆ ♇	3rd Quadrant (Houses 7–9)	
Western (Houses 4–9)	♃ ⚷	4th Quadrant (Houses 10–12)	☉ ☽ ☿ ♀ ♂ ♅

Part 3: Essential Dignities

Planet	Ruler	Exalt.	Trip.	Term	Face	Detri.	Fall	Score
☉ (in ♋)	☽	♃	♂	♂	♀	♄	♃	−5p
☽ (in ♉)	♀m	☽+	♀	☿	☽+	♂	—	+5
☿ (in ♊)	☿+	☊	♄	♃	♂	♃	☋	+5
♀ (in ♋)	☽m	♃	♂	☿	☿	♄	♃	−5p
♂ (in ♊)	☿	☊	♄	♃	♃	♃	☋	−5p
♃ (in ♒)	♄	—	♄	♄	♀	☉	—	−5p
♄ (in ♍)	☿	☿	♀	☿	☉	♃	♀	−5p
AS (in ♌)	☉	—	☉	♄	♄	—	—	—
MC (in ♈)	♂	☉	☉	☿	☉	—	—	—
⊗ (in ♊)	☿	☊	♄	♀	♂	—	—	—

Part 4: Dispositor Tree Diagram

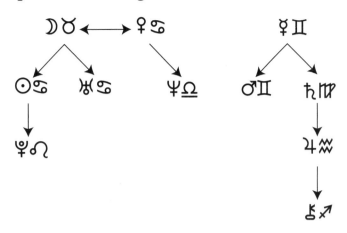

Now we've got something juicy to look at. Streep's chart is split between the planets that answer to her Moon/Venus mutual reception, and the planets that answer to her Mercury in Gemini. This split may also be the very thing that describes both Streep's exceptional method acting techniques, and the periodic accusations that her craft overshadows true spontaneity and freedom of emotional responses.

Looking at the Moon/Venus grouping first, we see that Streep is very much influenced by her feelings, with her Taurus Moon, and her Sun and Venus in Cancer. She has a pronounced tendency toward the nurturing, protecting, mothering approach to her emotional life, something that (thanks to her peregrine Venus in Cancer) may have a tendency to spill over into her romantic relationships as well. Streep's chart shows someone with a very strong and deep, albeit grounded, emotional foundation; someone who is likely to be attracted to the caretaker/caregiver role in her relationships (which fits being a mother of four quite nicely). The presence of Uranus, Neptune, and Pluto should not be ignored, however. While their influence will be far clearer when we look at Streep's aspects (in chapter 10), we can bear in mind that Streep's emotional makeup is likely to be a bit unusual, and quite powerful.

On the other hand, we have Streep's intellectual and active side, ruled by her Mercury in Gemini. Streep's Mercury is extremely well dignified, and in her eleventh house of friends and peer social relationships. We can safely assume that Streep has a very quick mind, and probably an insatiable curiosity about other people. Streep's Mercury directly supervises her Mars in Gemini and her Saturn in Virgo. Mars and Saturn together are the two hardest-working and most productive planets around. True, they need to be watched quite carefully because they can also cause no small amount of trouble, but if something needs to be accomplished, look to Mars (action) and Saturn (manifestation and structure). When these energies are filtered through Mercury in Gemini, one of the results can certainly be an actor or actress with exceptional technique and skill, one who is renowned for being hard-working and thorough, for building complex and well-rounded characters, and, thanks to the agile mimicry of Mercury, for giving virtuoso performances. Does this sound at all like Streep? Let us not forget that Mercury rules all languages (and dialects) as well. Mercury in Gemini can thus be described as an A-list actress who insists on creating a new accent for each character as part of her technique; and since Mercury in Gemini is a planet in rulership (and an A-list actress), who's going to say "no" to it?

If there's any doubt that Streep approaches her craft through her Gemini-ruled planets, including her Mars and Saturn, consider this: one of her more notable quotations about acting is, "The work will stand, no matter what." That sounds very much like Saturn and Mars talking, doesn't it?

Does this mean that Streep doesn't feel real emotions in her work? Of course it doesn't. The application of the "method" in acting involves creating a real world for a character and pulling emotional responses and emotional memories from the actor's own personal experience. Streep has a wealth of emotion to draw from, thanks to her Moon/Venus configuration, and her emotional nature is certainly quite visible in her professional life through her tenth-house Moon in Taurus. However, when she performs, she's using her Mercury in Gemini (backed, of course, by her Mars in Gemini and Saturn in Virgo) to recreate and mimic her emotional experiences in more structured and consciously controlled ways.

This split in Streep's chart would not only apply to her work, it would also impact other areas of her life. When we look at Streep's planetary aspects later on, we will see how she may have developed this separation as a defense mechanism initially, a way of diffusing some of the extremely intense emotions that she will experience courtesy of her Moon square Pluto. The aspects will also show how easily Streep can make the connection between experiencing her emotions, and breaking them down both to better understand them (so she can recreate them at will), and to distance herself from them so that she feels safe enough to deal with them.

Lastly (for now, at least), let's look at the relationship between Streep's Sun, Moon, Ascendant, and Part of Fortune. Streep's Sun in Cancer and Moon in Taurus will work quite well together, although, as we know from the dignities and dispositors, the Moon is very much the boss in this relationship. Streep will define herself and express her individuality through her emotional connections, the way she nurtures and protects others, and the way she in turn is nurtured and protected (Sun in Cancer). Her Moon in Taurus will encourage her to look for stability and solid foundations in all things, to help her ground the intense emotions that make up her life. Streep's Ascendant, however, is in Leo, and while she may try to keep her personal drama grounded and stable, she very much expects that the outside world will notice her and pay special attention to her, based on her value and worth as a unique individual. Streep may at times appear to be far more self-centered than she really is—both her Sun and Moon are very open and caring, while Leo rising wants to appear to be generous, but sometimes seems to only want to be the center of attention, regardless of the situation. This Leo Ascendant, however, allows Streep to shine as a performer, when it is time for her to be in the spotlight.

On the physical side, Streep's Ascendant is in the terms of Saturn, which is in Virgo in her chart. Streep's physical appearance is very reserved and restrained, controlled and serious—in short, very Saturn-like. No matter how spontaneous she may be, her physical appearance will always be influenced by the rigid, prepared, analytical, and structured energy of Saturn in Virgo.

Streep's Part of Fortune will help us understand how she can best synthesize the three different energies of her Sun, Moon, and Ascendant. Her Part of Fortune is in Gemini in her eleventh house. Gemini energy is extremely curious, playful, dual-natured, changeable, very mental, and not particularly fond of experiencing deep emotions. We've already seen how Streep's Mercury in Gemini (which rules her Part of Fortune) expresses itself through her ability to change and become a variety of different people in different situations, and through her exceptionally well-learned acting technique. Working with Gemini energy is the key for Streep to integrate her identity, her emotions, and her approach to the world.

So far, we've only scratched the surface of Sylvester Stallone's and Meryl Streep's charts. With the information we've learned up to this point, we could move on and interpret each planet by dignity, sign, and house, breaking things down and looking at their charts on a more specific, minute level—and I encourage you do so! The only way to learn how to interpret charts is to actually sit down and interpret them.

Ultimately, though, the secret to coming up with an accurate, synthesized chart interpretation is to start with the fundamentals—the elements, the modalities, and the quadrants. Look at the person's temperament. Look at the dispositor tree of the chart and see if you can find any repeated themes. The point of this lesson is to realize that we must start with the big picture before we start looking at little details in the chart. As we move through the rest of the lessons, we'll cover aspects and aspect patterns, the Moon's nodes, and retrograde planets, all of which can help to provide valuable information when interpreting a natal chart. The fundamental rule of chart interpretation, though, still holds true: any truly important theme will be repeated in many different places, in many different ways; and the most fundamentally important themes can usually be seen, at least in part, in the big picture.

8

The Aspects

By now, we're very familiar with the analogy of the planets being the actors, the signs being the roles that they play, and the houses being the scenery and setting for the action. The last piece of the puzzle is the aspects—how the different actors interact with each other, and the types of scenes they will tend to play out.

In this lesson, we're going to look at just about everything that was ever considered to be an "aspect" in astrology. We're going to include, of course, the more traditional angular aspects such as the conjunction, opposition, trine, square, sextile, and quincunx, but we're also going to look at some less familiar relationships, like antiscia and contra-antiscia, receptions, and parallels and contraparallels. Aspects are angular relationships between two planets, measured along the 360° circle of the ecliptic, and for the most part they represent the longitudinal (sign) relationship between two points. The exceptions to this are parallels and contraparallels, which are aspects of declination (distance north or south of the equator) rather than of longitude.

Whole Sign versus Harmonic Aspects

In ancient astrology, when precise measurements were not possible, aspects were counted by sign, not by degree. Although the Greeks certainly understood the mathematics behind the aspects—they were the ones who created them, after all—they took a much broader approach to the aspects than we do today. The Greeks worked only with the "major" aspects, which are also known as the "Ptolemaic aspects," because they were the ones mentioned in Ptolemy's book *Tetrabiblos.* These aspects included the conjunction (planets in the same sign—although the conjunction wasn't really considered an aspect), sextile (planets two signs apart), trine (planets three signs apart), square (planets four signs apart), and opposition (planets six signs apart). The Greeks weren't too concerned with the question of "orbs," but they did distinguish between aspects that were exact (aspects between planets in the same whole degree) and aspects that were not exact. Exact aspects were called "partile," and were considered to be quite powerful; aspects that were not exact were called "platic." Partile is not the same thing as having a 1° orb. Two planets at 5°00' and 5°59' Aries are in a partile conjunction, but two planets at 4°59' and 5°01' Aries are only in platic aspect.

The whole-sign approach to aspects has a very strong foundation because it's based on the fundamental relationship between the elements, modalities, and polarities. This predominantly elemental approach to aspects takes into account the nature of the signs and the relationship between those signs in interpreting an aspect, a technique that is still essential today. Conjunctions occur between planets in the same sign, and represent a unity of approach, a merging of energy. Oppositions occur between planets in the same modality (cardinal, fixed, or mutable), *and* in the same polarity (masculine or feminine). Squares occur between planets in the same modality (cardinal, fixed, or mutable), but in different polarities. Trines occur between planets in the same element (fire, earth, air, or water), and sextiles occur between planets in the same polarity, but in different elements and modalities. Quincunxes and semisextiles (inconjuncts), while not widely used until modern times, occur between two signs that have nothing in common by polarity, modality, or element.

In the 1600s, when measuring the positions of the planets became much more accurate, and also largely due to the influence and theories of Johannes Kepler, the concept of harmonics came into play. Kepler thought that aspects worked because the planets vibrated at the same frequency, and therefore resonated with each other. The harmonics were based on the division of the 360° circle by whole numbers. Conjunctions, 0° aspects, are first-harmonic aspects. Oppositions, 180° aspects, are second-harmonic aspects (360 divided by 2). Trines, 120° aspects, are third harmonics; squares (90°) are fourth harmonics; and sextiles (60°) are sixth harmonics. Kepler didn't stop with the Ptolemaic aspects, however. He is the "inventor" of the quintile (fifth harmonic, 72° aspect) and its complement, the biquintile (144° aspect, also fifth harmonic); as well as the eighth-harmonic aspects, including the 45° semisquare and the 135° sesquiquadrate.

When using harmonics, both in music and in astrology, the closer the two vibrations are to being exact, the more pronounced and powerful the harmonic is; also, the higher the harmonic, the more subtle the effect and the more precise the vibrations must be. This is where the whole question of orbs came about. The closer two planets are to the exact angle of the aspect, the more powerful and pronounced the harmonic effect is. The question becomes, however, at what point does the harmonic influence fade to insignificance? There is no answer to this question. The only rule of thumb is that based on the laws of harmonics (from physics): the widest "orbs" should be allowed for conjunctions (first-harmonic aspects), and then in decreasing order for oppositions (second harmonic), trines (third harmonic), squares (fourth harmonic), quintiles (fifth harmonic), sextiles (sixth harmonic), septiles (seventh harmonic), octiles (the eighth-harmonic series, including the semisquare and the sesquiquadrate), noviles (ninth harmonic), deciles (tenth harmonic), and the smallest orbs of all would be allowed for the twelfth-harmonic series, which includes the semisextile (inconjunct) and the quincunx. However, harmonics that are multiples of other harmonics (for example, 6th harmonic = 2nd x 3rd) are reinforced, and thus get wider orbs than the previous argument would indicate.

The Difficult Question of Orbs

Perhaps the biggest controversy involved with aspects is the question of "orbs"—the space within which an aspect is considered to be in effect. Orbs are one of the topics that astrologer Kim Rogers-Gallagher says should be avoided at all costs at an astrology cocktail party, and she's right. No hard and fast rules exist as to how exact an aspect must be in order to be effective. Astrologer Michael Lutin puts it best: "If you felt the aspect, it was in orb."

One thing that just about all astrologers will agree with is that the more exact the aspect, the more important it is. No matter how many degrees a given astrologer will allow for a conjunction, there's little question that a partile conjunction is far more powerful than one between two planets 6° apart.

The concept of assigning orbs to the aspects is actually a new one (invented by Alan Leo, and stemming from Kepler's work with harmonics), and one that, to my traditional way of thinking, makes no sense. The aspects aren't physical bodies, so how can they have orbs? Planets, on the other hand, are physical bodies: they radiate or reflect light, and most definitely have spheres of influence that extend both in front and behind them. Traditionally, it's the *planets* that have orbs, not the aspects.

Even here, classical astrologers couldn't agree completely, of course, but here are the orbs that William Lilly used:

Sun	15 degrees
Moon	12 degrees
Mercury	7 degrees
Venus	7 degrees
Mars	7 degrees
Jupiter	9 degrees
Saturn	9 degrees

Moiety

Moiety is a term that means "half-orbs," and was how aspect "orbs" were determined. The orb of each planet extends equally ahead and behind that planet. In other words, the 15° orb of the Sun extends 7½° in front and 7½° behind the Sun.

The "orb" for an aspect depends not on the aspect itself, but on the two planets involved. By adding up the moieties for the two planets, we can see how close together the planets need to be for their orbs to touch and therefore aspect each other. For a Sun/Saturn aspect, for example, the moiety of the Sun is 7½°; the moiety of Saturn is 4½°; so Sun/Saturn aspects have an orb of 12°. Moon/Saturn aspects, on the other hand, only have an orb of 10½°, because the moiety of the Moon is only 6°.

So what about the outer planets? Good question. Obviously, we can't look to the classical literature for their orbs, because the outer planets hadn't yet been discovered. I think we're probably safe in allocating at least a 6° orb to the outer planets (3° moiety)—and that may even be too conservative. This is just one of many parts of astrology that you have to discover on your own, based on your own personal experience.

Calculated points, such as the angles (Ascendant, Midheaven), the Moon's nodes, and the Part of Fortune, on the other hand, *have no orbs*. This is very important to remember. These points are not real—they are mathematically calculated, and while they are certainly important and sensitive points in the chart, they do not *make* aspects, they can only *receive* aspects. What this means is that a Mars/Moon aspect will impact both the expression of Mars and the Moon, but a Mars/Ascendant aspect will *only* affect the Ascendant. Also, because the angles, nodes, and parts don't have orbs, any aspects to these points must be within the moiety of the aspecting planet: for example, Moon/Midheaven aspects would have an orb of 6° only (the moiety of the Moon).

Interpreting Out-of-Sign Aspects

Remember that when we're dealing with aspects, we're looking at two factors: the sign relationship and the harmonic relationship. Sometimes they're in sync with each other, and other times they're not (the so-called "out of sign" aspects). Take, for example, the Mars at 1°00' Cancer and the Moon at 29°00' Pisces. The Greeks would have considered this to be a trine because *all* planets in Pisces are trine all planets in Cancer; but on a harmonic level, there's no question that these planets are square each other—with a 2° orb at that. So what's the deal? Are they trine or square each other? How about both?

An out-of-sign aspect is not going to function in the same way as an aspect that has both harmonic and sign elements. The harmonic force is undeniable —Mars and the Moon are going to be on less-than-friendly and comfortable terms in the above example; but because of the elemental connection between them, this square is going to be a bit more manageable than it will be in one more degree when the Moon enters Aries. Mars and the Moon are at cross-purposes here, certainly, but they also have enough common ground to ease the tension between them somewhat.

Without a doubt, the most powerful aspects are those that are supported both by the elemental relationship and by the harmonic vibration.

Waxing and Waning Aspects

Aspects are categorized as either "waxing" or "waning." This refers to the relative position in the cycle between the pair of planets. The faster-moving body always determines whether the aspect is "waxing" or "waning." "Waxing" aspects are aspects that occur when the faster-moving planet is ahead of the slower moving planet, and moving toward the opposition (which is the "Full" phase in the cycle). "Waning" aspects are aspects that occur when the faster-moving planet is behind the slower-moving planet, moving toward a conjunction.

Although the distinction between, for example, a waxing square and a waning square is subtle, many astrologers emphasize this difference. Waxing aspects tend to be slightly less conscious in nature—they tend to involve more reaction to a situation. Waning aspects, on the other hand, tend to be more conscious, and often indicate situations where we are more aware and in control. Again, this distinction is quite subtle, and only presented here in the interest of being extremely thorough (and satisfying my Jupiter in Virgo!).

Applying, Partile, and Separating Aspects

The last point to consider about aspects, before we finally look at what they mean, is whether an aspect is applying or separating. Applying aspects are forming—the two planets are within orb of each other and are moving toward the point when the aspect will be exact. Partile aspects, as we've already covered, are "exact" aspects—they occur between two planets in the same degree. Separating aspects are aspects that have passed the point of being partile or exact; the planets are still in orb of each other, but they are moving apart.

Partile aspects are unquestionably the most important and the most powerful aspects in the chart. Not only do they share the correct sign/element/modality/polarity relationship for the aspect, but they also are in extremely tight harmonic resonance with each other. Planets in partile aspect to each other *never* act alone. Any time one of the planets acts, the other is also triggered. For better or for worse, planets in partile aspect are joined at the hip.

Applying aspects are the next most important and powerful type of aspects. They represent energies that are growing. Applying aspects become more powerful and influential over time—they are energies that we experienced immediately after birth, and they leave very powerful and lasting impressions on us.

Separating aspects are the least important types of aspects—and the wider the orb, the less influential and important they are. They represent energies that had already happened when we were born, and that we only experienced the tail end of, exerting less and less influence over time.

Although most astrologers consider separating aspects to be less important than applying aspects, astrologer Michael Lutin makes an excellent case supporting the importance of separating aspects. Even though the aspect is separating by transit, we can still experience the aspect as applying through secondary progressions (a predictive technique that we will not be covering), and these experiences, which occur very early in our lives, are extremely significant.

The Aspects Defined

In the following sections, the aspects are discussed—just about all of them, in fact. Not all aspects are important, however! In the interest of thoroughness, I've simply worked through each of the harmonic series and defined each aspect as it comes up. Many of these you've probably never heard of and may never hear of again. The important aspects are the first harmonic (conjunction), second harmonic (opposition), third harmonic (trine), fourth harmonic (square), and sixth harmonic (sextile). These are the Ptolemaic aspects—the ones used by the Greeks and recorded by Ptolemy in the *Tetrabiblos*. To this list, I also add the quincunx, one of the twelfth-harmonic aspects. These are the aspects that form the backbone of natal astrology.

In addition to these "major" aspects, the eighth-harmonic series, which includes the semisquare and the sesquiquadrate, is also worth noticing: these are "hard" aspects and create tension and action. In general, they're more important when looking at transits than in natal interpretation.

The rest of the aspects are definitely "minor" aspects. They are not going to provide any essential information about the individual on their own; they will only reinforce patterns that are already prominent in the chart. Again, I'm covering them mainly because I have four planets in Virgo in my own chart, and I can't stand to leave out any details.

The First-Harmonic Aspect: The Conjunction (☌) (Major)

The conjunction was not even considered an aspect by classical astrologers; it was in a class by itself, and was far more important and powerful than any other planetary relationship. The conjunction is technically a first-harmonic aspect: the division of the circle by one, with the result of a 360° (0°) angle. Conjunctions represent a merging of the energies of the two planets. The two planets involved are united by the same sign motivation, and the closer they are to each other, the more connected the two planets are. Planets in close conjunction to each other can even seem to become a single unit, always acting together, and losing much of their individuality.

Conjunctions are "neutral" aspects in that the ease or difficulty of the conjunction depends entirely on the planets involved. Sun/Moon conjunctions tend to be quite easy, for example, representing, as they do, a unity between the individual's conscious and unconscious selves. Conjunctions to Saturn, on the other hand, can be more challenging.

Conjunctions have tremendous power in that they represent the beginning of a new cycle for the two planets involved. Conjunctions carry a great deal of creative energy and the initiating drive and force to start something new.

The Second-Harmonic Aspect: The Opposition (☍) (Major)

The opposition is a second-harmonic aspect: the 360° circle is divided by two, resulting in a 180° aspect. Oppositions are about balance and perspective. Two planets in opposition are directly across the chart from each other, and can "see" each other with the greatest amount of clarity and perspective. Planets in opposition are in the same polarity (masculine or feminine) and in the same modality (cardinal, fixed, or mutable). They are each motivated by the same core issues, but they approach the issues from different ends of the spectrum. With oppositions we often feel as if we have to choose between the two planets—we can express one or the other, but not both at the same time. Sometimes we project one of the planets onto other people—we don't express or accept the planet's energy as a part of ourselves, so thanks to the Law of Alchemy, we experience it from the outside. Ultimately, planets in opposition can learn to work together, to discover the common ground they share, and find a point of balance—one that doesn't require either planet to compromise, but rather that simply requires each planet to respect and acknowledge the other.

Oppositions are often considered to be "hard" aspects. Although they can be very challenging to work with, they do not encourage any action.

The Third-Harmonic Aspect: The Trine (△) (Major)

The trine is a third-harmonic aspect: the 360° circle is divided by three, resulting in a 120° angle. Trines occur between planets in the same element, and are by far the "easiest" and most flowing of the aspects. Trines represent gifts and talents—things that we are born with, and that will always be there for us. Trines do not require any effort whatsoever on our part, and while they certainly can be fun, restful, and extremely enjoyable, they are also exceptionally lazy. This is something that most of the older astrology books don't mention, because they're too busy describing how wonderful trines are; but just as with planets in rulership, having two or more planets trine each other is wonderful for the planets (they get along famously with each other), but it's not necessarily the best thing for the individual. For one thing, trines are *always* working, which can result in ruts and behavior patterns that are extremely hard to change; and because trines are so easy, we generally don't take full advantage of them. Trines represent talent that we don't necessarily have to work for, and talent that we don't have to work for often remains unexplored and unexpressed. The best thing for a trine is to also have a nice, difficult square to one of the planets in the trine, to encourage us to actually get out and do something with the trine energy.

The Fourth-Harmonic Aspect: The Square (□) (Major)

Squares are fourth-harmonic aspects (the circle is divided by four, resulting in a 90° angle), and are the first truly "hard" aspects. Squares occur between two planets in the same modality (cardinal, fixed, or mutable), but in different elements; so we've got two planets with the same core issues, but with completely different approaches to addressing those issues. It's not that the planets can't learn to work together; it's just that they always tend to butt heads first. Squares represent friction, conflict, and stress, and as a result of this discomfort, squares encourage us to actually get up off the couch and *do something* to alleviate the discomfort. The fourth harmonic relates to the plane of matter, and to action. Squares aren't terribly fun, but they are responsible for some absolutely wonderful accomplishments. The challenge with squares is to learn how to get the two planets involved to work with each other: they have to recognize that even though they've each got their own agendas (as seen by the element), they're ultimately concerned with the same issues (cardinal with identity, fixed with self-worth, and mutable with healing and completion), and if they can stop arguing long enough to realize that, they can come up with some very effective solutions.

The Fifth-Harmonic Aspects: The Quintile (Q) and Biquintile (Q^2) (Minor)

The fifth-harmonic aspects are the first of the "new" aspects proposed by Kepler, and are obtained by dividing the circle by five, resulting in a 72° angle (the quintile), and its double, the biquintile, a 144° angle. The fifth harmonic generally relates to creativity and to change. The quintile series seems to manifest primarily on the mental level, and hardly ever on the physical plane. Since these aspects don't seem to be responsible for either noticeable action or fundamental personality traits, most astrologers don't bother with them.

The Sixth-Harmonic Aspect: The Sextile (⚹) (Major)

Sextiles are sixth-harmonic aspects, and result from dividing the circle by six to come up with 60° angles. Sextiles are generally considered to be "soft" aspects, and occur between two signs in the same polarity (fire/air or earth/water), but in different elements and modalities. Sextiles represent *opportunities*, and, unlike trines, we have to pursue sextiles actively in order to activate them. The energy of sextiles does not flow automatically; however, once the two planets are triggered, they discover that they do indeed work well with each other, in a very supportive and encouraging manner. Of the "major aspects," sextiles are perhaps the weakest, because they *do* require activation. In and of themselves, sextiles represent balance and harmony, but it is just this balance and harmony that is responsible for the fundamental inertia of sextiles.

The Seventh-Harmonic Aspects: The Septile (S), Biseptile (S^2), and Triseptile (S^3) (Minor)

The seventh-harmonic aspects are the most recent additions to astrology, primarily because they are the only series of aspects that do not involve whole degrees. The 360° circle is not evenly divisible by seven, and the resulting aspects are rather unwieldy: the septile (51°25'43"), the biseptile (102°51'26"), and the triseptile (154°17'09"). Unless you're particularly good at math, you're not going to even notice these aspects without a computer to calculate them for you. The septile series of aspects are minor aspects that certainly have a "hard" testing quality about them. A single septile in a person's chart can safely be ignored, or interpreted as a curiosity; however, if an individual happens to have several planets linked with seventh-harmonic aspects, the septile series can become quite important to him or her personally. These individuals will be particularly sensitive to seventh-harmonic transits (which are next to impossible to spot without the aid of a computer). Essentially, the seventh harmonic has to do with spiritual lessons manifesting on the physical plane, something that rarely happens in a pleasant manner. While everyone else is paying attention to the fourth-harmonic and eighth-harmonic transits to their charts to see when and where the action will be in their lives, individuals with seventh-harmonic aspects also need to look at the seventh-harmonic (and fourteenth-harmonic) aspects, because for them (and only them), these aspects can be more powerful than squares.

The Eighth-Harmonic Aspects:
The Semisquare (∠) and Sesquiquadrate (⬚)
(Minor, but Important)

The eighth-harmonic aspects result from the circle being divided by eight, and include both the 45° semisquare aspect and the 135° sesquiquadrate aspect. Although these aspects are usually classified as "minor aspects" (if only because they are not whole-sign aspects, and were not documented by Ptolemy), being a part of the fourth/eighth harmonic scale, they're quite important. They don't have the raw power and force of squares, but they can be quite stressful, and are very much "action" aspects. Semisquares tend to be rather insidious because they often occur between two planets that are sextile by sign, and who should theoretically be working together quite well. Semisquares carry a certain amount of creative potential with them because of this elemental relationship.

Sesquiquadrates, which frequently occur in signs that are elementally trine each other, can carry both the talents and gifts of the trine, but also the inherent laziness of it as well. Sesquiquadrates are usually experienced as outside influences—we'll tend to project one of the planets on others and experience the energy through our relationships. The stress and tension of sesquiquadrates is often dissipated through verbal and mental activity, which is, after all, easier than actually taking action, and in keeping with the inherently lazy but creative energy of the elemental trine. Individuals with many sesqui-quadrates in their charts often have a very quick wit and a well-developed (if sarcastic) sense of humor.

The Ninth-Harmonic Aspects:
The Novile, Binovile, and Quadnovile (Minor)

The ninth-harmonic aspects result from dividing the circle by nine, and include the 40° novile (or nonile), the 80° binovile, and the 160° quadnovile. The ninth harmonic is used predominately in Eastern (Hindu) astrology, where it relates to perfection and to marriage. In Western astrology, the ninth-harmonic aspects are rarely used. The vibration of the number nine has to do with the testing that comes near the end of a cycle, to evaluate whether we are ready or not to progress onto the next level of our lessons.

The Tenth-Harmonic Aspects: The Decile and Tredecile (Minor)

The tenth-harmonic aspects result from dividing the circle by ten, and include the decile (or semiquintile), a 36° aspect, and the tredecile, a 108° aspect. The tenth harmonic combines the mental creative potential of the fifth harmonic with the balance of the second harmonic, and these aspects can be interpreted as weak fifth-harmonic aspects. Although the decile is almost never used, many astrologers who work closely with the 72° fifth-harmonic quintile aspect feel that the tredecile (which is the complementary angle to the quintile: 72° + 108° = 180°) is the key to unlocking the creative potential of the quintile aspect.

The Twelfth-Harmonic Aspects:
The Semisextile (⊻) (Minor) and Quincunx (⊼) (Major)

The twelfth-harmonic actually includes two very different aspects: the 30° semisextile (one-twelfth of the circle), and the 150° quincunx (five-twelfths of the circle) — both of which have at one time or another gone by the name "inconjunct." While both aspects share the common property of occurring between signs that have nothing at all in common by element, modality, or polarity, the two aspects are, in fact, quite distinct. Both are traditionally considered to be "minor" aspects, although most astrologers today agree that the quincunx is, in fact, a rather major aspect and should not be ignored.

The Semisextile

Let's start off by looking at the semisextile. The semisextile is usually categorized as being a weak, moderately easy aspect. Although the two signs involved have nothing in common, they are connected in that one sign evolves into the next, and therefore the two signs in the semisextile *do* work together, on at least a fundamental level. Saying that a semisextile indicates even a weak opportunity is probably pushing things a bit. Ultimately, planets that are semisextile each other are like roommates who, while they can share the same space and have no real animosity toward each other, at the same time live very different lives and don't have much in common beyond having the same address.

The Quincunx

On the other hand, we have the quincunx, which is most definitely *not* a minor aspect. Quincunxes are rather tricky, because all quincunxes are not created equal: some are much easier to resolve than others, as we will see. Generally, quincunxes are moderately stressful aspects. As with the semisextile, quincunxes occur between two signs that have nothing in common by element, polarity, or modality—but with quincunxes, these signs don't even "live together" in the way that semisextiles do. Planets that are quincunx each other are far enough apart that they can "see" each other clearly, as with an opposition; and indeed, quincunxes feel much like oppositions in that we want to try to balance the energy and expression of the two planets involved— but quincunxes don't have the common ground that oppositions do, and there can be no balance. With a quincunx, one or both of the planets will have to make a very uncomfortable adjustment in its expression in order to accommodate the other planet.

As I mentioned earlier, some quincunxes are easier to deal with than others because the signs involved have other connections besides the elemental and modal ones, as you can see in the table that follows.

The three types of connections, in diminishing order of strength, are rulership, antiscia, and contra-antiscia. Quincunxes connected by common rulership of the two signs (Aries/Scorpio and Taurus/Libra) are perhaps the easiest to resolve: both signs, and both planets in those signs, will look to the common sign ruler to settle all disputes. Quincunxes connected by antiscia are slightly less easy to resolve, unless the two planets in the quincunx are in the middle degrees of the signs, where the planets are actually antiscia to each other. (Don't panic, we're going to cover exactly what an antiscion and a contra-antiscion are in the next section.) Since a relationship by antiscia is considered to be quite a harmonious one, the planets in these quincunxes are able to work together more easily. It's rather the opposite with the contra-antiscia, though. When planets are quincunx each other in signs that are contra-antiscia to each other, near the middle degrees of the signs where the contra-antiscia would be in orb, the quincunx can get nasty, since contra-antiscia relationships are considered to be rather stressful in and of themselves. Finally, the planets may truly be quincunx each other (averse) when the signs have absolutely nothing in common (any quincunx involving either Leo or Aquarius).

Other Types of "Aspects"

In addition to the aspects already covered, planets can have other relationships to each other—and many of these were considered by the Greeks to be as important and valid as the "major" aspects.

Receptions

Receptions are based on the essential dignities of the planets, and on the planetary rulerships in particular. Mars, for example, is the ruler of Aries. Whether or not Mars happens to be in Aries, Mars will also rule or "receive" any planet that is in Aries. The ruling planet gives form and structure to the expression of the planet ruled—and the type of form and structure depends on the dignity and sign position of the ruling planet. The Moon in Aries, for example, is received by Mars, and the Moon will "look to" Mars for ways in which it can express itself. If Mars is in Capricorn, Mars is going to be far more structured and practical in its approach, and the Moon will pick up some of this energy (and perhaps even gain a degree of control over the impulsive energy of Aries). If, on the other hand, Mars is in Gemini, the Moon will tend to be less focused and even more impulsive, because Mars in Gemini is motivated to act and explore. In any case, when the Moon is in Aries, it is connected to Mars, regardless of whether or not the Moon and Mars are in aspect to each other.

SIGN	QUINCUNXES	RELATIONSHIP
Aries	Virgo	Antiscia (equally powerful)
	Scorpio	Rulership (Mars)
Taurus	Libra	Rulership (Venus)
	Sagittarius	Inconjunct (averse)
Gemini	Scorpio	Inconjunct (averse)
	Capricorn	Contra-Antiscia (equally rising)
Cancer	Sagittarius	Contra-Antiscia (equally rising)
	Aquarius	Inconjunct (averse)
Leo	Capricorn	Inconjunct (averse)
	Pisces	Inconjunct (averse)
Virgo	Aries	Antiscia (equally powerful)
	Aquarius	Inconjunct (averse)
Libra	Taurus	Rulership (Venus)
	Pisces	Antiscia (equally powerful)
Scorpio	Aries	Rulership (Mars)
	Gemini	Inconjunct (averse)
Sagittarius	Taurus	Inconjunct (averse)
	Cancer	Contra-Antiscia (equally rising)
Capricorn	Gemini	Contra-Antiscia (equally rising)
	Leo	Inconjunct (averse)
Aquarius	Cancer	Inconjunct (averse)
	Virgo	Inconjunct (averse)
Pisces	Leo	Inconjunct (averse)
	Libra	Antiscia (equally powerful)

Receptions by themselves aren't terribly strong "aspects," but what happens if we have the Moon in Aries while Mars is in Cancer? The Moon is ruled by Mars, and Mars is ruled by the Moon. This is called a "mutual reception," and is a much stronger connection between the two planets. Whenever two planets are in mutual reception to each other, they will work together and try to help each other; however, mutual reception does *not* change the essential dignity of the individual planets! How helpful the planets will be to each other depends on how dignified each planet is on its own.

Let's take, for example, Jupiter in Aries and Mars in Pisces. In a night chart, both Jupiter and Mars are at least dignified by triplicity, so they're in pretty good shape. In this example, Jupiter and Mars are going to be able to help each other—Mars will lend its drive and energy to Jupiter, while Jupiter will lend its luck and good fortune to Mars.

On the other hand, let's look at Mars in Capricorn and Saturn in Aries. Mars in Capricorn is in great shape in the sign of its exaltation. Saturn in Aries, however, is in terrible condition, in fall. Since the two planets are bound by mutual reception, they're going to be working together, but Saturn gets the best end of the deal by far. Mars in Capricorn is strong and able to "help" Saturn; but Saturn in Aries is going to be doing more harm than good with its attempts to "help" Mars. It may *mean* well, but for the most part, Mars would be better off if Saturn didn't try to return the favor.

Finally, let's take a common example: Mercury in Sagittarius and Jupiter in Gemini. Both Mercury and Jupiter are in detriment in this example, and neither one is able to be of any use to the other—in fact, they may tend to make the situation even more difficult. Jupiter in Gemini's "help" may simply make the problem bigger, and Mercury in Sagittarius' "help" will probably blow the little things out of proportion rather than being able to address the big picture. Even if Mercury and Jupiter aren't in degree aspect to each other, they're very strongly connected through the mutual reception. Astrologers J. Lee Lehman and Rob Hand call this situation "mutual deception," and it occurs between the complementary pairs of planets: Mercury and Jupiter, Venus and Mars, and the Sun/Moon and Saturn.

I have one final comment on mutual receptions: The current thinking is that the ancients only considered planets to be in mutual reception when the planets both receive each other and are in aspect to each other at the same time. The mutual reception on its own, without a supporting aspect, was evidently not considered a particularly strong connection.

Antiscia and Contra-Antiscia

Antiscia are solstice points. (Antiscia is plural; the singular is antiscion.) The signs are divided along the Cancer/Capricorn axis, and the antiscia are mirrored points across this axis. Antiscia points are equally strong: they correlate to days with the same amount of daylight. Antiscia are considered to be "soft" aspects and are usually interpreted in similar ways to trines and sextiles. Contra-antiscia, on the other hand, are points out of balance—the hours of daylight represented by one point are equal to the hours of nighttime at the other point. Contra-antiscia function as "hard" aspects and are usually interpreted as squares.

You may notice from the table that the fixed signs are all either antiscion or contra-antiscion to each other. This means that anytime two planets in fixed signs are square to each other, they also stand a good chance of also being either antiscia or contra-antiscia, which adds an even greater emphasis to the aspect.

Aspects in Latitude: Parallels and Contraparallels

All the aspects and relationships that we've covered so far have to do with the longitudinal or sign position of the planets along the ecliptic. The ecliptic is the plane of the Sun's apparent path around the Earth, and also the plane of the Earth's orbit around the Sun. The zodiac is usually considered to include a band of sky above and below the ecliptic. A planet's latitude is designated as the number of degrees north or south of the ecliptic. Planets that are conjunct by longitude may in fact be nowhere near each other in the sky because of their latitude (and/or declination, which is similar to latitude, only it's measured in terms of the Celestial Equator, not the ecliptic). Planets that are at the same latitude or declination (for example, Mars at 12° North and the Moon at 12° North) are parallel to each other. Parallels are conjunctions in latitude or declination. Planets at the same degree but in opposite directions (for instance, Mars at 12° North and the Moon at 12° South) are contraparallel to each other. Contraparallels are oppositions in latitude or declination.

In general, parallels and contraparallels are minor aspects and can be interpreted as weak conjunctions or oppositions. Parallels and contraparallels become important, however, when they reinforce longitudinal aspects between the two planets. In particular, when two planets are both conjunct *and* parallel to each other, then the faster-moving planet completely eclipses the slower-moving planet, an event known as an "occultation." Solar eclipses are simply occultations of the Sun and Moon—the Sun and Moon are both parallel *and* conjunct. (We'll cover eclipses in more detail in chapter 10). Occultations are *extremely* powerful conjunctions. They are somewhat rare, but worth noting when they do occur. Occultations are designated in the ephemeris with this symbol: ✝

ANTISCIA AND CONTRA-ANTISCIA (SOLSTICE POINTS)

DEGREES TABLE	
COL. #1	COL. #2
0	30
1	29
2	28
3	27
4	26
5	25
6	24
7	23
8	22
9	21
10	20
11	19
12	18
13	17
14	16
15	15
16	14
17	13
18	12
19	11
20	10
21	9
22	8
23	7
24	6
25	5
26	4
27	3
28	2
29	1
30	0

ANTISCIA SIGNS TABLE	
COLUMN #1	COLUMN #2
Aries	Virgo
Taurus	Leo
Gemini	Cancer
Libra	Pisces
Scorpio	Aquarius
Sagittarius	Capricorn

CONTRA-ANTISCIA SIGNS TABLE	
COLUMN #1	COLUMN #2
Aries	Pisces
Taurus	Aquarius
Gemini	Capricorn
Libra	Virgo
Scorpio	Leo
Sagittarius	Cancer

TO CALCULATE ANTISCIA AND CONTRA-ANTISCIA (SOLSTICE POINTS):

1. Round each natal placement (degrees/minutes) UP to the next WHOLE number (degrees only).

2. Look up the whole degree in COLUMN #1 of the Degrees Table. The degree opposite it in COLUMN #2 becomes the Solstice Point Degree for the Antiscia and Contra-Antiscia.

3. Look up the natal sign in the Signs Tables. The sign opposite it in the other column is the sign of the Antiscion or Contra-Antiscion.

EXAMPLE: If the Sun is at 29°45' Libra, then you would round it up to 30 whole degrees. 30 degrees in COLUMN #1 of the Degrees Table equals 0 degrees from COLUMN #2. Libra in the Antiscia Signs table equals Pisces, so the Antiscion of the Sun would be 0 degrees of Pisces. The Contra-Antiscion of the Sun would be 0 degrees of Virgo.

Figure 13. Calculating Antiscia and Contra-Antiscia (Solstice Points)

9

A Brief Look at
Natal Retrograde Planets

This chapter is entitled "A Brief Look at Natal Retrograde Planets" because a brief look is all that is really needed when it comes to natal retrogrades. Retrograde planets are certainly important to consider—but mostly in transit, as opposed to natal charts. Where natal retrograde planets become truly interesting is in secondary progressions, a predictive technique that we will touch on briefly at the end of this chapter, but which is not really a part of natal astrology.

Before we continue, it might help to review the mechanics of retrograde motion (we covered that in chapter 2, remember?). The planets, of course, never actually slow down and change direction in their orbits around the Sun. Retrograde motion occurs because we're observing the planets orbiting the Sun from our vantage point on the Earth, which is also orbiting the Sun, albeit at a different speed from the other planets.

So how do we interpret a retrograde planet? Traditionally, retrograde planets are thought to have difficulty expressing themselves in a conscious, direct, outward manner. Some astrologers believe that natal retrograde planets relate to past-life issues and lessons. Others interpret natal retrograde planets as representing personal psychological issues that the individual may have with respect to the retrograde planet. While I certainly agree that retrograde planets do not behave the same way as planets in direct motion, I propose a slightly different interpretation, one that at once combines many of the common elements of interpretation found in traditional astrology, and that also places them in a broader perspective.

Growth versus Evolution

As we experience our lives in the universe and learn our lessons both on a personal and on a soul level, two different cycles of lessons become evident. One cycle is the cycle of growth, which is usually straightforward and direct, encompassing lessons that are designed to be learned during the span of one lifetime. The other cycle is the cycle of evolution, which is often unusual and difficult to comprehend, and which encompasses soul lessons that usually require more than one lifetime to integrate and complete. These two cycles operate simultaneously—we are always working on both growth and evolutionary issues. Think of the cycles as spirals. The growth cycle follows the spiral along the most obvious path, and the completion of each circle finds us at almost the same point at which we started, only we're one rung higher up the spiral. The growth cycle follows the path the long way around, while the evolutionary cycle moves directly up the spiral, level by level.

Planets in direct motion are operating on the growth level. Planets in retrograde motion are operating on the evolutionary level.

The Moon's nodes spend most of their cycle in retrograde motion through the zodiac, and as we will see in the next chapter, the Moon's nodes relate to our soul path and soul lessons—lessons that are most definitely on an evolutionary level, and that require many lifetimes to integrate. The most compelling evidence of the evolutionary cycle in action, though, is the precession of the equinoxes and the Great Ages of Man.

The Precession of the Equinoxes (and Why We're Not in the Age of Aquarius)

To understand the precession of the equinoxes, we first have to realize that there are two different zodiac systems: the tropical zodiac (which is used in Western astrology) and the sidereal zodiac (which is used primarily in Vedic astrology). The ecliptic is a circle, with no beginning and no end. In order to divide it into segments so that we can measure and locate the relative positions of the planets, we have to agree on a point that represents the start and end of the circle. We call this point 0° of Aries. Of course, it's difficult to get anyone to agree on exactly *where* 0° of Aries is actually to be found.

The tropical zodiac takes 0° of Aries to be the vernal (spring) equinox in the Northern Hemisphere, the point where the plane of the ecliptic intersects the plane of the equator (and hence, when the Sun is directly overhead at noon, along the equator). This date fluctuates each year, but is usually around March 20 to 21. This point is taken to be 0° of Aries, and the rest of the signs are positioned at 30° intervals from this point along the ecliptic. The tropical zodiac follows the seasons, with the cycle beginning each year with the first day of spring (in the Northern Hemisphere, at any rate).

The sidereal zodiac, on the other hand, attempts to use the positions of the fixed stars to determine the starting point of the ecliptic at 0° of Aries. (Remember, sidereal = stars.) Ostensibly, in the sidereal zodiac, 0° of Aries corresponds with the beginning of the constellation of Aries. Since the constellations are human-made conventions, however, no one is able to agree on exactly where the constellation of Aries begins. The result is that many different sidereal zodiac systems exist and are in use today.

The reason that there is such a difference between the two zodiac systems is because of the wobble of the Earth's axis. The Earth's axis is not vertical; it's inclined toward the Sun at an angle of approximately 23½°, which is what creates the seasonal changes. As the Earth rotates and orbits the Sun, however, this axis wobbles, and slowly makes a circle around itself in the opposite direction. We can "see" this change because over the years, the positions of the fixed stars seem to shift, ever so slightly. So slightly, in fact, that one complete circle of the Earth's axis takes over 25,800 years to complete.

The result is an increasing difference between the spring equinox (0° of Aries in the tropical zodiac) and 0° of Aries in the sidereal zodiac. Each year, the spring equinox occurs at a slightly earlier point than in the previous year— it *precesses* (or moves backward) through the sidereal signs. Currently there is about a 23° difference between the tropical and the sidereal zodiacs, and the spring equinox occurs at about 6° to 7° of Pisces in the sidereal zodiac.

The precession cycle of 25,800 years is divided up into twelve Great Ages of Man, each of which lasts approximately 2150 years (the amount of time that the equinox occurs in each sidereal sign). Currently, we are still in the Age of Pisces, where we will remain until sometime in the year 2150 or so, when the spring equinox will occur at 30° of Aquarius, and the Age of Aquarius will actually begin.

Each of the Astrological Ages is related to significant evolutionary changes in humankind. The Age of Gemini brought the formation of a structured language system and the development of communication. The Age of Taurus saw the discovery of agriculture—humankind was able to make the transition from the hunter/gatherer mode of survival and actually put down roots (both literally and figuratively), staying in one place rather than wandering. This was the beginning of civilization, as tribes became villages, towns, and city-states. The Age of Aries, which followed, focused on warfare and conquest, as the newly formed civilizations fought for dominance; and during the Age of Pisces, we have seen the struggle and suffering of humankind in search of our spiritual connections with the universe, as seen most clearly through the rise and various declines of the Church. The Age of Pisces has also presented us with many opportunities to discover sacrifice, suffering, and martyrdom. The next evolutionary step for the human race is the Age of Aquarius, which is likely to see significant advancements in tolerance and equality among all creatures, with a common goal of creating a utopian society based on personal freedom and equality within the group.

Progression and Precession Cycles Through the Zodiac

As we will see, we learn different lessons moving from one sign to the next, depending on the direction in which we move—progressing through the signs relates to natural growth cycles, while precessing or retrograding through the signs relates to more evolutionary lessons.

The Progression Cycle

We begin the cycle at 0° of Aries—the point when we focus all our energy on separating from the collective unconscious, on breaking free and forming an individual identity. As Aries moves to Taurus, we begin to create a structure and container to house our newfound identity. Taurus seeks to put down roots, to ground, and to settle into steady growth, merging and identifying with the material world. As Taurus moves to Gemini, we begin to differentiate between ourselves and the rest of the world. We experience separation on an intellectual level and seek to make connections, to explore, to make sense of our surroundings. When Gemini becomes Cancer, we experience separation on a deeper, fundamental and emotional level. Cancer is the first point where we remember that we were once part of a collective where all our needs were met by definition, because we were a part of all that exists in the universe. In Cancer, we begin to discover our emotional and spiritual nature, and discover that we need help in order to meet our survival needs. As Cancer becomes Leo, the realization that we are separate from the group becomes stronger, as does our need to receive approval and attention from the group. In Leo, we seek this attention by reinforcing our individual identities and sharing our unique gifts. We seek to earn love and support because we are special. As we continue to grow and Leo becomes Virgo, we change our tactics, and rather than seeking approval because we are special, we seek approval because we are useful and willing to serve. In Virgo, we begin to remember what it feels like to be a part of something bigger than ourselves.

When Virgo becomes Libra, we discover that the group is actually made up of other individuals just like ourselves, with the same desires, gifts, talents, and needs. We narrow our focus from being of service to many, to trying to find balance and harmony while relating to other individuals. At the same time, we become increasingly self-aware, as we see ourselves and the repercussions of our actions reflected clearly back to us for the first time. As Libra transitions to Scorpio, we seek to deepen the relationship, to merge with other individuals on a fundamental emotional and spiritual level; to experience again, for a moment, at least, what it felt like to be without an individual identity, to no longer feel the separation and isolation that we have experienced for so long. Ultimately, the connection we experience through Scorpio is not enough, and as Scorpio becomes Sagittarius, we change our focus, seeking instead to relate to the universe as individuals, rather than relating to other individuals on a one-to-one basis. We seek to understand our role in the grand scheme of things, and as we do so, we begin to realize that we are responsible not only for ourselves, but also for helping and protecting the other members of the group; and at this point, Sagittarius becomes Capricorn. In Capricorn, we take on the roles of group responsibility, seeking to preserve and uphold the structure and integrity of society, to protect others, and to help everyone meet their fundamental survival needs; but ultimately, Capricorn becomes too addicted to the status quo, and becomes Aquarius. Aquarius energy looks not just at the

letter of the law, but more importantly at the spirit of the law. Personal freedom is of the utmost importance, and structures that no longer support the
greater good and freedom of the group are replaced with those that do. In
Aquarius, we step down from the role of leader and experience an intellectual
collective, where all members are equal and are equally responsible for themselves and for the other members of the group. As this connection and relationship deepens, Aquarius becomes Pisces, and the last vestiges of separation
and individuality dissolve as we return to the universe, merging once again
with all that is—until the point, of course, when the collective becomes too
limiting, and we must once again break away as individuals, as Pisces becomes
Aries.

The Precession Cycle

The precession cycle, too, begins at 0° of Aries. The difference, of course, is
that from this point of ultimate individuality and separation, we move back
into Pisces, taking our experiences as individuals, and letting them merge
once again into the collective energy of Pisces, sharing the knowledge and wisdom that we have gained. As Pisces evolves, the collective energy gradually dif-
ferentiates into individual segments in order to expand and enhance its
experience and understanding of itself. As these segments begin to solidify
into distinct, albeit entirely equal individuals, Pisces becomes Aquarius. The
ideal collective energy of Pisces is taken to a more abstract, intellectual level in
Aquarius, as the collective begins to explore the illusion of separation from
each other, and begins to take on and differentiate their individual identities.
As this exploration continues, the level of equality between the individual
members begins to shift, as certain individuals discover that they are able to
make more noticeable contributions to the integrity and safety of the group.
As clear leaders begin to emerge, Aquarius becomes Capricorn, and all individuals in the group begin to focus on how they, as individuals, can make
unique contributions to society, and be recognized and acknowledged for
their service. As the concept of individual identity continues to solidify, Capricorn evolves into Sagittarius, where the individuals seek a greater understanding of their role in the universe—a much broader perspective than simply
understanding one's role in the group and society structure. Sagittarius explores the philosophical, spiritual, and religious aspects of individuality, all
the while trying to discover once again the ultimate connection to the universe

that we experienced before we separated from the source. As Sagittarius becomes Scorpio, the quest for truth turns inward, and we begin to explore our unconscious, emotional, and spiritual nature, looking into the darkest corners of our souls and being transformed by the experience. In Scorpio, we also discover other individuals, and discover deep and healing emotional connections with them. As Scorpio evolves into Libra, we begin to take a more objective approach to our encounters with other individuals, and the focus shifts to one where balance and harmony is maintained, and where justice and fairness is pursued on a one-to-one basis, rather than as a function of society.

Our desire to relate to others, to balance and maintain harmony with them, naturally evolves into a desire to be of service to others, to give of the self in order to improve the quality of life for all, and this is the point where Libra becomes Virgo. As Virgo works tirelessly to discriminate, to improve, and to serve the greater good of humanity, we gradually begin to desire acknowledgment for our work. The point where we fully acknowledge our need for the approval and attention of others is the point where Virgo becomes Leo. Through Leo, we seek validation of our individual identities and recognition for the service, generosity, and love that we freely share with others. Soon, though, simple validation and acknowledgment are not enough: we begin to long for the nurturing and protective energy of the collective once again, and as Leo evolves into Cancer, we begin to actively seek out and strengthen our emotional bonds. Cancer is no longer conscious of the presence of other individuals; rather, Cancer seeks to reconnect with the source directly, and thereby once again experience all our needs being met. When the emotional approach no longer seems to work, Cancer becomes Gemini, which explores the fundamental nature of duality, searching for the ultimate connection, the common thread that will lead us back to the source. Gemini soon discovers that the universe is everywhere, and that we do not need to explore in order to connect with it. As Gemini becomes Taurus, we begin to center once again, to gather our resources, and to merge with the physical. As Taurus becomes more focused and intense, we approach the point where we are no longer aware of anything other than our own consciousness, and Taurus becomes Aries. Aries energy focuses on individual identity—and gradually reaches the point where we once again recognizes our true identity as a part of all that is, at which point, of course, Aries moves once again into Pisces, and the cycle continues.

And Precession Relates
to Retrograde Planets How, Exactly?

Retrograde planets are operating on an evolutionary cycle, rather than on a growth cycle. As such, their lessons are somewhat different from those of planets in direct motion. Now, planets in retrograde motion are only operating on the evolutionary level for relatively brief periods of time—these are opportunities to reflect, and to perhaps make rapid advancement along their growth cycles. Retrograde natal planets carry this energy, this noticeably different perspective, and therefore will tend to express themselves in somewhat different and perhaps unexpected ways.

Traditionally, a planet in retrograde motion is considered to be accidentally debilitated. I personally do not believe that this applies in natal interpretations (although it most certainly does apply in horary and electional astrology). What can have an impact on how easily a planet is able to express itself, however, is the planet's relative speed of motion. When planets are getting ready to change direction, they appear to slow down. This applies to any change of direction, retrograde or direct. When a planet is slow in motion, or stationary, the planet's energy becomes much more focused and concentrated in its expression. It's not so much that these planets have difficulty expressing themselves (although at times, this can appear to be the case), but more that these planets have a tendency to become obsessed with understanding certain situations and concepts with a level of thoroughness and intensity that is quite unusual for them.

Interpreting Natal Retrograde Planets

As a rule of thumb, the only retrograde planets that I personally interpret are the personal planets: Mercury, Venus, and Mars. The rest of the planets, Jupiter through Pluto, spend up to 5½ months of the year in retrograde motion; and because the growth lessons of these slower planets tend to take such a long time to unfold in and of themselves, the change in perspective and expression when they are retrograde in a natal chart is so subtle that it's hardly worth interpreting.

I do notice the outer planets when they are getting ready to change direction and are therefore slow in motion. This is very easy to see in the chart: any planet trine the Sun is slow in motion and has either just changed direction, or is preparing to change direction shortly. A waxing trine (the Sun 120° *ahead* of the planet and moving toward the opposition) means the planet is about to turn retrograde. A waning trine (the Sun 120° *behind* the planet and moving toward a conjunction with the planet) means the planet is about to turn direct.

Mercury Retrograde in the Natal Chart

Mercury, as you recall, relates to the functions of our mind—specifically to our lower mind. Mercury relates to how we think, speak, write, understand language, move, travel, and reason. But remember that before we can communicate with others, we first have to learn how to communicate with ourselves. The first function of Mercury is to allow us to describe the world, our perceptions, our entire reality, to ourselves, so that we understand it. Only then are we able to attempt to interact and communicate with others.

Individuals born with Mercury retrograde do not simply have different styles of communication from individuals born with Mercury in direct motion: they have an entirely different understanding of the universe—one that is rooted in an evolutionary perspective, rather than a growth-oriented one. Again, just because a planet is operating on the evolutionary cycle doesn't mean that we automatically get all the answers! Retrograde natal planets are no different from direct natal planets in that they allow us to grasp a single piece of the puzzle. Retrograde planets simply have a very different puzzle piece than direct planets do—one that, needless to say, won't fit where we might expect it to.

Far from having any learning disabilities, individuals with Mercury retrograde often have very quick minds and extremely sharp, if slightly offbeat, senses of humor. For the most part, the challenges they experience in learning how to reconcile their personal understanding of the world with the apparent perceptions and reality of other people, occur very early in life. While these struggles can certainly be significant, and occasionally even traumatic, after a time, like everything else, they become a learned skill, even a habit, and Mercury retrograde becomes a far less important issue to them. In a very real sense, while individuals with Mercury in direct motion only need to learn one language to be able to communicate with the world, those born with Mercury retrograde must simultaneously learn how to think, speak, and translate between two languages—the one that describes their individual perceptions, and the one that the rest of the world is able to understand.

Although no formal studies have been conducted, I do have a theory that individuals born with Mercury retrograde are significantly more likely to have some level of dyslexia than individuals with Mercury in direct motion. Dyslexia is far more than simply a tendency to reverse letters and numbers, and indeed, is frequently mild enough that it does not constitute any kind of a learning disability. However, dyslexic individuals quite literally have a different way of looking at the world—they have different patterns of focusing their eyes, for example, which is one of the reasons that they tend to transpose letters and numbers—and they are continually forced to translate their perceptions to match the perceptions of others.

Venus Retrograde in the Natal Chart

Venus retrograde in a natal chart indicates individuals who will take a somewhat different approach to their values, relationships, and social interactions than most people. Venus in the chart shows the things we appreciate and admire, the things we wish to emulate and relate to. Venus, you will remember, represents the forces of adhesion, of like attracting like. Individuals born with Venus retrograde tend to have a fundamentally different system of values from those around them. This can be quite a difficult challenge, particularly during adolescence, when feeling socially accepted is often the single most important goal in life, and when being at all different, especially when those differences affect social activities, can result in becoming an outcast.

Our understanding of Venus is evolving continually as we pursue our life-long searches for love and beauty, for things of worth and value that lift our spirits and raise our hearts. We don't really start forming our own individual value systems until adolescence, and individuals with Venus retrograde are usually highly aware that no matter how hard they try to fit in, they are not the same as their friends. Oftentimes, these individuals tend to be quite shy and avoid much of the social interaction and dating that their peers enjoy. This type of behavior is one of the reasons that Venus retrograde has a reputation for having difficulties socializing—but this is not the case at all.

For most of us, our system of values and the things we admire are shaped by our social interactions with friends and peers, and on a larger scale by society and the media. We are shown examples of what is considered beautiful by society, and most of us adopt these standards, to one extent or another. We socialize and interact with our friends and bond through common experiences, and these all help to mold, shape, and reinforce our individual sets of values. After a certain point, our values are more or less established, and rather than changing them to fit our current social situations, we instead begin to seek out social situations and relationships that support our value systems. For individuals born with Venus retrograde, this process is reversed.

Individuals born with Venus retrograde are born with a much stronger sense of their own individual values, although they are not able to understand these values or to discover them any sooner than individuals born with Venus in direct motion. These individuals are bombarded with the same information, values, and standards as everyone else; however, they tend to create their value systems through exclusion, rather than through acceptance. Individuals with Venus retrograde may not understand what they value, but they clearly understand what they don't value. Eventually, through the ongoing process of exclusion, these individuals achieve a clear understanding of what they do value, and at this point, they are able to seek out others who share these common foundations. The challenge, of course, is that this process of exclusion can make it difficult for these individuals to want to socialize or date as adolescents because they may tend to reject so many of the values held at the time by their peers. This means that these individuals may have to learn many fundamental social skills as adults, rather than as adolescents.

Mars Retrograde in the Natal Chart

Mars retrograde in a natal chart can be one of the more challenging energies to learn from. Mars is happiest when it is able to express itself in a forceful, direct, overt way. When Mars encounters obstacles, it fights them, and when Mars feels threatened, it defends itself aggressively. Individuals born with Mars in retrograde motion are exploring their desires, their motivations to take action and create movement in their lives, on a different level from most of the people they will encounter in their lives. Mars retrograde, whether in a natal chart or by transit, offers an exceptional opportunity for us to gain a better understanding of the struggle between our egos and our higher selves, and a chance to become more sensitive to which one is guiding our desires, choices, and actions at any given time. Mars, you will recall, is like the engine of our car, and doesn't care who's doing the driving, as long as it's moving forward.

Mars retrograde presents a challenge, however, because the ego is so fundamentally involved. All fear comes from our egos, and when we feel afraid or threatened, Mars comes to our defense. On a higher level, individuals with Mars retrograde in their charts have a fundamental inclination to channel their Mars energy toward higher purposes. They carry an inherent understanding of the dual nature of Mars as both creator and destroyer, and of the responsibility that our actions carry. Individuals with Mars retrograde are far less inclined to express the more aggressive tendencies of Mars, even when confronted or attacked, and herein lies the challenge of Mars retrograde.

One of the most common issues for individuals born with Mars retrograde is that of repressed anger. People born with Mars in direct motion generally learn to express their Mars, which can often involve angry, aggressive behavior, and then as they grow up, they learn that Mars' energy must be tempered and guided by their higher selves, rather than by their egos. People born with Mars retrograde, on the other hand, naturally seek to contain their Mars, and must instead learn how to express Mars' energy in healthy, appropriate ways. When these individuals are threatened, they may find it difficult to stand up for themselves and defend themselves. They still call Mars to defend them, but the energy of Mars is often directed more inward than outward. These individuals becomes angry at themselves for being violated and not addressing the wrong or defending themselves. This misplaced anger is frequently repressed rather than expressed (because, again, this would be the domain of Mars), and grows with each instance until finally the pressure becomes too great, and the combined force of all this anger explodes in an often inappropriate manner.

Although each of us must learn the same Mars lessons—when and how to defend ourselves with appropriate force—the majority of individuals born with Mars in direct motion learn how to contain and temper their anger, rather than how to release and express it. Individuals with Mars retrograde learn to accept that not all anger and aggression is bad, and that we not only have the right, but we also have the duty to ourselves to stand up and address situations and individuals that have violated our boundaries and injured us in some way. We are not entitled to vengeance; we are, however, entitled to justice.

Outer Planets Changing Direction in the Natal Chart

Having outer planets retrograde in a natal chart isn't terribly significant. Since it takes such a long time before we can begin to really understand the energies of Jupiter (12-year cycle), Saturn (29½-year cycle), Chiron (51-year cycle), and Uranus (84-year cycle), and our present life spans aren't nearly long enough to complete cycles of Neptune and Pluto, the difference in expression between these planets in direct motion and retrograde motion in a natal chart is far too subtle to attempt to interpret. If, on the other hand, a person is born at a time when one of these planets is getting ready to change direction (which, remember, happens whenever the Sun is close to being trine to these planets), then we have something worth considering.

The outer planets move slowly to begin with, and their energy tends to be more heavy and plodding than the faster-moving planets. When an outer planet is slowing down and changing direction, its energy becomes that much more intense, and therefore that much more significant as an influence on an individual's personality. The fact that, being trine the Sun, these planets will also be exerting a very direct influence on that person's core sense of self and identity is also an important consideration! Individuals born with one of the outer planets stationary (either direct or retrograde) will be working very closely with that planet as their teacher; and since this energy will be such a sensitive spot for them, the times each year when that planet changes direction in transit will tend to be felt quite strongly.

Secondary Progressions and Retrograde Planets

Ultimately, retrograde planets have their greatest importance and significance when working with secondary progressions, in conjunction with a natal chart. Secondary progression is a predictive technique that takes each day after a person is born and relates it to the trends and events that will occur in an entire year of that individual's life. For example, the positions of the planets on the fifteenth day after birth correlate to the fifteenth year of life, and so on. Although we won't be covering progressions in this book, they tend to relate to our inner growth and evolution more than to external events.

Because progressed planets move so slowly, any change at all in the progressed chart—planets changing sign or house, forming new aspects, and of course, changing direction either direct or retrograde—is an extremely significant event. Mercury goes retrograde every three months, and stays in retrograde motion for about eighteen days. In terms of progressions, Mercury is retrograde for about eighteen years, every ninety years. This means that the vast majority of individuals will experience some kind of directional change in their progressed Mercury during the course of their lives. Individuals born with Mercury retrograde will experience a shift before they are nineteen years old, when Mercury turns direct by progression, and they are "suddenly" more in step with the rest of the world. They still carry the energy of the retrograde Mercury, and still have their rather unique, evolutionary-based perceptions of the world, but now that their progressed Mercury has turned direct, they often find that they are better able to make the connections between their own perspectives and the perspectives of others. Communicating their perceptions becomes a much easier task.

For those individuals born with Mercury in direct motion who will experience Mercury turning retrograde by progression, this process is often responsible for a lengthy period of analysis, where they take a very close look at their perceptions, beliefs, and understanding of the world, and where they have the opportunity to develop an entirely new perspective and outlook.

Since Venus and Mars retrograde less frequently, and for longer periods of time, their direction changes in progressed charts are less common, but certainly not less significant. Mars stays retrograde for almost three months (in 1999, it was retrograde for seventy-seven days, which of course is seventy-seven years in terms of progressions). The outer planets retrograde once a year, but stay in retrograde motion for up to six months each. Having an outer planet retrograde in your chart isn't terribly significant; however, having an outer planet change direction by progression *is* significant, particularly when it occurs early in life (which is one of the reasons that I encourage you to pay attention to stationary and slow-moving planets).

10

Eclipses, Lunations, and the Moon's Nodes

The term "lunation" refers to any New Moon or Full Moon. The New Moon occurs each month when the Moon is conjunct the Sun, while the Full Moon occurs each month when the Moon opposes the Sun. At the New Moon, when the Moon and Sun are conjunct, they rise together and set together. The Moon is in the sky at the same time the Sun is, during the day—and because the Sun's light is so bright, we can't see the Moon. By the time the Sun has set and we can see the stars, the Moon has also set. At the New Moon, we cannot see the Moon in the sky at night at all. Since the Moon is the fastest-moving body in the sky, each month the Moon speeds ahead of the Sun, and as it separates from the conjunction with the Sun, the Moon begins to rise and set after the Sun does, and we can once again see the Moon in the sky in the evening.

You may have heard the term the "phases" of the Moon. These refer to the eight major points around the cycle between the Sun and Moon. The first phase, which lasts from the conjunction of the Sun and Moon to the semisquare between them (0° to 45°), is called the New phase. When the Moon makes a semisquare to the Sun, it has entered the crescent phase, which lasts from the semisquare to the waxing square (45° to 90°). In this phase, the Moon is visible until late in the evening. At the first square between the Sun and Moon, the First Quarter phase begins (and will last until the waxing sesquiquadrate (90° to 135°). At the First Quarter phase, the Moon rises at noon and sets at midnight. If the Moon is visible in the afternoon sky, it is a waxing moon. The next phase, which lasts from the waxing sesquiquadrate to the opposition (135° to 180°) is called the Gibbous phase. The Moon is approaching its brightest point, and continues to grow. At the Full phase, which begins at the opposition and continues until the waning sesquiquadrate (180° to 225°), the Moon rises at sunset, is directly overhead at midnight, and sets at sunrise, and so is visible for the entire night. As soon as the Moon passes the opposition to the Sun, it begins to wane, or to shrink. It is no longer ahead of the Sun in the zodiac, but rather behind it, rising later each evening and setting later each morning. If the Moon is visible in the morning sky, it is a waning moon. The Disseminating phase lasts from the waning sesquiquadrate to the waning square (225° to 270°), when the Last Quarter phase begins. During the Last Quarter phase (from the waning square at 270° to the waning semisquare at 315°), the Moon rises at midnight and sets at noon. The last phase is called the Balsamic phase, and this lasts from the waning semisquare to the next conjunction with the Sun (315° to 360°/0°). During the Balsamic phase, the Moon is less visible each night and then only in the early morning, as it now rises and sets just before the Sun.

Eclipses and the Moon's Nodes

The Moon, like all the other planets except for the Sun, has an orbit that is inclined slightly to the plane of the ecliptic (which, you will recall, is the apparent orbit of the Sun around the Earth, but which is actually the orbital plane of the Earth around the Sun). The points where the Moon's orbit intersects the plane of the ecliptic are called the Moon's nodes. The Moon's nodes are a pair of mathematical points that have an average retrograde motion of about three minutes of arc per day, and take about eighteen years to complete a full cycle of the zodiac (albeit in retrograde motion). The North Node (or the Ascending Node) is the point where the Moon's orbit intersects the ecliptic plane as it rises from below the ecliptic to above it, and the South Node (or the Descending Node) is the point where the Moon's orbit intersects the ecliptic plane as it descends from above the ecliptic to below it. The North Node (☊) is also sometimes known as the "Dragon's Head," and the South Node (☋) as the "Dragon's Tail"—but more on this later.

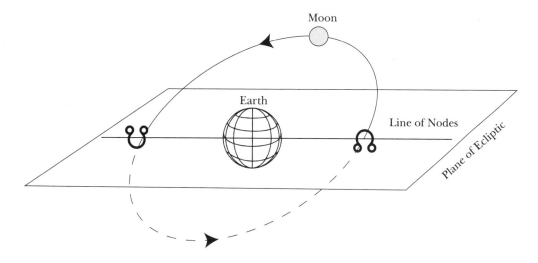

Figure 14. The Moon's Nodes

We're going to spend the majority of this chapter looking at how to understand and interpret the Moon's nodes. For now, we need to realize one more very important thing about them: the Moon's nodes are the transiting eclipse points. What this means is that any time a lunation occurs within 17° of the Moon's nodes, that lunation is either a solar or a lunar eclipse. A solar eclipse occurs when there is a New Moon conjunct one of the nodes, and a lunar eclipse occurs when there is a Full Moon conjunct one of the nodes. Eclipses always occur at least in pairs (one solar and one lunar), although occasionally, three eclipses can occur in a row, alternating solar, lunar, solar; or lunar, solar, lunar.

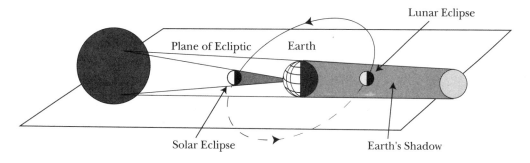

Figure 15. Solar and Lunar Eclipses

As you can see from the illustration, during a solar eclipse, the Moon's shadow is cast on the Earth, temporarily blocking out the light of the Sun in a very small area. During a lunar eclipse, when the Earth is between the Sun and the Moon, the Earth's shadow temporarily blocks out the light of the Full Moon. Although solar eclipses can only be seen from the specific location of the eclipse, lunar eclipses can be seen from anyplace in the world where the Sun has already set by the time of the eclipse.

Interpreting and Understanding the Moon's Nodes

The Moon's nodes are probably the most misunderstood points in astrology. Although few astrologers would dispute their importance in the chart, equally few astrologers could offer a modern, supportive interpretation of the nodes, what they represent, and why. Traditional astrology takes a fairly consistent view of the Moon's nodes. The North Node (*Caput Draconis,* which means the "Dragon's Head") was given a similar quality to the traditional interpretations of Venus and Jupiter, and was associated with all the good things we could possibly experience in our lifetime, including success, advancement, increase, and personal fulfillment. The South Node (*Cauda Draconis,* which means the "Dragon's Tail") was of the same nature as Mars and Saturn, and associated with huge, heaping amounts of what one would expect to come out of the tail end of a dragon. The traditional interpretations of the Moon's nodes pretty much boil down to "North Node *good*; South Node *bad.*"

As modern astrology moved away from the extremely fatalistic and often very negative traditional style of interpreting the planets, the Moon's nodes also received a face-lift of sorts in order to make working with them more empowering. The North Node became the processes and experiences that we must strive for in order to work with our karma and to grow in this lifetime; and the South Node gets promoted from evil incarnate to the point in the chart where we're most likely to take the easy way out and to rely on habit. The South Node is also related to the karma that we're working off in this lifetime. In other words, "North Node *good*; South Node *bad.*"

One of the difficulties in coming up with a truly comprehensive understanding of what the nodes represent in the natal chart is that the Moon's nodes are the only points in the chart that do not have an associated Western mythology. The associations of the dragon with the Moon's nodes comes from

Hindu mythology, and while working with this myth is a great help in understanding the nodes as they are used in Eastern astrology, it doesn't help come up with a Western, humanistic understanding of the nodes.

If we want to understand the energy of one of the signs, for example, we can simply break it down into its component parts. Is the sign cardinal, fixed, or mutable? Is it earth, air, fire, or water? When we combine our understandings of the elements and the modalities, we can easily come up with a very accurate understanding of the energy of each of the signs. In a similar vein, by examining the things that we can observe about the Moon's nodes and interpreting them individually, we're going to come up with a much more structured, comprehensive, and, above all, supportive approach to interpreting the Moon's nodes.

Let's review what we know about the Moon's nodes so far. The nodes are mathematical points that represent where the orbit of the Moon around the Earth crosses the ecliptic (which is the apparent path of the Sun around the Earth). The North Node is the point where the Moon's orbit rises above the ecliptic, and the South Node is the point where the Moon's orbit falls below the ecliptic. The North Node and the South Node are always exactly opposite each other in the chart.

This may not all be quite as obvious as elements and modalities, but just this simple physical description of the Moon's nodes can help us gain a more complete understanding of what they represent in astrology.

The Nodes Are Mathematical Points— They Are Not Physical Bodies

The Moon's nodes are mathematical points; they are not physical bodies. What this means is that the nodes do not emanate light. The nodes can *receive* aspects from the planets, but they cannot directly influence how a physical body expresses itself.

This also means that the nodes do not filter the energy of the signs. With the nodes, as with the angles, we have a pure expression of the energy and symbolism of the signs. Our experience of the energy of Aries, for example, is very different when we are experiencing Venus in Aries from what it is when we experience Mars in Aries. The personalities of the planets color the expression of the signs they visit. The nodes, however, do not change how the signs are expressed or experienced.

The Nodes Are Related to the Moon, the Sun, and the Ecliptic

The nodes are most closely related to the symbolism and processes of the Moon because they represent points on the Moon's orbit around the Earth; but the nodes also relate to the Sun because of their relationship to the ecliptic. In other words, the nodes are the points where aspects of the lunar and solar principles connect.

Let's look at the Moon first, and get a feel for what the Moon brings to this process. The Moon reflects the light of the Sun; it is passive, receptive, and feminine. The Moon responds, and produces emotions and feelings. The Moon is the container of our experience, providing form and location for the Sun's expression. The Moon relates to our conditioning, habits, vices, and learned responses; in other words, the Moon is our memory. The Moon is not just our memory of this lifetime, the Moon is our soul's memory, and the Moon is what our soul wants us to remember from other lifetimes. The Moon is our unconscious and our subconscious.

The Sun, on the other hand, is our conscious, active, life force. The Sun is our will, our power, and our sense of purpose. The Sun is the heart of our existence, and is the motivation for our life this time around. The Sun is how we are seen, how we shine, and how we express and project ourselves. The Sun is how we want to be a hero in our lives; it is how we want to become an individual.

The ecliptic, the apparent orbit of the Sun around the Earth, describes the path that our journey will follow in this lifetime. When we look at a natal chart, what we're actually looking at is a two-dimensional representation of the positions of the planets as viewed from the Earth, flattened to the plane of the ecliptic; in other words, in a chart, the ecliptic is the chart wheel itself. When we look at the positions of the planets along the ecliptic, we are looking at where along our journey we encounter these energies. The position of the Sun at birth shows the point where we chose to begin our quest for self-expression and self-realization in this lifetime. The ecliptic, the chart wheel, represents the actual course that we will follow.

Viewed in this way, the nodes represent the places in the chart where our past, our soul memories (the Moon), intersect with our current conscious experiences, and with our current cycle of lessons and growth. The South Node is the point where we are able to dip below the ecliptic into our past and access our memories from previous journeys. The North Node is the point where our past lessons intersect with our present journey, the point where we emerge from the past and move into new territory. It is the point where our past lessons come up into the light of conscious awareness and allow us to look at this piece of our past in an entirely new way.

Now the connection of the South Node to our past, our karma, and of the North Node to our future, or dharma, begins to make sense.

The Nodes Are Always in Perfect Opposition

Next, let's look at the opposition aspect. Planets are said to be in opposition when they occupy points across the wheel from each other, at an angle of 180°. Traditionally, oppositions were considered "hard" or "challenging" aspects, but fortunately, this opinion has been largely updated.

When I look at oppositions, the keywords I start with are "balance" and "perspective." (Others also use "compromise," but I find that limiting. To me, "compromise" means that each person has to give up something they want in order to get something they want. "Balance" just means that there is agreement and harmony.) The thing about oppositions is that both planets really "want" the same thing, they just approach it from different ends of the spectrum. If we can get each planet to see things from the other's point of view, then we can find that middle ground where they can work together and both get what they want. This process is made easier by the fact that being directly across from each other, the two planets can "see" each other easily, and are able to gain greater perspective on the big picture.

Putting It Together

In other words, the key to the nodal axis is to get the South Node and the North Node to work with each other, right? Not quite. The nodes are not planets, they are mathematical points in the chart. This doesn't make them any less important than a physical body, it just makes them a bit different to work with. The planets, remember, represent physical urges (for want of a better word) and drives that we all have. We can choose either to work with our Mars, for example, or to ignore it. Either way, we're going to be very aware of its presence in our charts. When Mars is activated by transit, or when transiting Mars triggers activity in our charts, we feel it. If we choose to become aware of it, and own it, we can learn to use the energy in the most constructive way possible. If we don't, we're still going to experience it.

The nodes, on the other hand, have to do with the spiritual or soul lessons that we can encounter in this lifetime. The nodes are where the path of our soul development intersects with the path of our physical experiences. Since we're presently incarnated on the physical plane, that is where our focus naturally lies. If we don't choose to work with the nodes and their lessons on a conscious level, we are probably not going to be very aware of how they manifest.

In order to really work with and experience the nodes, we have to become consciously aware of our spirituality, of our soul connection and our connection to the universe. We have to accept that we came here with a lesson that we chose to work on in this lifetime, and we have to be ready to ask what that lesson might be. Are we learning it now? Of course. But the soul path lesson is far more subtle than a Mars transit.

The nodal axis is not our spiritual path in this lifetime. What it is, or rather, what it can be, is a spiritual compass, pointing us in the right direction. The nodes show us where our spiritual path and our soul lessons intersect with our physical path, and they are the points where we can most easily align our physical selves with our spiritual path.

So, with the nodes, it's not just about perspective and balance, it's about learning how to consciously work with and integrate the lessons, gifts, and experiences indicated by the North and South Nodes. The nodes can tell us what we have to work with, and can show us what direction to go in to experience our lessons and to look for our true path in this lifetime.

The South Node

The South Node, then, sheds light on our past. By its location in the chart, the South Node represents the types of experiences and memories that our soul wants us to have in this lifetime to help us on our developmental path. If our soul has gone to all the trouble of bringing up these experiences, shouldn't we pay attention to them? Would a soul filled with love and light intentionally send us back into the material realm with only excess baggage? Of course not.

The South Node represents gifts to us from past lives. The lessons, skills, talents, and abilities that we struggled so many years to master and acquire are still available to us through the South Node. The South Node is our soul's report card; it tells us what subjects we have passed. The South Node says, "Congratulations, you have passed Gemini Level I." For "incompletes" and less impressive marks, look to Saturn for further instruction and retesting, not to the South Node.

Now, just because we can now look at the South Node in a more positive light doesn't mean that the traditional warnings about the South Node being a "trap" don't have merit. Every planet and point in the chart has a highest potential, as well as a potential trap. With the South Node, the trap is to mistake summer vacation for graduation. We may be able to take a break, but we're still in school. So long as we are incarnated on the Earth, we are here to learn.

Even though the South Node represents lessons and skills that we have learned, used, and often mastered in the past, it also is an indication that we still have more to learn about them in this life. We may have learned the skills *too* well, and limited our growth in other areas. We may have misused the information in the past, learning the letter of the lesson, but not the spirit; or it may merely be time to learn how to use the skills in a different way, to expand our mastery. In any event, for higher education, we look to the North Node.

The North Node

The South Node is not alone in being long overdue for a revised interpretation. True, the trap of the South Node is a tendency to stick with what is familiar, which can mean that we miss the opportunity for growth, and repeat old patterns. Also true is the fact that the way to avoid the trap of the South Node is to work with the North Node, which is why the North Node got such a great reputation. The North Node, though, also has a trap: the tendency to want to turn our backs on the past in the single-minded pursuit of growth and new experiences.

The temptation of the North Node is to forget where we've been, and to focus only on where we are headed. The North Node, after all, brings success, happiness, abundance, luck, and freedom from the patterns and habits of the past. The North Node is the spiritual equivalent of the trip to the Bahamas that we've always wanted to take; and just like that trip to the Bahamas, the trap of the North Node is that it makes us feel that much as we want it, we probably can't afford it. The North Node seems to say, "You can get to the Bahamas, but you have to leave your nice, comfortable boat and swim there on your own. Oh, and by the way, there are probably sharks in the water." The trap of the North Node is just as dangerous as that of the South Node. We buy into the idea that we have to sever our ties to the past to create a new future.

We dive into the water to swim out to the Bahamas, get part of the way there, and either get too tired or too scared of the sharks in the water, and hurry back to the comfort and familiarity of our boat, the *S.S. South Node.* If we've *really* bought into the trap of the North Node, we may feel like spiritual failures on top of it all.

Obviously, this is not an interpretation of the nodes that is very supportive. My intention is not to bash the North Node, only to point out that the traditional interpretation of the nodes encourages us to stay away from the South Node in order to reap the rewards of the North Node, and that is just *not* what it is all about. The true process of the North Node is not about turning our backs on the past. The North Node is about taking stock of the past, honoring it, working with it, building on it, and learning how to use it in a new way.

For example, the North Node Sagittarius/South Node Gemini axis doesn't tell us that we're done with Gemini and now have to learn Sagittarius. Instead, it tells us that we are now going to learn how to use our Gemini experiences in a Sagittarian way. It tells us that part of our path, part of our lesson in this lifetime, is to recognize that there *is* a point of balance between Gemini and Sagittarius, and finding it will be a key to our spiritual growth and development. By working with both the North Node and the South Node, we get to take the boat with us to the Bahamas, instead of having to swim there.

Interpreting the Nodes

Before we can begin to integrate and interpret the nodal axis, there is one more factor to consider: the houses. And the single most important thing to remember about the houses is that *the houses are NOT the same things as the signs.* Every book on the Moon's nodes that I have come across makes the same assumptions and claims that the North Node in Aries is the same thing as the North Node in the first house. This is simply not the case. Remember that the signs are the roles the actors play, and the costumes they wear. The houses are the scenery, the locations, the places where the actors go to play out their roles. The signs represent the underlying motivations and the evolutionary lessons that we must learn. The houses represent the areas of life and of experience where we are most likely to encounter these lessons. The signs, then, are the "what," and the houses are the "where." The house placement of the nodes does not in any way change the fundamental lessons and gifts of the nodal axis, it simply shows where in our lives we need to look to find these lessons and gifts.

The houses, too, have their lessons, and like the lessons of the sign axis, the house axis teaches the importance of balance and perspective. The opposing houses, like the opposing signs, represent areas of our lives that we must learn to integrate and harmonize. Just as we may tend to get a little too comfortable with the gifts of the South Node, we may also tend to focus more on the areas of our lives represented by the house of the South Node. Moreover, we may also occasionally focus too much on the North Node, or spend too much time involved in the affairs of the North Node's house, and forget to draw on the support and resources of our South Node. Because the houses represent the places where we will naturally encounter the nodes, if we want to work with our nodes, we can simply devote time to activities that relate to the house in question, and we will thus naturally encounter our nodes.

When interpreting the nodal axis then, the first and most important factor to consider is the sign axis of the nodes. What do the two signs have in common? All opposing signs share some common theme; they simply approach it from very different perspectives. Next, look at the sign placement of the South Node and the North Node within this axis. What are the gifts that the South Node offers? What are the best and most wonderful expressions of the sign of the South Node? How can working with the North Node balance and enhance the gifts of the South Node? By exploring these questions, we can discover some of the lessons of the specific nodal axis. Now, take this understanding and look at the house placement of the nodes to learn more about where in our lives we will be able to experience and encounter these lessons.

Finally, let's try to put things into perspective. Remember that the nodes are not physical bodies, and because they are not physical bodies, they operate on a far more subtle level than the planets do. Unlike the planets, the nodes do not play a very big part in the development of our individual personalities. The nodes, however, are the key to understanding more about what our spiritual purpose is in this lifetime. Sometimes the nodes are closely connected with the planets in our chart, and the connection between our physical life and our spiritual path is obvious. Sometimes the nodes seem to exist on their own, separate from the rest of the action in our chart. Whichever way they appear to be linked with the other elements in our chart, the nodes can help us step back and see beyond the limitations of our time on Earth, and once again glimpse the bigger picture of the evolutionary journey of our souls.

That being said, let's take a quick look at the different lessons of each of the nodal axis combinations.

The Aries/Libra Nodal Axis

The Aries/Libra nodal axis is the axis of identity. The purpose of this axis is to learn to develop a sense of self as an individual within the context of relating to other individuals. Both Aries and Libra seek to create a greater expression and develop a greater understanding of the self. While Aries defines the self through expression of individuality, Libra defines the self through relating with other individuals, and therefore by exploring and defining boundaries.

The function of Aries is to begin, to pioneer, and to create new life. Aries breaks away from the collective consciousness of Pisces when the infinite connection to everything becomes too limiting. In order to be able to continue to evolve, a part of the infinite separates and forms the illusion of an individual identity: this is the process of Aries. Aries is a trailblazer because Aries must push past all boundaries and shatter all limitations in order to express an individual identity. Aries is a leader because Aries is not comfortable being led or limited by others. Aries is courageous, inspirational, enthusiastic, original, and independent; however, Aries is entirely focused on expressing the self, and is therefore entirely ignorant of the presence of other individuals, and, more to the point, ignorant of the fact that its actions have repercussions that will affect and impact other people.

Libra, the sign opposite from Aries, is as naturally aware of other individuals as Aries is ignorant of them. Libra fully understands the responsibility of being an individual, and seeks to maintain balance and harmony in all aspects of one-to-one relationships. Ultimately, Libra seeks to restore the balance between the self and the universe, the collective source of creation that it left when it formed its individual identity through the process of Aries. Through relating to and harmonizing with others, Libra is able to further define and strengthen its sense of personal boundaries. Libra is truly collaborative, and can be charming, diplomatic, artistic, creative, objective, and entirely fair and impartial. Libra is very aware of personal responsibility, and has a strong sense of justice. This understanding of the burden of responsibility for its actions and the need for balance can become Libra's greatest challenge, however. When keeping the peace becomes the most important objective, Libra can begin to sacrifice personal boundaries and individual needs in order to avoid a potential conflict. When every decision, every action, will have a direct and equal reaction, not making a decision and not taking action can appear to be the safest way to maintain harmony. The result is that Libra can become either calculating and manipulative, or passive and reactive, denying its own individual needs.

The Aries/Libra nodal axis teaches us that we must learn to develop our individual identities and yet maintain them in relationship to others. We must learn to develop appropriate personal boundaries and maintain them in relationship to others. At the same time, once those boundaries are defined, we have an obligation to ourselves to fully express our individual identities. We must learn to what degree we must be selfish and be allowed to express our individual needs and desires, and at what point we must learn to compromise with others.

North Node in Aries/South Node in Libra

The South Node in Libra carries the gifts of balance, harmony, beauty, and a fundamental appreciation for the finer points of relationships. The trap of the South Node in Libra, however, is a tendency to want to maintain the harmony in relationships at all costs, and to deny all individual needs that could upset the dynamic of the relationship. The lesson here is to learn to work with the North Node in Aries, to explore and express our individual identities, while still maintaining an awareness of the dynamics of interpersonal relationships. The North Node in Aries teaches that it is not enough to simply have balance in a relationship: we must maintain balance while fully expressing our individuality at the same time.

North Node in Libra/South Node in Aries

With the South Node in Aries, expressing our individuality is something that comes quite easily. The gifts of the Aries South Node include decisiveness, leadership, and a passion for life. The trap of the South Node in Aries, however, is being ignorant of the needs and boundaries of others. Working with the North Node in Libra will teach us how to balance our individual identities with the other individuals in the world. Through relationships, we can learn that we end where others begin, and become more consciously aware of our individual boundaries, which in turn reinforces our sense of individual identity. The North Node in Libra also teaches us how to take responsibility for how our actions affect other individuals.

The Taurus/Scorpio Nodal Axis

The Taurus/Scorpio axis relates to the universal cycles of birth and death, of growth and destruction. The purpose of this axis is to learn to surrender to the natural cycles of life, and to be open to change when change is necessary. As fixed signs, both Taurus and Scorpio are concerned with sustaining and maintaining, and with the core issue of self-worth. Taurus seeks to sustain and maintain on the physical and material plane, and represents the building side of the axis. Scorpio, on the other hand, seeks to sustain and maintain on the emotional and spiritual plane, which necessitates the tearing down of physical boundaries; and therefore, Scorpio represents the destructive side of this axis.

The purpose of Taurus is to sustain and maintain, to stabilize and support the sense of individual identity and initiation that comes from Aries. Taurus reinforces the sense of self through the physical and the material. Taurus defines the self through physical experience and finds validation through the five senses and all forms of interaction with the material plane. Through working with the physical, Taurus seeks to build a structure that will support its sense of individuality and separation from others that it first experienced through Aries. Taurus, however, can become too focused on the material, the physical, and the practical. The very things that helped to support and define its new sense of self can easily become the things that limit and confine it, and hinder its ability to truly grow. Taurus can become attached to the physical and the material, and can lose the ability to distinguish between the true, eternal self and the physical manifestations and extensions of the self.

The purpose of Scorpio, on the other hand, is to break down these illusions, to strip away all the concepts that we have used to confine and define our true selves, beginning with the physical, and ultimately ending only when the ego, the core of our illusions of separation, has been killed, at least temporarily. Scorpio seeks to reinforce its emotional and spiritual self-worth by experiencing deep and transformational connections with others. When we let our egos die, we can merge with another individual on a deep emotional and spiritual level, and at least for a moment, experience a profound sense of connection to something bigger than ourselves and a reminder that we are truly all connected and part of all creation. Scorpio can get carried away in the same way as Taurus, however, and become obsessed with a continual process of destruction and transformation. Scorpio is often tempted to explore all its hidden fears, each and every one of its buried emotions, and be transformed by this experience. Scorpio doesn't care about the external turmoil that this inner journey tends to create because, for Scorpio, the only true reality exists on the inner, emotional, and spiritual levels.

The Taurus/Scorpio axis relates very strongly with the Greek myth of Persephone. Persephone, the daughter of Demeter, the goddess of the spring, was kidnapped by Hades, the ruler of the underworld. Demeter was so upset that she punished the world—nothing would grow, and for the first time the world experienced fall and winter. Ultimately, Demeter was able to gain the return of her daughter, but because Persephone had eaten six pomegranate seeds while she was in the underworld, she could never truly leave and was bound to Hades forever. An arrangement was made wherein Persephone would spend six months of the year with Hades in the underworld, and six months of the year with Demeter aboveground. When Persephone is in the upper world, we have spring, the rebirth of life, and everything begins to grow again. When Persephone is in the underworld, we have fall and winter, things begin to die, and the earth is barren until the next spring when the cycle begins again.

True growth occurs in cycles, and in order for us to be able to continue to grow, a part of us must first die. The Taurus/Scorpio nodal axis teaches us how to get in touch with these cycles, to understand when it is time to put down roots and grow, and when it is time to tear down some of what we have created, so that we can eventually rebuild structures that will allow us to grow even more.

North Node in Taurus/South Node in Scorpio

The South Node in Scorpio brings the gifts of transformation, spirituality, and healing. Individuals with the South Node in Scorpio are very familiar with the process of death and transformation. They bring with them their experiences in the underworld, as it were. The trap of the South Node in Scorpio, however, is that these individuals may become too obsessed with change. They may actually fear change, and so rather than have changes occur to them, they may have learned to initiate change themselves. For these individuals, the North Node in Taurus teaches that it is time for them to leave the underworld, return to the surface, and begin to build again, to put down roots, to plant seeds in the ground. The South Node in Scorpio can ensure that they won't ever get too addicted to the status quo, but the North Node in Taurus teaches that for now, it's time to build and to grow, not to change.

North Node in Scorpio/South Node in Taurus

Individuals with the South Node in Taurus, on the other hand, bring the gifts of stability, creativity, being grounded, and of growth into this lifetime. They have learned well how to create a solid foundation, and how to build on that foundation slowly and steadily to create an integrated sense of self. The trap of the South Node in Taurus, however, is that these individuals may be quite addicted to this illusion of structure and extremely resistant to change; in fact, the idea of change may positively terrify them. Change, of course, is exactly what is required for these individuals. They have taken the Taurus energy as far as they can, and it's time to let some of it die to clear the way for new growth. The North Node in Scorpio teaches that it's time for Persephone to return to the underworld, and it's time for these individuals to let certain parts of themselves die so that other parts can continue to grow.

The Gemini/Sagittarius Nodal Axis

The Gemini/Sagittarius nodal axis is the axis of the mind. The purpose of this axis is to learn how to balance the lower mind with the higher mind; the immediate environment with the cosmos; knowledge and information with truth and understanding. Gemini explores the world, gathering information, making connections, focusing primarily on the fundamental nature and expressions of duality. Sagittarius, on the other hand, seeks the unifying thread, the single idea, the great truth that connects all creation with the creator.

The function of Gemini is to explore the environment and to make connections between different elements. Gemini relates to all forms of language and communication because words are simply ways of drawing a connection between ideas and objects. Gemini is fascinated by everything and has an absolutely insatiable curiosity about the world. Gemini is constantly gathering information and ideas, and exploring every possible facet and permutation of any situation. Inherent in the energy of Gemini is the concept of duality—Gemini will explore both extremes of any situation in an attempt to understand how the two opposite concepts relate to each other. Gemini, however, is so completely focused on the details that it lacks any kind of perspective. Gemini is always gathering information, but lacks the focus and attention span to make use of the raw data, to discover common themes, and to discover where the details fit in the bigger picture.

Sagittarius, on the other hand, is entirely concerned with the big picture. Sagittarius energy is focused and one-pointed, and always dedicated to discovering the ultimate truth. While Gemini explores the lower mind, Sagittarius operates on the level of the higher mind, in the realms of theory and philosophy, spirituality, and theology. Where Gemini seeks to explore duality, Sagittarius wants to resolve it, integrating the opposite sides into a unified whole. Sagittarius is symbolized by the centaur, which merges our dual animal and human nature. Even though Sagittarius has focus where Gemini does not, Sagittarius, too, can lose perspective and become so obsessed with discovering the truth that it can adopt the idea that the end will always justify the means. While pursuing an understanding of the laws of the universe, Sagittarius can often forget the laws of humankind, inadvertently hurting the feelings of other individuals who may have different perspectives on their own personal truths.

The Gemini/Sagittarius nodal axis teaches us to find a balance between the lower and higher minds. We must always maintain our curiosity and flexibility, but it must also be guided by a higher understanding and philosophy. Searching for an understanding of universal truths is important, but we must also discover how to apply these truths on a smaller scale in our daily lives—we must be able to communicate them to ourselves and to others. Knowledge must always be tempered with understanding and perspective.

North Node in Gemini/South Node in Sagittarius

The gifts of the South Node in Sagittarius include a core understanding of our individual relationship to the universe and to society. The South Node in Sagittarius gives us a very strong belief system, a fundamental and unifying philosophy of life that can be a great help in expressing and reinforcing our individual identities. The trap of the South Node in Sagittarius, however, involves adhering too rigidly to this belief system, and not being receptive to other people's ideas and beliefs. The trap of the South Node in Sagittarius can result in a "holier than thou" attitude, as well as a tendency to "talk the talk, but not walk the walk."

While the South Node in Sagittarius most certainly has important information to share with the world, the only way to effectively communicate this information is by working with the North Node in Gemini. The North Node in Gemini will teach us how to apply the Sagittarius beliefs to our daily lives and environment; and perhaps most importantly, through exploring the issues of duality that are always a part of Gemini energy, the South Node in Sagittarius can help us discover that universal truth can appear in many different forms, and express itself in many different and often contradictory ways.

North Node in Sagittarius/South Node in Gemini

The gifts of the South Node in Gemini include an insatiable curiosity about the world, a quick mind that is open to all forms of new ideas, and a playful, youthful outlook. The South Node in Gemini loves variety and is always searching for new ideas and information. The trap of the South Node in Gemini, however, is a lack of focus and a difficulty in integrating the vast stores of information accumulated. The South Node in Gemini can be very much a "jack of all trades and a master of none." The key to balancing this energy is to work with the lessons of the North Node in Sagittarius, and to look for the common thread that links the dual concepts. Gemini already looks for connections, and the Sagittarius influence simply helps Gemini look for connections on a broader and much larger scale. Gemini collects information, but working with the focus of Sagittarius, that information can be catalogued and synthesized. Working with the Sagittarius North Node takes the Gemini information and distills from it an understanding about how the universe works, and our role in the greater scheme of things.

The Cancer/Capricorn Nodal Axis

The Cancer/Capricorn nodal axis is the axis of responsibility. The purpose of this axis is to learn how to find a balance between our responsibility to take care of ourselves, and our responsibility to take care of others in the form of our duties to our families and to society. Both Cancer and Capricorn are concerned with responsibility and with meeting our fundamental needs in life. Cancer is concerned with making sure that our emotional and soul needs are met—that we feel nurtured, safe, and emotionally protected. Capricorn is concerned with making sure that the structures and laws of society are formed and maintained, so that everyone is protected and supported. Although the more obvious need for balance between Cancer and Capricorn has to do with our personal/family obligations versus our professional obligations, within each of these signs is also the inherent need to find a balance between being selfish and selfless. Both signs struggle with the lesson that before we can take care of others, we have an obligation to take care of ourselves, and that we must always come first.

Cancer is where we seek to feel a sense of emotional and spiritual connection, to once again experience the safety and comfort we felt before we separated from the universal consciousness. On the highest level, Cancer understands that because we are all connected and part of all that is, when we nurture and care for others, we are also nurturing ourselves; and when we are being nurtured, we are also nurturing others. Because there are truly no boundaries, no separations between us, there is no difference between giving love and receiving it. Cancer, however, does not always operate on this level, and all too often, it forgets the truth of our connections to each other, and buys into the illusion of ego and separation. When this occurs, Cancer can become obsessed with having its personal emotional and security needs met. This can manifest as exceptionally needy and dependent behavior, or as the eternal caretaker, the person who is always giving and never allows anyone else to give back in return, for fear that if he or she stops giving, others will not give back.

Capricorn, on the other hand, is concerned with the needs of society rather than the needs of the individual. Being an earth sign, Capricorn operates on the material and practical level, and is motivated by structure and support, whether these are physical (in the form of shelters), or social (in the form of laws and guidelines for acceptable behavior). In its highest manifestation, Capricorn understands our connection to all creation as well, and therefore understands that when we take responsibility for protecting the structure of society and meeting the physical needs of others, we are also meeting our own physical and material needs; but Capricorn can also become ego-involved and focused only on personal gain and ambition, pursuing power and influence for its own sake at the cost of personal and individual happiness.

The Cancer/Capricorn nodal axis teaches us about our responsibilities to ourselves and to others. We must at once learn to find a balance between our family obligations and our responsibility to be contributing members of society. In each case, we must also learn what it means to be truly selfish—a concept that currently has a very negative connotation. Being truly selfish simply means being responsible for making sure that our individual fundamental needs are being met before we devote any of our resources to helping others meet their needs. Until we can help ourselves, we cannot be expected to help others. Once we are able to help ourselves, however, then we do have an obligation to assist others, not simply by meeting their needs for them, but by helping them discover how they can take personal responsibility for their lives, and begin to meet their needs on their own.

North Node in Cancer/South Node in Capricorn

The South Node in Capricorn offers the gift of a strong sense of self-reliance, personal responsibility, and practicality. Capricorn is the builder of the zodiac, and the South Node in Capricorn indicates advanced skills in the manifestation of one's desires and ideas. The trap of the South Node in Capricorn, however, is the belief that relying on other people for help and forming emotional connections is a sign of weakness. Individuals with the South Node in Capricorn may have little time for personal concerns or for emotional and spiritual issues, and may distance themselves from these types of situations by taking on jobs, careers, and responsibilities to others that consume much of their time and energy, leaving little time left for a personal life. This energy can be balanced by working with the lessons of the North Node in Cancer, which encourages these individuals to let down some of their walls and open their hearts to emotional connections. Oftentimes, the most difficult part of this for these individuals is to accept that they don't always have to be responsible and in control—that they can let down their guard and allow other people to take care of them. Ultimately, of course, in order to be truly responsible for ourselves as individuals, we must experience these emotional connections in our lives.

North Node in Capricorn/South Node in Cancer

The gifts of the South Node in Cancer include compassion, warmth, sympathy, and the ability to form and maintain nurturing, emotionally supportive connections with other individuals. The trap of the South Node in Cancer, however, is the tendency to become overly dependent on others on an emotional level. This can manifest as being needy and always relying on the support and attention of others, or it can manifest as becoming the eternal caretaker, always worrying about taking care of other people and helping them, whether they have asked for assistance or not. In either case, the key is to work with the energy and the lessons of the North Node in Capricorn, which first and foremost teach self-reliance and personal responsibility. Although we certainly want to maintain our gift of being open and available on an emotional level, the North Node in Capricorn can help us discover how we can take responsibility for our own lives and our own needs, and can free us from being dependent on the energy and attention of others for our survival. The North Node in Capricorn can also help us understand that when we are asked to support and nurture others, we must do so in a ways that help them discover their own self-reliance, not in ways that make them dependent on us for their survival.

The Leo/Aquarius Nodal Axis

The Leo/Aquarius nodal axis is the axis of group dynamics. The purpose of this axis is to learn to find a balance between prominence in the group and equality in the group. Both Leo and Aquarius are fixed signs and are thus concerned with self-worth, and both signs are very much related to our ability to express and receive unconditional love. Leo expresses love from the heart on an individual basis, while Aquarius expresses love on a more abstract and mental level, offering perspective and compassion for all humanity. True unconditional love comes when the head and the heart are balanced, a lesson that we can learn from the Leo/Aquarius nodal axis.

Leo seeks to express itself from the heart in a warm, open, generous, and creative way, and to share its unique identity with others. Leo seeks to earn its rightful place in the group by giving freely of itself, by opening its heart, loving others, and receiving love and acceptance from them in return. Leo does not always operate on this highest level, however, and when the ego becomes involved, Leo can become very dependent on the approval and attention of others, and may tend to seek constant validation of its unique and individual identity. Leo's desire to shine and share its warmth with others can quickly become a need to be in the spotlight continually. When this happens, Leo's generosity can become conditional and motivated by the need for validation and attention, rather than coming from a place of unconditional love and acceptance.

Aquarius, on the other hand, seeks acceptance by the group based on equality. Aquarius is an entirely group-oriented energy, and rather than operating on an individual level, Aquarius identifies with the group as a separate entity. Aquarius is capable of putting the needs of the group ahead of the needs of any individuals in the group, and because of this, Aquarius energy can contribute greatly to the overall safety and quality of life of the entire group. In its highest manifestation, Aquarius energy works tirelessly to ensure that the structures and rules that protect and support the group continue to provide the greatest degree of personal freedom within the group. Aquarius truly believes that everyone is created equal, with the same rights and privileges, and that everyone deserves the same chance to live their lives in the way they choose to. Aquarius, however, can easily lose sight of the fact that the group is made up of individuals, each of whom is unique. While Aquarius has a great love of humanity, Aquarius often has difficulty relating to people on an individual basis. Objectivity and perspective can be taken to the extreme, to the point where they ultimately prevent Aquarius from expressing any true compassion.

Working with the Leo/Aquarius nodal axis teaches us how to relate to humanity both as a group identity (through Aquarius), and on an individual level (through Leo). Unconditional love requires a balance between these two points of view. It must come from the heart, and is best shared on an individual basis, but it must also be tempered with perspective from the head, and the understanding that everyone is equally deserving of love and acceptance.

North Node in Leo/South Node in Aquarius

The South Node in Aquarius brings gifts of personal freedom and tolerance of others. The South Node in Aquarius can easily identify with the greater needs of society and willingly takes part in efforts to change and improve the world for the benefit of everyone, thanks to its gift of selfless dedication to humanity. The trap of the South Node in Aquarius, however, is letting the head rule the heart. Aquarius can become too abstract and too idealistic, finding it easier to be compassionate toward strangers and groups, than toward individuals and friends. Ultimately, the trap is to believe that the good of the group is more important than the good of the individuals that make up that group. Working with the lessons of the North Node in Leo will balance this energy, because the North Node teaches us to come from the heart. The contributions that Leo makes to the group are personal and individual, unique expressions of individual identity. While Aquarius gives to the group as a whole, Leo gives to the group one individual at a time. The North Node in Leo can help the South Node in Aquarius understand that it's not just that everyone in the group is equal: it's that everyone in the group is equally special and unique—and each individual deserves to be acknowledged and appreciated for his or her contributions to the whole.

North Node in Aquarius/South Node in Leo

The gifts of the South Node in Leo include the ability to give selflessly to others, to open the heart with warmth and generosity, and to embody and express love. The South Node in Leo is a tremendous store of creativity and honesty, and can provide courage, strength, and self-assurance. The trap of the South Node in Leo, however, is to become dependent on the acknowledgment and approval of others for Leo's generosity and love. The South Node in Leo can express an almost pathological need to be the center of attention, and may continually seek approval, acknowledgment, and validation from others for how special and unique it is. This trap leads to entirely self-centered behavior, pride, and frequently to childish behavior. The way to avoid this trap is, of course, to work with the lessons of the North Node in Aquarius. Aquarius energy can help Leo see the bigger picture, to focus less on itself and more on how it can become a part of something bigger. Aquarius can also help Leo understand that becoming a member of the group does not necessitate the loss of individual identity. On the contrary, the group is made up of other individuals, each making their own unique contributions toward a common goal.

The Virgo/Pisces Nodal Axis

The Virgo/Pisces nodal axis is the axis of matter and spirit. The purpose of this axis is to learn how to balance between discrimination and assimilation, and between isolation and integration. Virgo and Pisces are both mutable signs, and are concerned with healing and completion, and ultimately with perfection and improvement. Virgo operates on the physical plane, while Pisces operates on the spiritual plane. While we are incarnated on Earth, we must continually work to find the point of balance between our physical world and our true spiritual identity. We must discover how to bring spirit into matter, and matter into spirit.

Virgo is concerned with perfecting the physical universe through competence, analysis, discrimination, and adaptability. Virgo excels at all forms of quality control, thanks to outstanding analytical capabilities, an attention to detail, and ultimately a genuine desire to serve the greater good of humanity by being of service to others. Virgo seeks to adapt both itself and the world in its never-ending search for perfection. Virgo must learn, however, that perfection is as much about the process as it is about the end result. Virgo has a tendency to become overly critical of both itself and others. Obsession with details can result in a loss of perspective that makes any real progress and improvements difficult. Virgo's dedication to service must also be balanced with a strong sense of individual identity; otherwise, Virgo may tend to make needless sacrifices, believing that sacrifices are required to be truly of service.

Pisces, on the other hand, seeks the perfection and healing of the spirit that will occur when we once again become one with the cosmic consciousness and all creation. Pisces seeks the higher spiritual truth that we are all one, and operates by forming connections, dissolving boundaries, and transmuting all negative emotions and pain. By helping free others of these fear-based obstacles, Pisces encourages others to advance along their own spiritual paths. Pisces, however, can become so obsessed with the spiritual and emotional realms that it pays little attention to the physical world and, as a consequence, finds it increasingly difficult to function in a responsible manner. Pisces can also fall into the ego trap of the martyr or the victim. Instead of releasing the pain and negativity it absorbs from others, Pisces may tend to hold onto it, mistakenly believing that its personal suffering will help others evolve spiritually.

The Virgo/Pisces nodal axis teaches us how to balance our physical world with our spiritual world. Each of these realms is equally important, and ultimately, through working with the Virgo/Pisces axis, we can begin to understand how they are a part of each other. We can learn to spiritualize our daily lives and routines, and at the same time, we can learn to anchor and ground the spiritual energies in our lives.

North Node in Virgo/South Node in Pisces

The South Node in Pisces brings with it the gifts of compassion, spirituality, and the ability to heal and transmute negative emotions and pain. The South Node in Pisces indicates a fundamental understanding and appreciation of the ways in which we are all connected to each other. The trap of the South Node in Pisces, however, is to use spirituality as an escape and a way to avoid the lessons and responsibilities that come with being incarnated in a physical body. When the South Node in Pisces denies the physical, it begins to take on the role of the victim and the martyr, and the more suffering it experiences on the physical plane, the more determined it will become to attempt to escape through mystical experiences and spirituality. The North Node in Virgo teaches us that we must learn to bring spirit into matter. Rather than attempting to escape the physical, we must instead learn how to perfect and improve the physical world by applying the South Node in Pisces' gifts of compassion, spirituality, and healing in practical, tangible ways in our daily lives.

North Node in Pisces/South Node in Virgo

The South Node in Virgo brings with it the gifts of a sharp, analytical mind, the ability to discriminate, isolate, and evaluate, as well as an appreciation for the rewards of service, of being able to contribute something of value to society. The South Node in Virgo has a tremendous understanding of the material and physical plane, and on many levels has mastered the art of perfecting and improving the world for the betterment of everyone. The trap of the South Node in Virgo, however, is the tendency to focus on the physical plane exclusively. The South Node in Virgo can become obsessed with details and become overly critical. The South Node in Virgo can also become entirely too dependent on the left-brain, logical, deductive approach to the world. The service that the South Node in Virgo performs is entirely in the physical and material plane, and the more focused the South Node in Virgo becomes on proving its competence and skill, the emptier it will ultimately feel. The North Node in Pisces teaches us that we must learn to see the world in terms of how connected everything is, as well as how different things are. Where Virgo discriminates, Pisces integrates. More than that, the North Node in Pisces balances the left-brain functions of the South Node in Virgo by opening the door to a higher spiritual connection. The North Node in Pisces can teach compassion and forgiveness, and go a long way toward softening the critical approach of the South Node in Virgo. Most of all, the North Node in Pisces can help us understand that there must always be a higher spiritual purpose to our service: that everything we accomplish on the physical plane is simply an aspect of our work on the spiritual plane.

11

Aspect Patterns

Aspect patterns are configurations of three or more planets that each aspect each other or are connected by a common aspect. The Grand Trine, T-Square, Yod, and Stellium are all examples of aspect patterns and, along with several others, will be discussed in detail shortly. The key to an aspect pattern, in fact, what makes an aspect pattern, is that the planets involved are so closely linked to each other that whenever one of the planets is triggered by transit, progression, or direction, all the other planets in the configuration are also activated at the same time. Planets in aspect patterns function as units, always working together.

Interpreting, understanding, and working with aspect patterns is very complicated. Simply understanding how a single aspect between two planets may manifest is challenging enough: with aspect patterns, anywhere from three to six or more planets must be synthesized. The general level of confusion about aspect patterns is increased because aspect patterns are usually pretty easy to spot in a chart, and because they seem to be so important. It's impressive to be able to tell someone, "You've got a Grand Cross in your chart," and if that individual actually does have a Grand Cross, it is certainly a very important factor to consider; but when it comes time to explain exactly what that means, many astrologers, particularly newer astrologers, come up short.

Before we look at what each of the aspect patterns signifies and how to interpret them, we first have to set some guidelines as to what makes an aspect pattern and what doesn't.

Aspect Patterns Can Only Be Formed by Physical Bodies

The only points in the chart that can be used to make up an aspect pattern are physical bodies. Personally, I would limit that even further to only include the planets, and perhaps Chiron, excluding any and all the other asteroids, but that's a personal choice; however, the Ascendant, the Midheaven, the Moon's nodes, the Vertex, the East Point, the Part of Fortune, and any other mathematical point in the chart should not be considered when determining an aspect pattern.

Physical bodies both make and receive aspects from other physical bodies. When Mars trines Jupiter, there is a flow of energy from Mars to Jupiter, and from Jupiter to Mars; both planets are affected and influenced by the aspect. Mathematical points in the chart (including the angles, the Moon's nodes, and the Arabic Parts or Greek Lots) can only *receive* aspects from physical bodies; they do not *make* aspects. Mars trine the Ascendant will influence the Ascendant, coloring how that individual appears to others, and how that individual interacts with the world. It will not, however, influence the expression of that individual's Mars. Fixed stars, for the purposes of aspect patterns, should likewise be regarded as sensitive points in the chart, and nothing more. They can *make* aspects (usually by conjunction only), but they do not *receive* aspects.

For example, let's take the Moon in Taurus, Mars in Capricorn, and the Sun in Virgo. Each of these planets is trine the other two; the energy cycles endlessly between the three planets, with no beginning and no end. However, if instead we take the Moon in Taurus, Mars in Capricorn, and the Ascendant in Virgo, the energy either begins with the Moon, moves through Mars, and expresses itself through the Ascendant, or else it begins with Mars, moves through the Moon, and expresses itself through the Ascendant. Rather than being a Grand Trine, it's simply a Moon/Mars trine with a very natural outlet for expression.

Aspect Patterns Require Very Small Orbs

Aspect patterns are so powerful because of the harmonic resonance they carry. When any planet in the pattern is triggered, all the other planets are also triggered, either directly or indirectly.

So what the heck does all of this have to do with using small orbs for aspect patterns? Quite simply, part of the power of an aspect pattern comes from the harmonics of it. With a true aspect pattern, when one planet is triggered, so are all the others. Look at aspect patterns like a guitar. If you pluck one string on a guitar that has been properly tuned, all the other strings will also vibrate because of the harmonics; however, if the guitar is not properly tuned, the other strings will not respond. The tighter the orbs in the aspect pattern, the better tuned the guitar is. Another reason for this is that many aspect patterns involve harmonic aspects (a Grand Cross has two oppositions (second harmonic) and four squares (fourth harmonic)). If the orbs are too wide, some of the aspects will not be present, and some of the strings (to stick with the guitar example) won't vibrate.

This is particularly clear when the triggering planet is one of the outer bodies. A person with a T-Square or a Grand Cross with a 1° orb is going to experience transiting Pluto triggering all of those planets at the same time. Extend that orb to 5°, and the effect is quite different: the pressure of transiting Pluto will trigger the planets in sequence, but not simultaneously, and it may take a year or more for all the planets to be activated.

Aspect Patterns Must Be in the Correct Signs

One of the cans of worms opened by the harmonic approach to aspects is the creation of an "out-of-sign" aspect. The ancients would have considered a planet at 29° of Cancer and one at 1° of Scorpio to be trine each other, even though they are only 91° apart, and from a harmonic standpoint are most certainly square each other. "Out-of-sign" aspects are very different from "in-sign" aspects. In the above example, even though the two planets would certainly have a very active and stimulating relationship on a harmonic level, because they are in the same element, they still have common ground and share a connection that will tend to mitigate the "butting heads" feel of an "in-sign" square.

With aspect patterns, unless the orbs are *very* tight, as in the above example, they must be in the "correct" signs, because the other factor that contributes so strongly to the power of aspect patterns is the elemental influence. In fact, as we will see shortly, the elemental influence and interactions often provide the key to understanding and interpreting an aspect pattern in the first place.

Interpreting the Aspect Patterns

Once you have determined that you actually have an aspect pattern to interpret, the first step to understanding it is to forget that it's an aspect pattern. Although it's true that with aspect patterns the whole is very much greater than the sum of the parts, in order to even begin to understand the whole, you first have to understand each of the parts individually. Interpreting and synthesizing an aspect pattern is as challenging and as complex as synthesizing an entire chart. The only consolation here is that real aspect patterns tend to be the key to understanding the rest of the chart, and usually spell out the major themes of the chart quite clearly.

Each aspect pattern has a different feel to it, and this is important to keep in mind as you look at each of the individual planets involved, and then again at each of the individual aspects, trying to find the common theme between them. Since no aspect pattern is ever perfect, it's best to start with the tightest and most exact aspect, and work from there. Just as an aspect pattern can set the theme and tone of a chart, the most exact aspect in that pattern can set the theme and the tone of the aspect pattern.

Aspect patterns are entirely a product of modern astrology and have no foundation at all in classical astrology. Astrologers who are strictly "traditional" astrologers don't pay any attention to aspect patterns. I consider aspect patterns to be somewhat rare because they do require such tight orbs; however, I include them in my interpretations because when they do occur, the harmonic resonance is quite powerful, and the pattern most definitely merits consideration in its own right.

Now that all the disclaimers are out of the way, let's take a look at the different aspect patterns and try to make sense of them.

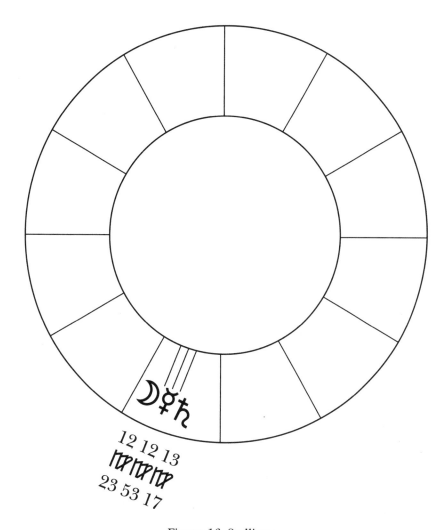

Figure 16. Stellium

Stellium

A Stellium is technically a group of three or more planets that are conjunct each other. Since it is a first-harmonic (conjunction) aspect pattern, the orbs allowable for a Stellium can be quite generous. The textbook definition of a Stellium would be three planets at the same degree of a sign, as in the Sun, Mars, and Jupiter each at 12° of Virgo (or each within a 1° to 2° orb of this point). Stellia can also consist of two planets that, while they are too far apart to be considered to be conjunct each other, are each conjunct a third planet that forms a sort of link and connection between the three planets. (In other words, the Sun at 1° of Virgo, Mars at 6° of Virgo, and Jupiter at 11° of Virgo; the Sun and Jupiter are too far apart to be conjunct, but since each of them is conjunct Mars, the three planets are linked.) Because Stellia are whole-sign aspect patterns, even having three or more planets in the same sign could be considered a Stellium. (Three or more planets in the same *house*, however, is not a Stellium.)

Needless to say, the closer the conjunctions are, the stronger and more powerful the effect of the Stellium will be. Also, in general, the personal planets are considered far more significant than the outer planets. An entire generation was born with Pluto and Uranus conjunct in Virgo; everyone born between August 22 and September 20 in the years 1964 through 1968 will have at least Sun, Uranus, and Pluto in Virgo. The outer planets represent universal forces, and while simply having personal planets in the same sign as outer planets may indicate a certain resonance with the generational influences, it generally doesn't indicate a significant impact on an individual's personality. What is significant, however, is when a personal planet is closely conjunct an outer planet (either on its own, or as part of a Stellium). This indicates a very strong link between that planet's function and the universal unconscious forces. Through that personal planet, the individual is tied into cycles and energies that are entirely beyond his or her control; the individual is both at the mercy of these forces, and also able to channel and express them in a very personal way, helping others experience and understand the energies of universal change.

When considering Stellia, the most important thing to keep in mind is that an individual with a Stellium—even only a Stellium by sign—will have a very strong emphasis on, and experience of, the energy represented by that sign. Although we all have all twelve signs in our charts, there are less than twelve major bodies, and therefore it is not possible to have a planet in every sign. We each experience the full range of energies represented by the twelve signs; however, we will tend to be more familiar with, and more focused on, the energy of the signs that contain planets. When three or more planets are in the same sign, the energy and lessons of that sign become extremely significant to that individual.

If the planets in the Stellium are actually conjunct each other, this intensity and focus grows to encompass more than a mere affinity for the experiences and energy of a particular sign. The closer the planets are to being conjunct, the more tightly unified the planets become, and the harder it becomes to separate the different needs and drives of the planets. In very tight Stellia, the planets almost seem to fuse together, and act as a unit, almost a "superplanet" that can often become the driving force in a person's chart.

As an example, let's look at individuals with the Moon, Mercury, and Mars in the same sign, but not conjunct each other. With this type of Stellium, these individuals will have the same approach, the same motivation for how they feel and react (Moon), communicate (Mercury), and take action (Mars). If, on the other hand, the Moon, Mercury, and Mars are all conjunct each other, the three planets will tend to act as a unit. These people might, for example, find that they always have to express their feelings and desires and have great difficulty holding back what they feel or think. Every thought and feeling will tend to require some action on their part, because every time their Moon or Mercury is used, so is their Mars. The manner, style, and motivations of these expressions would, of course, depend on the sign in question.

The key issue with Stellia is one of balance. Individuals with a Stellium often find that they tend to devote a large percentage of their time and energy to the types of activities that stimulate and allow them to express their Stellium, by both sign and house. What is important, then, is for these individuals to make a conscious effort to find some balance and perspective in their lives, which they can do by choosing to explore the energy and activities represented by the sign and house opposite from their Stellium. This will tend to be easiest when there are planets transiting opposite the Stellium, although obviously it can be done at any time.

Grand Trine

The Grand Trine is a third-harmonic aspect, and occurs when three planets are in the same element (fire, earth, air, or water), each forming a trine to the others. A Grand Trine forms an equilateral triangle, and in sacred geometry, the equilateral triangle is said to represent the level of pure being. In this manner, a Grand Trine is similar to a planet being in a sign it rules: when a

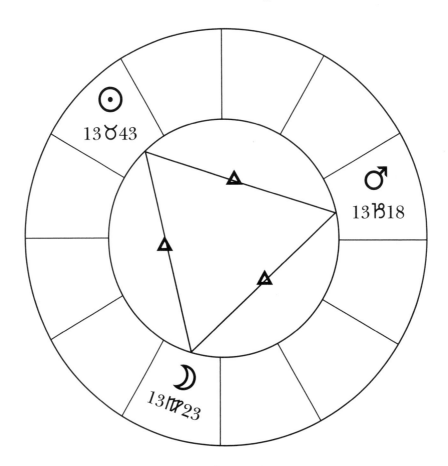

Figure 17. Grand Trine

planet is in its rulership, it is operating on the level of pure being and on its own terms. While this may be good for the planet, it's not always easy for the individual to integrate this energy. A Grand Trine, then, is the pure expression of an element.

Trines in general, and Grand Trines in particular, have a reputation for being wonderful, positive, enjoyable aspects. This reputation is not entirely deserved, however. Each aspect has its own nature and function, and no one aspect is better or worse than any other. The nature of the trine is ease and harmony, and trines represent a constant, open, and effortless flow of energy between the two planets (or three planets in the case of a Grand Trine). Trines do certainly indicate talents, and they are certainly comfortable aspects, because they are always there, always operating, and never require any conscious effort to maintain. The challenge with trines comes when we try to control or stop the flow of energy, to change the patterns of behavior encouraged by the trine. This is even more difficult with a Grand Trine, because the three planets are linked in a closed circuit of energy that is able to build up a tremendous amount of momentum.

Grand Trines can often feel like too much of a good thing. Because they are so easy and comfortable, and because they truly represent the easy way out, they can discourage us from exploring and developing the more challenging areas of our charts and of our lives. On top of that, we have a tendency to take Grand Trines for granted; trines are notoriously lazy, and Grand Trines often represent vast untapped potential. The talent is there, the creativity is there; what is missing is the drive to make use of it. Grand Trines often seem to illustrate the maxim "what we obtain too cheaply, we esteem too lightly."

There are four different types of Grand Trines—one for each element.

Fire

Grand Trines in fire tend to be extremely active. The element of fire expresses itself through action and activity. Individuals with a Grand Trine in fire may always be on the go, and also must learn not to overextend themselves. The element of fire, like a flame, will burn as hot as it can until all its fuel is gone. A Grand Trine in fire can often contribute to an impulsive nature; it can also indicate a tendency toward absolute honesty, since the fire signs can only express their true nature and are incapable of deception. Grand Trines in fire can be very intense, and emphasize the tendency of the fire signs toward expansive and sometimes explosive expressions of joy or anger. Individuals with a Grand Trine in fire must learn to conserve their energy and to explore the full range of emotional expression, rather than simply expressing the most intense and primal emotions.

Earth

Grand Trines in earth, on the other hand, tend to be the least active. The element of earth is associated with the material plane, and individuals with a Grand Trine in earth will tend to be very grounded and practical in their approach. Earth signs enjoy structure, routine, and security, and a Grand Trine in earth is the most likely of the Grand Trines to become addicted to certain behavior patterns. Earth signs are extremely sensual and enjoy all the physical pleasures and creature comforts that the material world has to offer. A Grand Trine in earth seems to say that if it feels good, then do it, and this aspect pattern can generate a wide range of excuses and rationalizations that make changing bad habits that much more difficult (such as quitting smoking or sticking to a diet). Although a Grand Trine in earth can indicate creative and artistic talent, as well as the ability to realize and manifest ideas in a tangible way, the challenge to actually take action, rather than to indulge in comforting activities, is always present.

Air

The element of air relates to the mental and social realms. Individuals with a Grand Trine in air tend to be extremely social and relationship-oriented. Air signs are all about making connections, about forming ideas, and about expanding our understanding of the world. All the air signs are double signs, and therefore all the air signs have an inherent understanding of duality and seek to find the balance between opposites, to discover the connection between them. With a Grand Trine in air, an individual would tend to have a very active mind, and to be most comfortable operating in a detached, objective, and theoretical manner. While air signs enjoy a wide variety of social contacts and exchange of ideas, they are not comfortable with emotions, particularly with the more intense and powerful ones. Air prefers to move quickly along the surface, rather than exploring too deeply. Grand Trines in air prefer talking about things and thinking about them to actually taking any action, and because of the swift-moving nature of the element of air, these individuals may tend to have a rather short attention span. It may be less that they find it difficult to focus on one task for any length of time, and more that they don't see any need to do so (another rationalization, courtesy of a Grand Trine).

Water

The element of water relates to the emotional and spiritual realms. Individuals with a Grand Trine in water tend to be extremely sensitive to emotions, both their own and those of others. The water signs operate on the deepest, the most unconscious, and ultimately the most transformative levels. Individuals with a Grand Trine in water are likely to trust their instincts and their intuition, and to make choices and take action in their lives based on how they feel. These individuals tend to be very in tune with the spiritual and psychic realms. The planets involved in the Grand Trine will largely determine how openly these individuals are able to express their feelings; but whether or not they feel comfortable wearing their hearts on their sleeves, individuals with Grand Trines in water go through life feeling everything intensely. This depth and intensity of emotion, however, can often result in oversensitivity and excessive emotional drama. Individuals with Grand Trines in water may be at their best when there is a crisis, when someone needs help and someone is there to care for them (and either role is perfectly acceptable to individuals with a Grand Trine in water). These individuals may tend to attempt to create a crisis, however, in order to experience the healing, transformational, and emotional energy.

Kite

A Kite is a Grand Trine that has a fourth planet opposing one of the three planets in the Grand Trine. While the fourth planet forms an opposition to one of the planets, it also sextiles the other two planets. Kites will always be in the same polarity, either "feminine" (earth and water) or "masculine" (fire and air).

Kites can be considered to be Grand Trines with some perspective. The opposition is quite helpful in encouraging individuals to actually take advantage of the gifts and talents offered by the Grand Trine. Oppositions, however, are not action-inducing aspects, so even with a Kite, there is no guarantee that the individual will fully exploit its potential. The opposition gives the Kite a sense of direction and focus. The Grand Trine has no beginning and no end, and can be thought to be constantly spinning its wheels. With a Kite, the planet in the Grand Trine that is being opposed becomes the focal point, the leader of the aspect pattern, if you will. The opposing planet forms a kind of anchor, a reference point allowing the lead planet to see a clear direction and purpose. The two sextiles from the remaining two planets to the opposing planet offer the individual the opportunity to activate the channel created by the opposition.

In theory, a Kite is structured so that all the creative energy and creative potential of the Grand Trine can be honed and focused and find expression

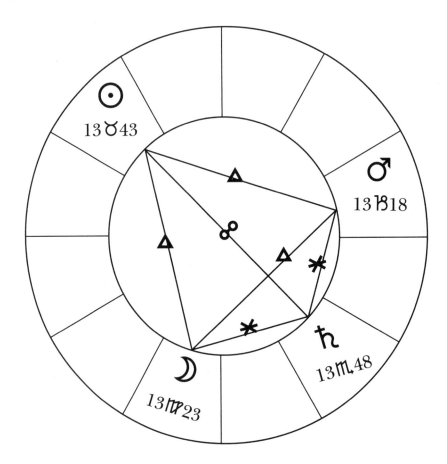

Figure 18. Kite

through the axis of the opposition, with the primary point of release being through the planet, sign, and house of the focal planet of the Grand Trine. In practice, a Kite is still a "soft" aspect pattern and lacks any real internal motivation to take action. The main difference between a Kite and a Grand Trine is that individuals with a Kite may be aware that they could be doing more with their talents, while individuals with a Grand Trine generally lack that perspective and awareness. The awareness provided by the opposition, however, does not guarantee any action.

Kites tend to express themselves more efficiently when stimulated by a hard aspect, because of the built-in sense of direction and perspective; but as is the case with most "soft" aspects, once the pressure is off, the tendency is to settle back into the most comfortable and least taxing routine.

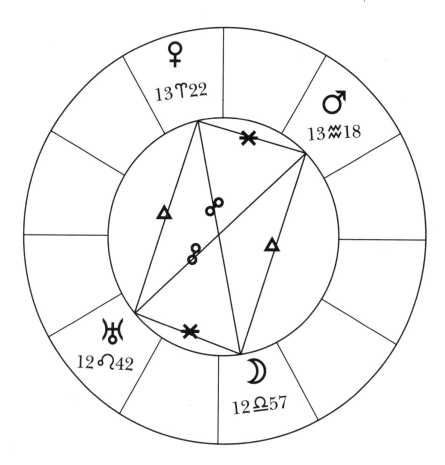

Figure 19. Mystic Rectangle

Mystic Rectangle

A Mystic Rectangle is formed when two pairs of oppositions are sextile each other. The result is an aspect pattern that includes two sextiles, two trines, and two oppositions. A Mystic Rectangle also occurs in either the "masculine" (fire and air) or "feminine" (earth and water) polarities. This is another "soft" aspect pattern in that it does not generate friction, discomfort, or a need to take action. What a Mystic Rectangle does offer, however, is an extremely strong sense of balance and structure, of harmony between the four planets involved. Finding this balance is not a given—it will still take conscious effort and awareness. However, working with the trines and the sextiles will help make more sense of, and find the point of integration for, the two oppositions.

Working with a Mystic Rectangle takes some practice because in order for it to hold up, all four planets must be working together and supporting each other. It is common for individuals with Mystic Rectangles to struggle with the two oppositions, seesawing back and forth between the opposing planets. Once the point of balance has been found, however, it becomes increasingly easy to maintain, and a well-integrated Mystic Rectangle can be the most un-flappable of aspect patterns. For individuals who have integrated a Mystic Rectangle, it represents a core of strength for them, and a solid foundation that can be a great gift in handling whatever else life throws at them.

Grand Sextile

The Grand Sextile is a sixth-harmonic aspect pattern and is formed when six planets are sextile each other. Grand Sextiles must be in either earth and water, or in fire and air ("feminine" or "masculine" polarities), and consist of six sextiles, six trines, and three oppositions. Grand Sextiles also contain two Grand Trines, six Kites, and three Mystic Rectangles. Although Grand Sextiles are not unheard of, because they involve six planets, they are quite rare.

The Grand Sextile represents tremendous creative potential, but at the same time, because it is such a self-contained, balanced, and harmonious con-figuration, it contains absolutely no inherent motivation to take any action or to explore and fulfill the potential it represents. Even more than with the Grand Trine, the Grand Sextile requires an external stimulus to get it to take action. However, because there are so many more planets involved in a Grand Sextile, and because so many planets would be receiving a simultaneous stim-ulus from a transit, progression, or direction, the ultimate response may tend to be far more diffuse and ultimately less productive than it would be with a Grand Trine. The natural inclination of the Grand Sextile is to return to a point of balance and equilibrium between the six planets, and almost any ac-tion produced will be aimed at this result.

Using only whole-sign transits (progressions, directions, etc.), there are only two different types of transits to a Grand Sextile: passive and active. A "passive" transit would be one through a sign in the same polarity as the Grand Sextile (for example, if the Grand Sextile were in earth and water, any transit through any of the "feminine" signs—the earth and water signs—would

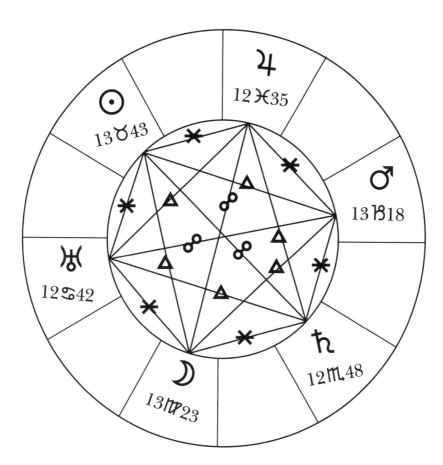

Figure 20. Grand Sextile

be considered "passive"). Passive transits simply re-emphasize the Grand Sextile pattern by conjuncting one of the planets and forming trines, oppositions, or sextiles to all the other planets. "Active" transits, on the other hand, are transits through the opposite polarity of the Grand Sextile (so if the Grand Sextile were in earth and water, any transit through any of the "masculine" signs—the air and fire signs—would be considered "active").

Active transits to Grand Sextiles will always form a transiting T-Square and a transiting Yod. The release point to these two transiting aspect patterns is identical: the point opposite the transiting planet. Under other circumstances, this type of transit would certainly encourage very direct and specific action to alleviate the pressure it represents; with a Grand Sextile, however, there are so many "soft" aspects to each of the triggered points that much of the discomfort (which is what motivates us to get up off the couch and do something) is diffused.

Grand Cross

A Grand Cross consists of four planets in the same modality (cardinal, fixed, or mutable) that form four squares and two pairs of oppositions. The Grand Cross is a fourth-harmonic aspect pattern. The number four relates to the cross of matter; it is the number of form, structure, and the physical world. A Grand Cross includes one planet in each of the elements: fire, earth, air, and water. Because the Grand Cross is composed of squares and oppositions, it is an aspect pattern that is concerned with both action (squares), and perspective and balance (oppositions).

A Grand Cross is classified by its modality, and each type of Grand Cross has its own specific feel and interpretation. One thing that all three types of Grand Cross share, however, is that they are all fundamentally stressful configurations. Squares generate action because they are uncomfortable aspects; the tension builds, and once it reaches a certain point, we do something, we take action in order to release some of the pressure. Squares can be either constructive or destructive, but because they are a fourth-harmonic aspect and are related to the world of form and structure, squares usually require some sort of physical, external act of expression.

Squares, particularly very tight squares, are very difficult aspects to ignore. A Grand Cross does offer a solid foundation, a core structure and strength that can be a tremendous resource; however, finding the point of integration and balance to be able to take advantage of this gift can be quite challenging. The key, of course, comes from working with the two oppositions. When the opposing planets are balanced, then they are exerting the same amount of pressure on the planets that square, creating a solid foundation. When the oppositions are out of balance, however, the structure cannot hold, and the squares take center stage again. Focusing on what the core issue of each modality is (cardinal signs are concerned with identity, fixed signs with self-worth, and mutable signs with healing and completion) can help us discover what all four of the signs in the Grand Cross have in common and, therefore, can also help us discover the point of balance and strength.

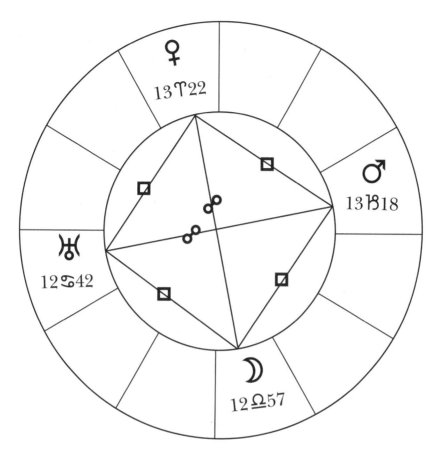

Figure 21. Grand Cross

Cardinal

Cardinal signs are all concerned with the question of identity, whether it be the ability to impulsively express ourselves (Aries), our emotional identity (Cancer), our social and intellectual identity (Libra), or the tangible manifestation of our identity (Capricorn). The cardinal Grand Cross, then, is essentially an identity crisis. The four planets involved are each trying to define and express a facet of who we are, except that each of them is operating on a different level and from a different perspective. Cardinal signs are about taking action; they are initiating and often very impulsive. The challenge with a cardinal Grand Cross is that whenever it is triggered, all four planets want to take action simultaneously, and each in its own direction. This can lead to these individuals either feeling pulled apart and overextended, or else feeling a building sense of frustration because of an overwhelming need to take action, and no clear direction or understanding of what type of action they need to take. The key with the cardinal Grand Cross is to maintain an awareness that whatever the stress and pressure seem to be about, at the core, the question is one of identity. When we stay focused on who we are, and understand that the need to take action relates to a need to further define, express, and experience our sense of individuality and identity, we will have an easier time choosing how to channel the energy.

Fixed

The fixed signs are all concerned with the question of self-worth. Fixed signs follow the cardinal signs, and their purpose is to sustain and maintain what the cardinal signs created and initiated. Because of this, fixed signs tend to resist all outside efforts to initiate change. When the fixed Grand Cross is triggered, the first inclination is for each of the four planets to dig in its heels, take a stand, and resist every external influence. The energy of the fixed Grand Cross tends to be initially focused on resistance, on maintaining things exactly as they are, rather than on taking action and initiating any kind of change; however, once the fixed Grand Cross starts taking action, it is very hard to stop or to convince to change its course. The fixed Grand Cross is like a steamroller: when it's stopped, it's hard to get it moving, but once it's moving, it's very hard to stop.

Because the fixed signs are so fundamentally concerned with self-worth, individuals with a fixed Grand Cross may tend to take all affairs related to the planets and houses in their fixed Grand Cross very personally, and on an unconscious level equate any external triggers with attacks on their sense of self. Giving in and taking action, or making any kind of a change, can be experienced as a fundamentally demoralizing act, one that to a certain extent lessens their sense of self-esteem. Individuals with a fixed Grand Cross must learn how to become more flexible and less resistant to change, particularly when the suggestion to change comes from others.

Mutable

Mutable signs are concerned with healing and completion. When placed under pressure, planets in mutable signs tend to scatter, dissociate, and disperse. The biggest challenge for an individual with a mutable Grand Cross is to maintain focus and coherence, and to learn how to maintain a sense of balance and co-ordination. Individuals with a mutable Grand Cross must learn how to juggle, how to keep all the balls in the air at all times with respect to the planets in the Grand Cross and the houses where these planets reside. Mutable signs are extremely flexible and adaptable. What tends to happen, however, with a mutable Grand Cross, is that whenever it is triggered, the first response of each of the planets involved is to change, adapt, and avoid whatever obstacle has just been presented. While it may certainly be appropriate to respond by adjusting the energy and approach of one of the four planets, when all four planets simultaneously adjust, it's very much like the juggler dropping all the balls at once.

T-Square

The T-Square consists of three planets in the same modality, and includes two squares and one opposition. A T-Square is simply a Grand Cross with a missing planet. A T-Square functions quite differently from a Grand Cross, however. Instead of forming a potentially stable structure, a T-Square is far less stable; all the pressure is placed on the planet that receives the two squares, the apex planet. T-Squares, then, have a built-in focus that the Grand Cross lacks, and they can often become extremely productive and a key motivating force for an individual.

The apex planet of a T-Square is the key. This is the planet that is the driving force, and also the planet that is under the most pressure. Squares, remember, are action aspects; the apex planet, receiving two simultaneous squares, is under a great deal of pressure to act. In order for this planet to act in a focused and productive manner, however, it needs an anchor. The "empty leg" of the T-Square is where this anchor is found. Some astrologers consider this point (the point opposite the apex planet) to be the "release point" of the T-Square. I don't consider this to be an accurate description. A T-Square is about moving forward and taking action with the apex planet, not about diffusing or redirecting that action. What an awareness of the opposing point offers is an anchor of sorts, and a reference point to ensure that the path and direction of the action taken is true. When a planet transits this point, creating a temporary Grand Cross, it often indicates an opportunity to unleash the power and energy of

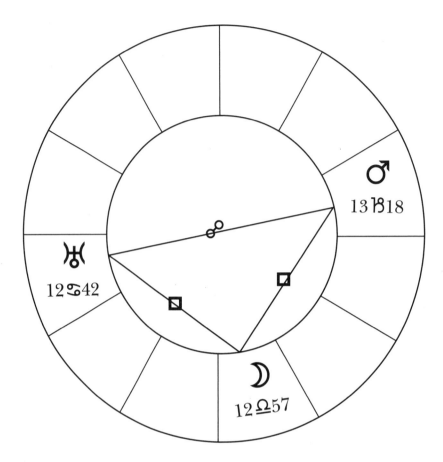

Figure 22. T-Square

the T-Square in a very focused and directed manner, because the transiting planet provides the awareness of balance for the apex planet, and at the same time triggers the two squares.

When considering a T-Square, pay close attention to the element of the sign that the apex planet occupies. This will help describe the kind of action that the T-Square will tend to generate (fire = physical, tangible, identity-oriented; earth = material, practical; air = mental, social; water = emotional, spiritual). The house positions of the planets, and of the apex planet in particular, are also extremely important. This will show where the stress will tend to come from (the house axis that contains the opposing planets) and where it will tend to manifest and need to be addressed (the house of the apex planet).

A T-Square forms a right triangle, and in sacred geometry, right triangles operate on the level of what the Greeks called *Nous,* which is the realm of the spirit and of the higher self and higher guidance. Because they are also isosceles triangles, T-Squares also operate on the mental/emotional level (what the Greeks called the "soul" level), and therefore can be quite challenging and stressful configurations. The key to working with a T-Square is to learn how to tap into the higher levels of guidance, and to discover different and more supportive ways of releasing the stress and pressure of the squares by taking action through the apex planet.

Cardinal

As with the cardinal Grand Cross, the cardinal T-Square is concerned with the question of identity. The sign of the apex planet will indicate where the point of focus and integration will be (Aries = individual identity; Cancer = emotional identity; Libra = social identity; Capricorn = accomplishments and tangible, material expressions of identity). Also, as with the cardinal Grand Cross, impulsiveness is a very prominent concern with a cardinal T-Square. Planets in cardinal signs need to take immediate action. They do not like to be told to wait, and they will do their own thing rather than waiting to be led by someone else. The cardinal T-Square is by far the most active of the T-Squares, but it is not necessarily the most productive. The challenge with this pattern is to get the three planets to work together, rather than each going off and doing their own thing (which inevitably conflicts with what the other two planets want to be doing). An awareness of the empty leg and house can provide some much-needed balance and guidance for a cardinal T-Square. Once all the planets are pointed in the right direction, as it were, taking action and moving forward is automatic. The hardest part is learning to control the impulsiveness of the cardinal planets long enough to get them to work together.

Fixed

The apex planet in a fixed T-Square, being under the greatest pressure, will also tend to be the planet and area of life in which the individual is the least flexible and has the most resistance to change. Opposing planets in fixed signs tend to find a certain amount of stability, if only because neither planet is willing to budge; but as they butt heads, they tend to discover some common ground, and will usually come to some sort of a cease-fire agreement. With a fixed T-Square, however, this cease-fire between the opposing planets may seem only to exist because each planet has decided to confront the apex planet as a common enemy. Fixed signs, remember, are all concerned with self-worth, with maintaining and sustaining who we are. Ultimately, the apex planet of a fixed T-Square will need to take action and to change—something that fixed signs are perfectly happy to do, so long as they feel that the action or the change was their idea and not something that is prompted by any outside influence. The lesson of the fixed T-Square is one of flexibility, particularly with respect to the planet, sign, and house that make up the apex of the T-Square.

Mutable

With a mutable T-Square, as with a mutable Grand Cross, the challenge is focus and coherence. All three planets are concerned with healing and completion, and all three planets will tend to adapt and to avoid direct confrontation. The apex planet in a mutable T-Square is the one that will tend to scatter the most, because this is the planet that is under the most pressure. Oppositions are more passive aspects, and planets in opposition in mutable signs, because of their natural tendency to adapt, are the most likely to find the point of balance and harmony, and therefore be the most comfortable with the opposition aspect. Working with the opposing point, and maintaining an awareness of the energy and lessons of the opposing sign, is particularly important with a mutable T-Square, because this can provide a sense of focus and direction for the apex planet.

Yod

The Yod, also known as the "Finger of God," is a twelfth-harmonic aspect pattern that consists of three planets, two of which sextile each other, and the third which forms a quincunx (150° aspect, which is five-twelfths of a circle) to each of the two other planets. The planet forming the two quincunx aspects, called the apex planet, must also be the fastest-moving of the three planets in order for the configuration to be a "true" Yod. In other words, Pluto (the slowest-moving planet) can never be the apex planet, while the Moon (the fastest-moving planet) can never be one of the base planets.

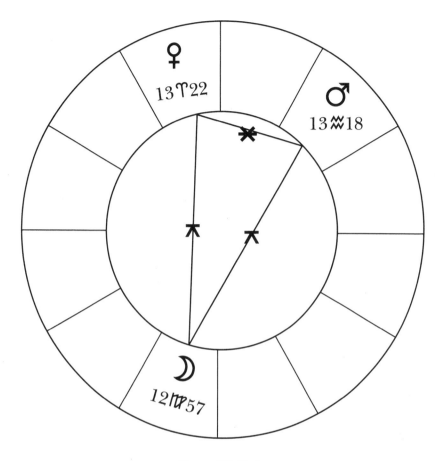

Figure 23. Yod

To understand a Yod, we first have to understand the quincunx aspect. Quincunxes occur between signs that have nothing in common by polarity, modality, or element. Even though the two planets have nothing in common with each other, they do have an undeniable connection. Since they feel so different, the natural tendency is to try to find a point of balance between them, as would happen with two opposing planets; however, since the two signs don't have any common ground between them, there is no point of balance with a quincunx. This energy can become quite frustrating, and the most common urge with a quincunx is the feeling that some sort of an adjustment must be made. In order to resolve the tension, one of the two planets is going to have to act in a manner that is contrary to the nature of its sign, which is both difficult and uncomfortable.

Remember that all quincunxes are not created equal. Some quincunxes have an easier time finding a point of balance because the two signs are linked in other ways—either by common rulership (Aries and Scorpio are both ruled by Mars; Taurus and Libra are both ruled by Venus), by antiscia (solstice points; signs that are equally "powerful"; these are signs that mirror each other across the 0° of Cancer/Capricorn axis), or by contra-antiscia (signs that are equally rising, signs that mirror each other across the 0° of Aries/Libra axis). Some quincunxes occur between signs that truly have nothing in common, and are considered to be "averse." This was covered in more detail in chapter 8.

Yods tend to represent a crisis in timing. What usually happens when a Yod is triggered is that we tend to react too quickly with the first sextile planet, and then we tend to wait too long to respond with the second sextile planet. The release point, the time when it is truly appropriate to take action, is the point opposite the apex planet, which is also the midpoint of the sextile. When a Yod has been integrated, and when we actually learn when and how to respond with it, the sextile planets tend to work together to stimulate a significant shift in how the apex planet functions.

A Yod forms an acute isosceles triangle, which means, from a sacred geometry standpoint, that this aspect pattern operates on what the Greeks called the "soul" level, but which refers to what we would consider the mental/emotional/astral plane. Quincunxes and sextiles are not "action" aspects, and Yods tend to manifest more as mental discomfort than as anything physical. With Yods, we often feel that we are missing some crucial understanding, a single piece of information that would help us transcend the frustration and the subtle but very irritating sense that things are not quite as they should be. When a Yod is integrated, and when we eventually learn how and when to take action when it is triggered, we can often catch a glimpse of that higher understanding as the energy of the sextile pushes the apex planet toward a higher, more cosmic perspective.

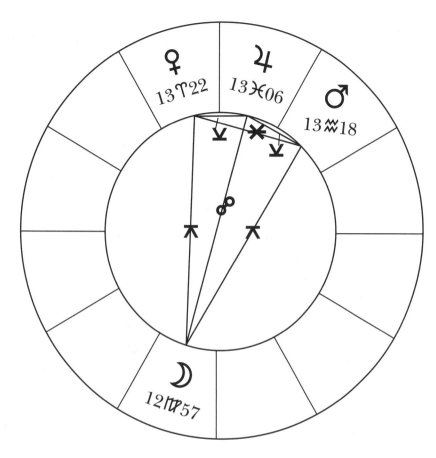

Figure 24. Boomerang

Boomerang

The Boomerang is one of the newer aspect patterns. I believe it was named by astrologer Marion March. Essentially, the Boomerang is a Yod with a planet at the release point, opposing the apex planet, and forming two semisextiles with the base planets. As is the case with the opposition that makes a Grand Trine a Kite, the opposition in the Boomerang helps provide a much-needed sense of perspective and balance to the aspect pattern. The difference here is that while the opposition in the Kite doesn't necessarily change the overall feel of the aspect pattern, the opposition in the Boomerang does.

The extra planet in the Boomerang helps take a lot of the guesswork out of the Yod. The quincunxes still create the feeling that some adjustment is needed, and they still create the feeling that there should be a point of balance between the two planets, when in fact there is none. The difference here is that in addition to receiving two quincunxes, the apex planet in a Boomerang also receives an opposition, which does have a true point of balance. As long as the individual is able to remain aware of the opposition, they are far less likely to suffer the problems of bad timing and missed opportunities that are so prevalent with the Yod.

The two semisextiles formed by the opposition are also invaluable in helping integrate the different energies of the quincunxes. The opposing planet creates a more concrete awareness of the balance point in the configuration.

On a higher level, the division of the triangle by the opposition splits the isosceles triangle of the Yod (which operates entirely on the mental/emotional plane) into four separate triangles. The result is that the Boomerang not only operates on the mental/emotional plane where the Yod exists, but also in the physical and material realm (enabling more concrete action) and on the level of what the Greeks called *Nous,* which is where we encounter our higher selves and higher guidance. The sacred geometry of the Boomerang offers assistance in integrating the conflicting elements, and can lend support in getting the most out of the lessons presented by the aspect pattern.

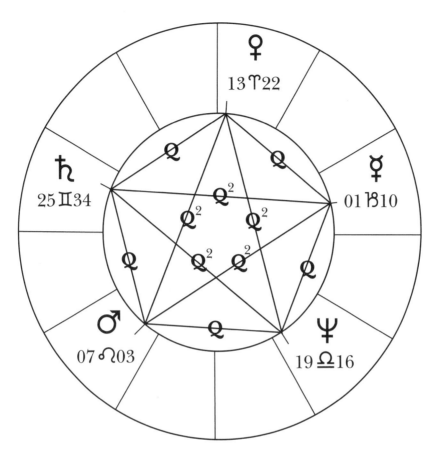

Figure 25. Grand Quintile

Grand Quintile

The Grand Quintile is formed when five planets are quintile (72°) each other. This is a fifth-harmonic aspect pattern, and consists of five quintiles and five biquintiles (144° aspects). This is perhaps the rarest of the aspect patterns simply because it requires five planets that can be 72° apart. The Sun, Mercury, and Venus are basically limited to occupying only one position of five because Mercury can at most be 28° from the Sun, and Venus can at most be 46° from the Sun. Mercury and Venus can, theoretically, be as far as 74° apart, and could form a quintile aspect, but this is an exceedingly rare occurrence. At least one quintile between outer planets would almost certainly be required for a Grand

Quintile, and the windows of opportunity for these cycles are both relatively brief and very infrequent.

The Grand Quintile is an aspect pattern that is entirely dependent on the harmonics because the quintile is not a whole-sign aspect. For this reason, the orb for a Grand Quintile would probably have to be less than 3° for each aspect.

Since this aspect pattern is so rare as to be practically nonexistent, interpreting it involves a lot of theory and guesswork. The fifth harmonic, which would be resonating with tremendous intensity here, relates to creativity, freedom, and change. In numerology, the number four represents the material world, the first manifestation of form and structure; the number five is the life energy, the creative spark that animates the form. Quintiles have been associated with both great creative power, and with unthinkable destructive force. Charlie Chaplin and Adolph Hitler are two examples; they were born very close together, and they both have strong fifth-harmonic activity in their charts.

Although I personally do not consider the quintile to be a particularly major aspect, because to me it seems to operate on the mental and intellectual plane, and therefore does not necessarily translate into any kind of action (as the fourth- and eighth-harmonic aspects do), I would have to guess that individuals with a Grand Quintile in their chart would feel compelled to be constantly in motion. The potential here would be perhaps to be fully immersed in the ebb, flow, and constant change that is life. I would also guess that the need to create and to destroy, to discover and participate in the natural cycles of life, would be extremely strong.

12

Synthesized
Chart Interpretation

Believe it or not, we now have all the information we need to create a synthesized, comprehensive interpretation of any birth chart. All that is required now is practice. Appendix A is a Natal Chart Interpretation Worksheet that will help guide you through the interpretation process. We've used the steps in this worksheet already in chapter 6, when we first looked at the charts of Sylvester Stallone and Meryl Streep, and in this chapter we'll finish our interpretations of these two charts, and also look at the charts of two more individuals: Evita Peron and Woody Allen.

Even without taking the newer information into account (retrograde planets, aspects, the Moon's nodes, and aspect patterns), we were able to come up with some pretty good chart themes for Stallone and Streep simply by looking at the elements, modalities, hemispheres, and dignities of the planets. To this, we can also now add the lessons and themes of the nodal axis, any aspects or aspect patterns involving key personal planets, and any stationary planets in the chart. When we've taken all of these factors into consideration, we can truly come up with the major themes for the individual's chart, and always working from this foundation, we can then synthesize and interpret the individual elements of the chart with an understanding of how they all fit into the big picture.

Interpretation Example 1:
Sylvester Stallone, Continued

We'll continue where we left off with Sylvester Stallone, and take a look at the aspects and aspect patterns in his chart, which appears in figure 11 on page 187.

The most exact aspect in Stallone's chart is the applying conjunction between his Mercury and Pluto in Leo, with an eighteen-minute orb. The way that Stallone communicates will be exceptionally powerful, to say the least! He naturally taps into the transformational, destructive, cosmic energy of Pluto, and when he communicates, he expresses, at least in part, our unconscious need for change. Pluto, remember, shows where the world needs to change, what needs to be destroyed because it has outlived its usefulness—although we are not always aware of this on a conscious level. Individuals who have strong aspects to Pluto become agents of change and transformation, and Stallone does so through his writing and communication. Again, we must look at Stallone's image here—he's practically an archetype of the warrior, Rambo, the one who is responsible for mass destruction ultimately in the name of progress and growth. Stallone understands well the power that words and ideas carry.

Part 5: Aspects and Aspect Patterns

	☉	☽	☿	♀	♂	♃	♄	⚷	♅	♆
☽	□ 8°30' S	☽								
☿		Q 0°29' S	☿							
♀		✶ 0°41' S		♀						
♂	✶ 4°39' S	∠ 1°49' A	⊻ 0°40' S		♂					
♃	□ 3°55' A	☌ 4°35' S		✶ 3°53' S		♃				
♄		□ 3°48' A			∠ 1°07' S		♄			
⚷	□ 1°11' A	☌ 7°19' S				☌ 2°56' S		⚷		
♅		△ 3°35' S		✶ 2°53' S	△ 1°00' A		△ 1°00' A		♅	
♆				∠ 1°07' S						♆
♇		Q 0°10' S	☌ 0°18' A		⊻ 0°59' A					

Aspect Patterns

Stellium

Ψ♎ ⚷♎ ♃♎ ☽♎

Since we already know how important Stallone's Sun, Moon, and Venus are from the dispositor tree, let's see if they have any other connections by way of aspects (which, of course, they do). Stallone's Moon is in a partile sextile to his Venus—this is a very strong, harmonious connection between these two planets. On the other hand, Stallone's Moon is just leaving a square to his Sun (8°30' orb, separating), and while this energy is certainly diminishing, it's still within moiety for the Sun and Moon, and it represents a certain amount of animosity and friction between these two planets. His Venus and Sun do not aspect each other.

These aspects between the Sun, Moon, and Venus change the dynamics of the committee somewhat, don't they? The Moon seems to have a pretty clear agenda, and may be able to enlist the help of Venus (which the Sun disposes) through the Moon/Venus sextile, to overrule the Sun and "win" the conflict. The emotional nature of the Sun will have a very difficult time being expressed because the Moon/Venus voting block doesn't want to be upset with intense emotions: the Moon in Libra wants beauty, balance, and harmony, and Venus in Leo simply wants attention and appreciation.

This theme is repeated several times, in fact. Effectively, Stallone has a Stellium of planets in Libra (Moon, Jupiter, Chiron, and by extension, Neptune), which places a great emphasis on the Libra energy of relationships, harmony, and balance above all; and Stallone's Sun in Cancer has either squared or is squaring each of these planets. The strongest energy, of course, comes from the Sun square Chiron and the Sun square Jupiter, but the Sun/Moon square is still very much in effect, and the Sun/Neptune square is gone, but not forgotten. In each of these instances, the conflict is one of identity because the squares are in cardinal signs; and in each of these instances, the core issue is how emotional connections can be expressed while maintaining balance and harmony in relationships. Emotions tend to be messy, and, as an air sign, Libra would rather ignore them and focus on surface appearances. Stallone's Sun is also in his seventh house of relationships, so even without the struggles from the aspects, he will tend to attempt to discover his identity in terms of how he relates to other individuals. Chiron and Jupiter in Libra squaring his Sun will make sure that he has some very specific life lessons along the way that will ultimately force him to look at the true nature of balance and emotional connections in relationships (and on a rather large and public scale, thanks to Jupiter being so close to the Midheaven).

How might this conflict manifest in Stallone's life? Ultimately, it will tend to surface in his public image—nobody wants to see Rambo cry. Stallone will tend to struggle, looking for ways to express his true self, which is fundamentally emotional. His Sun, however, doesn't have an easy outlet to express itself to the outside world. His Moon not only limits how his Sun can express itself, but also, since his Moon is on the Midheaven, it gets to express itself freely and in a very public manner.

Let's finish up our look at Stallone's chart by seeing how these influences may impact and affect some key areas of his life.

Work and Finances

When looking at questions involving money, jobs and career, we will focus on the second house (personal resources and finances), the sixth house (daily routines, jobs, coworkers), and the tenth house (public life, life path, career). Stallone's second house is empty, with Capricorn on the cusp, so his personal resources are ruled by his Saturn, which is in Cancer and has just crossed the cusp of his eighth house. Saturn in Cancer is in rather poor shape, being both in detriment and peregrine. Stallone certainly won't come by his fortune easily—he'll have to work hard for it (Saturn); and because of the peregrine nature of Saturn, it may take him a while to figure out how to handle his resources. The fact that Saturn is in the eighth house of other people's money indicates that his personal finances may tend to come from other people (for example, the public buying tickets to his films). Because Saturn is in such poor shape and in the eighth house, which also relates to financial managers, Stallone must be very careful about whom he trusts to manage his money.

With Gemini on his sixth-house cusp of work, and Uranus in the sixth house, Stallone will need a tremendous amount of variety and intellectual stimulation in his daily routines. He will not be a person who will ever be comfortable working a nine-to-five job at the Department of Motor Vehicles! Gemini on the sixth-house cusp can indicate a person who has many different jobs, or many different job duties. Stallone's Mercury is in Leo in his eighth house, and so we can also say that in any job situation, it will be very important to him that he be appreciated and acknowledged for his work and creativity. He will tend to want to be the star, and may find working in a team environment both challenging and uncomfortable.

Stallone's Midheaven is in Libra, a sign that relates to the fine arts, music, mathematics, and the law, and one that is well suited to a career in the film industry. Stallone's Moon and Jupiter are both conjunct his Midheaven, indicating that his career had better allow him to express his feelings and emotions in a very big way, and also that he's very likely to have a rather high-profile position where many people know who he is. Also, Libra is ruled by Venus, which also happens to be in Leo in his eighth house—yet another indication that Stallone needs to find a career where he's going to be adored and appreciated for his creativity and generosity.

Love and Relationships

Lastly, let's look at Stallone's relationship patterns as seen in the chart. The most important planet when it comes to relationships, of course, is Venus. Stallone's Venus in Leo indicates that while he will tend to be very warm, generous, open, and loving in his relationships, he will also need a tremendous amount of attention, support, and acknowledgment from his partner. The Moon, which shows our emotional nature and our safety and security issues, is equally important in these matters. From Stallone's Moon in Libra, we know that he is not comfortable with deep emotional connections, and feels safest when things at least appear to be balanced and harmonious. The Descendant (the seventh-house cusp) shows the type of person we're attracted to on a conscious level. Stallone's Descendant is in Gemini, ruled by his Mercury in Leo. He will be attracted to partners who are intelligent, social, charming, witty, young (or at least young at heart), and who are not looking for deep emotional involvement, because Gemini, an air sign, is as uncomfortable with emotions as Libra is. The last point we can look at when considering relationships is the Vertex, which acts as a kind of unconscious Descendant. Stallone's Vertex (which is not shown in the chart) is in Leo, and on an unconscious level he's attracted to individuals who are as warm, giving, expressive, and generous as he is—but who will also share his need to be the center of attention at all times. With Venus in Leo ruling his fifth house of love affairs and in the same sign as his Mercury in Leo ruling his seventh house of more committed relationships, he won't have much trouble moving from one type of relationship to the other—and both types of relationships are going to have the same Leo issues associated with them.

So what might Stallone's relationship patterns involve? Well, with so much Leo energy associated with his relationships (Venus in Leo, Mercury in Leo ruling his Descendant, Vertex in Leo), perhaps the biggest issue is that he will either need to learn that he can't always be the center of attention and that he must be willing to share the spotlight with his partner, or else he will need to look for partners who are willing to make him the center of their lives. The challenge here, of course, is that the partners who truly want to focus their energy and attention on him are also likely to want to form deep emotional bonds with him, which is another significant relationship issue for Stallone. He's *capable* of these emotional connections, of course (his Sun is in Cancer, after all), but they take considerable time, effort, and trust. If they happen too quickly, his Moon will perceive them as a threat, and he'll become defensive and try to protect himself.

Interpretation Example 2: Meryl Streep, Continued

Now let's pick up where we left off with Meryl Streep, and look at her aspects as well. Streep's chart appears in figure 12 on page 195.

Part 5: Aspects and Aspect Patterns

	☉	☽	☿	♀	♂	♃	♄	⚷	♅	♆
☽	∠ 1°19' A	☽								
☿			☿							
♀		⚹ 4°01' A		♀						
♂			☌ 1°27' A		♂					
♃	⚻ 0°11' S					♃				
♄	⚹ 0°51' A				∠ 1°51' S	⚻ 1°02' S	♄			
⚷				⚼ 0°48' A	☍ 4°36' S	⚹ 4°21' A	□ 3°39' A	⚷		
♅	☌ 0°01' A	∠ 1°20' A				⚻ 0°12' S	⚹ 0°50' S		♅	
♆		⚻ 1°59' S	△ 2°06' A		△ 3°33' A					♆
♇	∠ 0°51' S	□ 0°27' A							∠ 0°53' S	⚹ 2°27' S

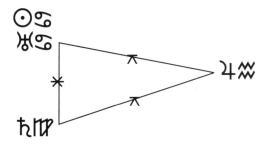

Aspect Patterns

Yod

The most exact aspect in Streep's chart is the applying conjunction between her Sun and Uranus with less than a one-minute orb (an aspect that is both partile and *cazimi,* which means "in the heart of the Sun," a condition considered to be a very substantial accidental dignity). Uranus in Cancer represents the new and disruptive ideas that relate to women's roles in society, and with her Sun so fundamentally fused with Uranus in Cancer, Streep was bound to become a living embodiment of this energy. After building her career on roles featuring strong, unique women in difficult and unexpected situations, Streep continued to shatter the preconceived roles of women, this time specifically in Hollywood, by turning forty and *still acting.* Before Streep came along and broke with convention, actresses over forty couldn't find work anywhere. Thanks to Streep's drive and persistence, this revolutionary idea (at least for Hollywood, anyway) has taken root, and paved the way for other actresses who are no longer ingenues such as Susan Sarandon, Jane Fonda, and Cher (to name but a few), and who are turning out some exceptional performances. Streep's pioneering path is also reflected in her Aries/Libra nodal axis. Streep's North Node in Aries is in her tenth house, conjunct her Midheaven, indicating that her spiritual and soul lessons in this lifetime will involve exploring and expressing her individual identity in a very public way, while drawing on the foundation of her balanced, personal and private relationships.

Let's consider how this energy would impact Streep on a more personal level. It's one thing to succeed by breaking with convention; it's quite another to have to live one's life always pushing the envelope in one way or another. Streep's Sun in Cancer needs to be able to experience and form emotional connections, to nurture and be nurtured; however, her Uranus in Cancer will make sure that these connections don't last too long, are disrupted by tragedy, whim, and miracles, and are ultimately forced to take very different paths from those they might otherwise take. Since this energy is fused with her Sun, her core sense of self, Streep will tend to thrive on this type of crisis. Coping with disasters, with the unexpected, will put Streep in her element.

Streep's Moon is quite challenged by some rather intense aspects, as well. First and foremost, with her Moon in a partile and applying square to Pluto, she will be experiencing and dealing with some seriously intense, powerful, and potentially destructive emotions. Moon/Pluto aspects embody an energy that our culture prefers to ignore: the destructive power of women. Our society encourages women to express only the life-giving, nurturing, protecting part of the female archetype, denying the darker, though equally necessary, side. Shakespeare understood this when he wrote that "Hell hath no fury like a woman scorned." With her Moon square Pluto, Streep is always tapped into the collective unconscious need to destroy and transform all that is old and outdated; and individuals with close aspects between personal planets and Pluto will always become agents of change, transformation, and destruction. In Streep's case, she will always know how terrible and destructive her emotions can be, and she will always be exceptionally sensitive to the power and control of others. Pluto is usually experienced as the unstoppable forces that try to control, change, and destroy us—and with Pluto square her Moon, Streep may never feel truly safe. She must be ever-vigilant against Pluto's energy as she tries to protect the things dearest to her heart.

The Sun and Uranus semisquare Streep's Moon, and Neptune quincunx her Moon don't exactly support a general sense of emotional security and stability, either! They do, however, reinforce the fact that Streep is a person who is at least familiar with crisis, and whether or not she actually enjoys the many disruptions that life has to offer, she is going to feel the safest, on the most familiar ground, when her world is falling apart.

So where is her escape valve? Remember, we know from the dispositor tree diagram that Streep has a very strong separation between the chaos and intensity of her emotions, and the objective, calculating technique that filters through her Mercury in Gemini and allows her to communicate the world to others and to herself. Is there a connection between these two halves of her chart?

When faced with a series of difficult and stressful aspects, always look for a harmonious aspect to any of the planets in the hard aspects—this will represent the escape route, the way that the individual will tend to channel the pressures of the squares and quincunxes. In Streep's case, her escape valve is the sextile between her Sun/Uranus conjunction in Cancer and her Saturn in Virgo. This is, in fact, the only strong link between her emotions and her mental faculties. Streep will naturally look to Saturn for support and structure to help her deal with her current emotional crisis. Saturn will approach the matter from an analytical and objective perspective, thanks to the Virgo influence, and then pass this information along to Mercury in Gemini (since Mercury rules Virgo). Gemini is an air sign, and will force Streep to take yet another step back from the emotional turmoil and view the situation from a more objective, logical, and flexible standpoint. The result is that Streep quickly learned how to keep a cool head in a crisis, and how to distance herself from her pain and emotional stress, at least long enough to fulfill her responsibilities in the situation (Saturn again).

This connection is also how Streep is able to access her emotions and feelings for use in her acting—Mercury sends the request down through Mars and Saturn, Saturn accesses the appropriate emotional experiences through the Saturn/Sun sextile, and then Streep is able to recreate the appropriate feelings on cue.

Love and Relationships

As we turn now to look at Streep's relationship patterns, we first need to look at an aspect pattern in Streep's chart that will involve her relationships: a Yod, whose apex planet is Jupiter in Aquarius conjunct the Descendant. Saturn in Virgo, the planet that rules both Streep's Jupiter and her Descendant, is also involved in the aspect pattern, as are her Sun and Uranus. Technically, for the configuration to truly be a Yod, the apex planet must be the fastest-moving planet, and Jupiter indeed is the fastest of the three primary planets, Jupiter, Saturn, and Uranus. That the Sun is also involved as a base planet doesn't invalidate the configuration, because even if the Sun were not conjunct Uranus, then Jupiter, Saturn, and Uranus would still form a true Yod.

We've already seen how important Streep's Sun/Saturn sextile is in helping her cope with the emotions in her life and bridging the gap between her emotional nature and her objective, logical mind. With Jupiter added to the picture (and in the process, her Descendant), Streep will also try to channel her own personal issues into her efforts to care for others, particularly in one-to-one relationships. For Streep, relationships will be associated with the most significant areas of her own personal growth because of Jupiter being conjunct her Descendant. The Aquarius influence makes these experiences at once compassionate and dispassionate. Aquarius is famous for its love and compassion for humanity, and for its simultaneous difficulty in relating to people on an individual basis.

Yods frequently relate to a crisis in timing, more than anything. The uncomfortable energy of the two quincunxes can be balanced and alleviated by activating the planets in the sextile; however, we tend to act too quickly with the earlier planets, and too late with the later planets. Streep's earlier planets are her Sun and Uranus in Cancer, which means that her first reaction will often be to become emotionally involved in a new relationship, and perhaps to immediately assume her mothering and protecting role. She will then also tend to bring the objectivity and perspective of her Saturn in Virgo into the picture too late to maintain a true sense of balance in the relationship. The release point of this configuration, the point where the Sun, Uranus, and Saturn should be activated together, is actually her Ascendant in Leo. The key then for Streep is to learn how to be more selfish in her relationships—perhaps to wait before she becomes involved in another crusade to save someone, to make sure that becoming involved is both appropriate and in her own best interest. This theme is also repeated in her nodal axis, as one of the key lessons for the North Node in Aries is to learn how to affirm and express one's individuality, and not to deny or compromise it in order to maintain a relationship.

With Streep's Descendant in Aquarius, ruled by Saturn, she will consciously be attracted to more stable, responsible individuals. To be sure, these individuals will tend to have their own very personal causes and agendas, and are quite likely to be very concerned with human rights and protecting individual freedoms. Her partners may tend to be far less in the public eye than she is, and, in fact, one of the things that Streep may find attractive is the fact that her partners have no desire to be in the spotlight or the public eye. As Streep's

Saturn is in Virgo in her second house, she will tend to consider her partners a very valuable personal resource, and may rely on them for support and to reinforce her sense of self. Aquarius, as we noted above, is an air sign, and is therefore more concerned with theoretical applications than it is with emotional connections. On a conscious level, Streep is going to be the most attracted to partners who seem to have little drama in their lives.

Of course, with her Venus in Cancer, Streep is going to need a certain amount of emotional connection in her relationships. Finding a partner who can remain objective and keep a cool head amidst the periodic emotional upheavals that may tend to be a fundamental part of Streep's life is very important, of course; but this partner must also be capable of sharing those emotions with Streep. With her Moon in Taurus and Venus in Cancer, Streep absolutely requires a partner who is emotionally available to her.

Streep's Vertex, which is not shown in the chart, is at 18° of Sagittarius, in her fifth house of children and love affairs. On an unconscious level, Streep may tend to carry a fantasy of a partner who will ride up on his white horse and carry her off to a life of adventure and excitement. While she may consciously be looking for the objectivity and stability of Aquarius, on an unconscious level, she is looking for a partner who has passion and drive, and the courage of his convictions.

Work and Finances

Streep's second-house resources are ruled by her Sun in Cancer, and her sixth-house routines are ruled by her Saturn in Virgo—two planets that already figure quite strongly in the rest of her chart. Her Sun, which rules her personal resources, is in the eleventh house of shared creativity and group activities, indicating that her fortune will come through working with others and through collaborative efforts. Capricorn on the sixth-house cusp indicates that Streep expects to work very hard and follow a structured, established routine in her approach to her work; and since the ruler of her sixth house (Saturn in Virgo) is in her second house of resources, her ability to be responsible and to do whatever is required is an extremely valuable resource to her. Finally, Streep's Midheaven is in Aries, ruled by Mars in Gemini in the eleventh house. Again, we see her career involving many other people and collaborative efforts (both from the eleventh house and from the Gemini influence), although ultimately what the world will see will be Streep as an individual, since Aries energy is about individuality and identity. No matter how many writers, actors, producers, and directors are there to support Streep's performance on the screen, ultimately, the only thing that we really notice and remember is her.

Interpretation Example 3: Evita Peron

Evita Peron (née Eva Duarte) was an actress who became a politician's wife and a cultural icon in Argentina. Her story has been popularized most widely in America by the musical *Evita*.

Eva was the fifth child born to a prosperous Buenos Aires family. Her father was very influential in the conservative government in place at the time, but when Eva was born in 1919, the political climate had started to change dramatically. As her family's power and influence began to wane, they moved several times, seeking better opportunities, but always returned to Buenos Aires. Eva's father was killed in a car accident when she was eight years old, and although the legends surrounding Evita's story detail how her family was rejected and barred from his funeral (an event that planted the seeds of her hatred of the upper and middle classes), her surviving siblings vehemently deny that this ever occurred. In any event, with the death of her father, the family's prosperity was most certainly at an end, and survival became a difficult struggle. During this time, Eva would play with homemade costumes, already showing her inclination toward a life in the theater.

Eva's acting career began in Buenos Aires in the 1930s. She toured with a number of theater troupes and eventually landed roles both in radio and film. By the early 1940s, she was an extremely well-known and popular icon in Argentina. In the political arena, Argentina's government was on the verge of collapse, and as a result of a military coup, the president was ousted, and Colonel Juan Peron took over the National Department of Labor. As part of a national relief effort for a devastating earthquake in San Juan, Eva Duarte was invited to participate and take up collections for the needy. She and Peron began a romantic relationship, one that also shared common political goals—both Eva and Peron were dedicated to supporting and defending the rights of the working class.

Peron and Eva were married, and Peron was selected as the Labor Party's candidate for president—and Eva accompanied him on his campaign, greeting people, handing out buttons, and supporting her husband. She had taken her first significant step into the political arena. When Peron was elected president, Eva took on a new role: Evita, who for the first time in Argentine history, took an active role in politics and stood by her husband's side as a representative of the people of Argentina. Evita continued her work with the labor unions, as well as her work with the needy, and she also reached out to the women of Argentina.

Evita's social work and outreach to the common citizen was designed to help her understand and represent the needs of the common people and to help her communicate these needs to Peron, who could then act on them. Evita was instrumental in the fight for women's rights, and ultimately for granting women the right to vote; and once women could vote, Evita became a significant political force. At the height of her popularity, she considered running for the position of vice president, alongside her husband. Although she certainly carried the popular vote, her failing health forced her to withdraw, and she died from cancer soon after the election.

Although Evita was responsible for significant social change in Argentina, she was also widely criticized for her raw ambition and political aspirations. Certainly, she had reached a level of power and influence that no woman had ever achieved in the history of Argentina.

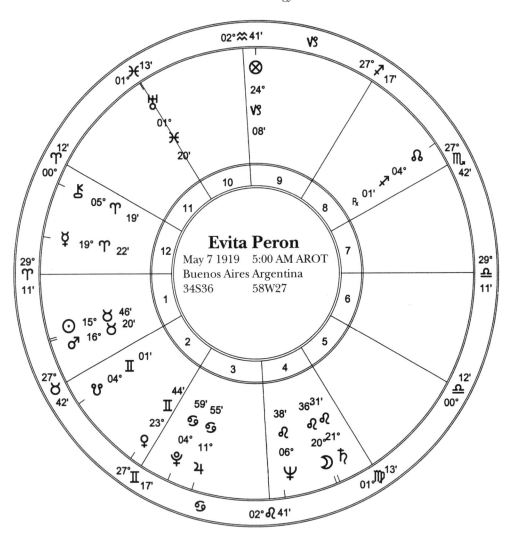

Figure 26. Evita Peron's Natal Chart

Part 1: Elements and Modalities

Element/Modality	Personal Planets	Personal Points (Angles)	Outer Planets
FIRE	☽☿♄	AS ♌	⚷♆
EARTH	☉♂	⊗	
AIR	♀	MC ☋	
WATER	♃		♅♇
CARDINAL	☿♃	AS ⊗	⚷♇
FIXED	☉☽♂♄	MC	♆
MUTABLE	♀	☊☋	♅

Part 2: Temperament

Hemisphere	Planets	Quadrant	Planets
Northern (Houses 1–6)	☉☽♀♂♃♄♆♇	1st Quadrant (Houses 1–3)	☉♀♂♃♇
Southern (Houses 7–12)	☿⚷♅	2nd Quadrant (Houses 4–6)	☽♄♆
Eastern (Houses 10–12, 1–3)	☉♀♂♃⚷♅♇	3rd Quadrant (Houses 7–9)	
Western (Houses 4–9)	☽♄♆	4th Quadrant (Houses 10–12)	☿⚷♅

On an elemental level, Evita has a strong influence in fire, as well as some earth, but she has a noticeable lack of both air and water in her chart. Passion and intensity would be quite natural for her; perspective and objectivity, however, may be qualities that she somewhat lacks. One aspect of fire seems to have played out very clearly in her life: she was full of action and drive, and she burned very brightly—but she also burned out very quickly. Her tendency to push herself to her physical limits and beyond ultimately contributed to her health crisis and death.

This is not to say that Evita didn't have considerable stamina, particularly with four planets in fixed signs, most notably the Sun and Mars, the two most action-oriented planets, in Taurus. The rather stubborn approach to life that comes with an emphasis in fixed signs, however, can often contribute to those individuals being absolutely convinced that they can keep up their strenuous use of energy indefinitely; and, of course, one of the more fundamental issues associated with the fixed signs is that of self-worth and self-esteem. When we factor in that Evita had only one personal planet in a mutable sign (Venus in Gemini), and combine it with the four personal planets in fixed signs, we can safely assume that Evita was not a person who welcomed change in her world. When we consider that both her Sun and Moon, in particular, are in fixed signs, we can reason that she would instinctively interpret any external suggestions to change or to adapt as personal attacks, and defend her position vehemently and passionately.

With eight planets below the horizon, we can assume that Evita would tend to be more introverted than extroverted, something that doesn't quite seem to fit with the very public life she led. Consider, though, that one of her more public planets is Mercury in Aries, which, we will see, is one of the focal points in her chart. Also, as public a figure as Evita was, she maintained a very private side. "Evita" was simply another acting role for her, another mask that she could wear in public. Evita also has eight planets in the Eastern Hemisphere of her chart, which indicates that she would tend to be very self-motivated.

Evita has an emphasis in both fire signs and fixed signs—a combination that perhaps gives her chart a strong Leo signature, one certainly supported by her Moon and Saturn in Leo. Some themes we might want to look for would thus include warmth, passion, and generosity, as well as the traps of Leo: pride, arrogance, dependence on others, and a need to be constantly appreciated, acknowledged, and validated as an individual.

Part 3: Essential Dignities

Planet	Ruler	Exalt.	Trip.	Term	Face	Detri.	Fall	Score
☉ (in ♉)	♀	☽	☽	♄	☽	♂	—	−5 p
☽ (in ♌)	☉	—	♃	♃	♂	♄	—	−5 p
☿ (in ♈)	♂	☉	♃	☿+	☉	♀	♄	+2
♀ (in ♊)	☿	☊	☿	♄	☉	♃	☋	−5 p
♂ (in ♉)	♀	☽	☽	♄	☽	♂−	—	−10 p
♃ (in ♋)	☽	♃+	♂	♃+	☿	♄	♂	+6
♄ (in ♌)	☉	—	♃	♃	♂	♄−	—	−10 p
AS (in ♈)	♂	☉	♃	♄	♀	—	—	—
MC (in ♒)	♄	—	☿	♄	♀	—	—	—
⊗ (in ♑)	♄	♂	☽	♂	☉	—	—	—

Part 4: Dispositor Tree Diagram

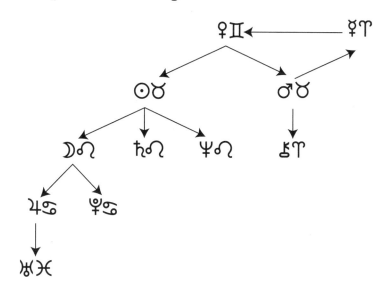

One of the reasons that I selected Evita Peron as an example chart is that the key to her chart, the central themes and issues that form the context for being able to interpret the chart as a whole, is not immediately obvious. In the other charts we've interpreted so far, we were quickly able to find core issues that helped guide us in our approach to interpreting the individual elements of the chart.

Evita's dispositor tree doesn't seem to be much help in finding the way into her chart. As we found with Sylvester Stallone's chart, Evita's chart seems to be run by a committee consisting of Mercury, Venus, and Mars. Evita's committee, however, has a very different power dynamic from that in Stallone's chart. All three of Stallone's ruling planets were peregrine, and therefore equally ineffective. Evita's chart, on the other hand, is ruled by Mercury with dignity by term, a peregrine Venus, and a Mars that is not only peregrine, but also in detriment. This is all very important information and is worth interpreting in detail. However, this information does not appear to be the key that we're looking for, so we will set it aside for the moment, and move on.

At this point, the next logical step is to take a close look at the foundations of the chart: the Sun, Moon, and Ascendant. Whatever other themes may be present in a chart, whatever other issues individuals may face in their lives, the Sun, Moon, and Ascendant form the core of their individual identities. It so happens that when we look at Evita's Sun and Moon, we will find some important clues to the key to her chart; but in order to completely interpret her Sun and Moon, we need to consider her aspects at the same time.

Part 5: Aspects and Aspect Patterns

	☉	☽	☿	♀	♂	♃	♄	⚷	♅	♆	
☽	□ 4°49' S										☽
☿		△ 1°14' S									☿
♀		✶ 3°07' A									♀
♂	☌ 0°34' A	□ 4°15' S									♂
♃	✶ 3°50' S										♃
♄	□ 5°45' A	☌ 0°55' A	△ 2°09' A	✶ 2°12' S	□ 5°10' A						♄
⚷		⚼ 0°14' S					⚼ 1°12' A				⚷
♅											♅
♆								△ 1°19' A			♆
♇		∠ 0°36' S					∠ 1°31' S	□ 0°20' S	△ 3°39' A	⚻ 1°38' A	

Evita's Sun is applying to a conjunction with her Mars in Taurus. Evita's Moon in Leo is applying to a conjunction with her Saturn in Leo. While Evita's

Moon is separating from a square to her Sun and Mars, her Sun and Mars are simultaneously applying to a square to her Saturn. This, as they say, is juicy. Let's break this down and look at each individual planet before we put it back together and see how powerful and important this configuration is in the chart.

Evita's Sun is peregrine in Taurus. The Sun in Taurus is motivated to explore and express its identity through creating lasting and valuable structures in the physical realm. The Sun in Taurus operates though tangible experience, and Evita would be very aware of the physical aspects of her life—both the creature comforts she enjoyed later as her success grew, and the harsher reality and poverty she endured as a child. Taurus energy is very slow-moving and methodical, and the Sun in Taurus tends to wander, looking for ways in which it can shine and express itself, something it must ultimately learn to do a little bit at a time, rather than all at once. Being a fixed sign, Taurus does not like change, and the Sun in Taurus in particular likes to focus on steady, natural, methodical progress and consistent growth. Evita's Sun, however, is conjunct her Mars in Taurus, and so her identity is fundamentally linked with her need to take action.

When the Sun is conjunct Mars, identity is no longer something that can simply be. The things we desire, the ways that we focus our energy and take action, become the ways in which we define and express our sense of individuality. Inaction, then, is a slow, draining death for these individuals. They must always have some goal, some project in progress—if they do not have somewhere to focus their energies, they will lose sight of their identity.

Now, Evita's Mars is in Taurus, where it is both peregrine and in detriment. Mars is perhaps the most frustrated in Taurus, because Taurus is the slowest sign in the zodiac and has the greatest inertia. Mars likes to see rapid progress and instant results, but while in Taurus, Mars is forced to build things one brick at a time. Just because Mars is in detriment in Taurus doesn't mean that it's weak. The challenge for Mars in Taurus is that it generally tries to apply its strength toward speeding things up rather than toward building a stronger foundation. Particularly when the ego gets involved, Mars in Taurus tends to spend a great deal of time banging its head against the wall and pounding its fists in frustration because things aren't moving as quickly as it would like.

For Evita, then, it would never be enough for her to simply express herself as an individual—she would tend to define her individuality and her identity through the tangible things she created. She would always have some goal in mind, and most often, these goals would involve the accumulation of material wealth and security. On a fundamental level, her identity and worth as an individual would be directly related to how much she had accomplished and accumulated in the material world.

Evita's Moon in Leo is also peregrine, not that the Moon finds Leo too uncomfortable. Leo allows the Moon to express a full range of emotions and passion (although, as is the case with all the fire signs, Leo tends to gravitate toward variations on intense joy and extreme anger); and the Moon in Leo is also capable of expressing and receiving love. The challenge of the Moon in Leo is that it often needs a constant stream of appreciation, attention, and validation from other people in order to feel safe and secure. The Moon in Leo has to learn how to survive without relying so completely on the energy and focus of others—we cannot live our lives as the center of attention. On the other hand, when the Moon in Leo is receiving enough adoration and praise, it can become quite regal in its approach and expression. Evita was unquestionably Argentinean royalty, receiving the worship of the public, and sharing her love and generosity in return.

Evita's Moon doesn't work alone, however, because it is conjunct her Saturn in Leo. Saturn is, of course, the planet of structure and limitation, and the Moon can certainly be supported in its expression by the appropriate boundaries. Since conjunctions represent a blending of the energies of the two planets, the relative ease or difficulty of the conjunction depends a great deal on the dignities of the planets involved. Saturn in Leo is both peregrine and in detriment—an indication that the relationship between Saturn and the Moon is not going to be a terribly supportive one.

Being able to express the creative, generous, loving, and special nature of Leo is extremely important to Saturn. Since Saturn is so concerned with responsibility and structure, and with being right, Saturn in Leo tends to be overly cautious and often hesitates before sharing with others, for fear that what it has to offer, what it has created, is not good enough. Saturn in Leo is in detriment, and planets in detriment operate on the mental/emotional plane. What this usually means is that when we have a planet in detriment, we tend to worry obsessively about the affairs of that planet. Saturn in Leo works very hard to create and truly wants to share a unique expression of the self with the world—but Saturn in Leo also wants to make sure that it has worked hard enough at it and will earn any rewards and attention.

Essentially, the Moon in Leo is motivated to express its unique creativity, to prove that it is special and deserving of the support and attention of others—something the Moon in Leo believes it requires in order to survive. Saturn in Leo conjunct the Moon basically tells the Moon, "You're not special enough," and, "You have to work harder to prove your worth." With Saturn conjunct her Moon, it wouldn't be enough for Evita to simply be in the spotlight: she would have to be in the spotlight because she had earned her place there and truly shared something of value with the world.

Evita's Ascendant is in Aries, ruled by Mars in Taurus (conjunct her Sun) in the first house. Her approach to the world will tend to be passionate, honest, impulsive, and direct. Most of all, when she goes out into the world, it is to express her identity. Because Mars in Taurus rules her Ascendant, and is also both conjunct her Sun and in her first house, she's not going to be satisfied with any old way of expressing herself. She is going to look for ways to make a lasting impression on the world. Remember that Evita defines her identity based on the things that she has created and sustained in the physical world.

This is further supported by Evita's Part of Fortune in Capricorn, the sign motivated to create a material expression of our identity, and also ruled by Saturn in Leo in Evita's chart. Capricorn relates to taking responsibility both as individuals and as members of society. Evita's Part of Fortune is in her ninth house of organized religion, higher learning, spirituality, and dreams. Her greatest success was becoming the "spiritual leader of the nation," as she was called when her death was announced to the republic.

We've already established that Evita has some pretty strong fundamental identity and self-worth issues; and they get even stronger when we consider that her Sun/Mars conjunction is square her Moon/Saturn conjunction. This configuration would create tremendous pressure for Evita—the constant need to build, to create things of value and of use, and at the same time to be recognized for her contributions. Her entire sense of self, both conscious and unconscious, would be bound up in how much she believed she had accomplished in her lifetime. The primary ways that she would evaluate her progress would be to look at what kinds of lasting changes she had initiated, and how much she was being recognized and lauded by others for her efforts. This is quite a lot of pressure, and it naturally will be looking for an escape—an easy and hopefully creative and constructive way to express itself.

Fortunately, Evita's chart does have that built-in escape valve. When the pressure builds up between her Sun/Mars and Moon/Saturn, it will express itself through her Mercury in Aries (which is trine her Moon/Saturn conjunction), and through her Venus in Gemini (which is both sextile her Moon/Saturn conjunction, and also sextile her Mercury in Aries). *Now* we've got a context to take another look at Evita's dispositor tree, since we now understand just how Mercury, Venus, and Mars will operate in her chart.

Let's look at Mercury first. Mercury in Aries is always going to speak its mind. Aries energy is so direct and impulsive that Mercury in Aries often says things without thinking them through completely. It's long on passion and intensity, but once the passion of the words has cooled, Mercury in Aries often has trouble completing its initial train of thought, or supporting its arguments in a methodical, well-reasoned manner. Evita's Mercury will express her Moon/Saturn conjunction energy very strongly. Even though Saturn is in rather poor condition, the trine between Mercury and Saturn helped Evita apply structure to her thoughts, and provided a platform that supported her as she used her passion and gift of public speaking to change forever the political and social structure in Argentina.

Venus in Gemini is responsible for the more playful aspects of Evita's life, and can be directly related to her attraction to the stage and her successful career as an actress. Venus in Gemini is nothing if not charming, and fueled by both the warmth and generosity of the sextile to the Moon and Saturn in Leo, as well as by Leo's need to be loved and appreciated, Evita's social skills would have been both valuable resources to her (as her Venus is in her second house), and also quite strong. She was certainly not above using her romantic and social connections to advance her career, and ultimately to offer her the opportunity to express her love and generosity and her need to build and create on a very grand scale.

The "committee" that rules Evita's chart consists of her Mercury, Venus, and Mars. Of these three planets, only Mercury has any dignity (by term), while Venus is peregrine, and Mars is both peregrine and in detriment. Term is not a very strong dignity, so while Mercury's ideas are going to count for a lot, they're still going to be modified thanks to Venus and Mars. The way this might work is that Mercury receives the pent-up energy from the Sun/Mars and Moon/Saturn who tell Mercury to think of a way to express its identity that will be practical and grounded, and at the same time make enough of a difference that people will respond with love and adoration. Mercury then looks to Venus in Gemini, who makes the ideas more attractive and palatable and less aggressive, and who also brings up the whole issue of duality. Venus in Gemini looks to Mars in Taurus who says we need to take some concrete action with this— and if there are two sides to the issue, then we have to pick one and fight for it. Mars in Taurus then looks back to Mercury in Aries, who will use words and communication to fight to bring about the new growth.

Work and Finances

Evita has Taurus on her second-house cusp of personal resources, and has Venus in Gemini both ruling the second and in the second house. Virgo is on her sixth-house cusp of daily routines and work, ruled by Mercury in Aries in the twelfth house; and Aquarius is on Evita's Midheaven, governing her life path, and ruled by Saturn in Leo in her fourth house. The fact that Virgo, the sign of service, relates to Evita's sixth house is no surprise—Evita fought hard for the rights of workers and laborers in Argentina. She was, in fact, their voice and their advocate, helping them fight for their rights through her Mercury in Aries. Also of no surprise is her Midheaven in Aquarius. Evita was able to embody some of the highest and most noble energies of Aquarius as she fought for changes in the very fabric and structure of Argentina. With the ruler of her Midheaven being Saturn in Leo, she took a very personal interest in her good works, always keeping in direct contact with the people she fought to help. Her fundamental approach and goals were also very practical: a job, medicine, and housing. Through her charity, passion, and dedication, she most certainly earned the love and adoration of an entire nation.

Interpretation Example 4: Woody Allen

Woody Allen is best known for his off-the-wall humor which revolves around his neurotic, Jewish, New Yorker persona that he first created doing stand-up comedy in Greenwich Village. Allen further honed his skills writing gags for television shows, and ultimately broke into films when he wrote and acted in *What's New Pussycat,* followed by his directorial debut with *Take the Money and Run.* Over the next thirty years, Allen would refine both his comic skill (writing screenplays, books, and a successful Broadway play or two), and his filmmaking abilities, winning three Oscars in 1977 for *Annie Hall.* Allen, however, remained very private and very much a New Yorker. Instead of flying to California for the Academy Awards, he stayed in New York so that he wouldn't miss his regular session with his jazz band (where he plays the clarinet).

Recently, however, Allen's private life began to overshadow his artistic contributions. Allen was already divorced once before he met and eventually married his first leading lady, Louise Lasser. After his marriage with Lasser ended, Allen began a long-term relationship with his next leading lady, Diane Keaton. Keaton left him for Warren Beatty, and in 1980, Allen began his much-publicized relationship with Mia Farrow (who also became his leading lady in his next eleven films). Farrow already had nine children when she began her relationship with Allen; after having one more child with Allen and adopting two more, this brought the total to twelve. In 1993, Allen's relationship with Farrow's adopted daughter, Soon-Yi Previn, became public, leading to accusations of child abuse and a bitter custody battle which, it seemed, was conducted as much in the media as it was in the courts. Allen was eventually cleared of all abuse allegations, and he and Soon-Yi married in 1997.

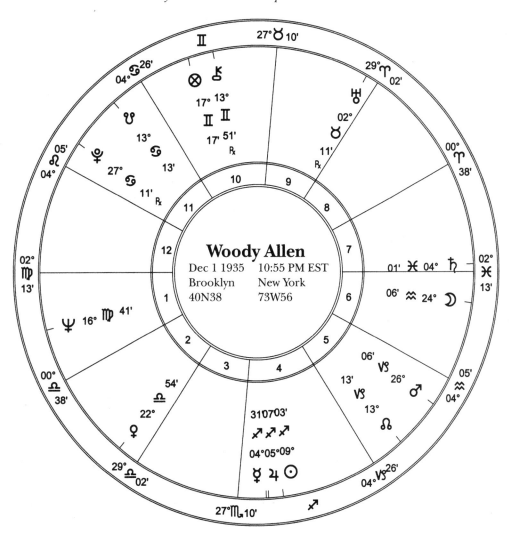

Figure 27. Woody Allen's Natal Chart

Part 1: Elements and Modalities

Element/Modality	Personal Planets	Personal Points (Angles)	Outer Planets
FIRE	☉☿♃		
EARTH	♂	AS MC ☊	♅♆
AIR	☽♀	⊗	⚷
WATER	♄	☋	♇
CARDINAL	♀♂	☊☋	♇
FIXED	☽	MC	♅
MUTABLE	☉☿♃♄	AS ⊗	⚷♆

Part 2: Temperament

Hemisphere	Planets	Quadrant	Planets
Northern (Houses 1–6)	☉☽☿♀♂♃♆	1st Quadrant (Houses 1–3)	♀♆
Southern (Houses 7–12)	♄⚷♅♇	2nd Quadrant (Houses 4–6)	☉☽☿♂♃
Eastern (Houses 10–12, 1–3)	♀⚷♆♇	3rd Quadrant (Houses 7–9)	♄♅
Western (Houses 4–9)	☉☽♀♂♃♄♅	4th Quadrant (Houses 10–12)	⚷♆

One of the first things to notice about Allen's chart is how his approach to the world differs from his inner nature. Allen has a reasonably strong fire emphasis with his Sun, Mercury, and Jupiter all in Sagittarius, as well as both his Moon and Venus in air signs. He only has one personal planet in earth (Mars in Capricorn), and one personal planet in water (Saturn in Pisces). Ordinarily, we would consider that with a lack of emphasis in earth, Allen would tend to be a bit impractical and lack a solid foundation—and on a personal level, this will prove to be very much the case. Both his Ascendant and Midheaven are in earth, however, so his approach to the world will be very grounded and practical.

Where Allen has an unquestionable lack is in the element of water. Making emotional connections will require a conscious effort for him—particularly since the only water he has in his chart is being limited by Saturn. Allen's preferred modes of operation will be on more abstract levels. Fire is quite passionate, of course, and air is very objective, and both elements are far more inclined to operate in the mental and left-brain arenas than in the emotional and right-brain arenas where water is the most comfortable. Furthermore, Allen's Moon and Venus, the two planets that embody the majority of our emotional and relationship functions, are both in air signs and will tend to be far more interested in relating on the mental and social levels than they will be in forming deep emotional bonds. With Virgo on his Ascendant, Allen's approach to the world is going to be very left-brained, thanks to Virgo's practical, logical, and analytical energy.

Allen also has a very strong emphasis in mutable signs in his chart, with his Moon the only personal planet in fixed signs. He is likely to be very flexible and adaptable, and very concerned with healing and completion. He does have both Venus and Mars in cardinal signs, so he's able to initiate things as well, although this would not be his strong suit. The relative lack of fixed energy and emphasis on mutable energy can often indicate individuals who have difficulty sticking with any one project for any length of time, usually because they have so many different projects going on simultaneously, and their energy and attention is being spread too thin. When pressured, Allen will have a tendency to scatter his attention and lose focus. He may also have a very strong aversion to any kind of conflict, and will do whatever he can to avoid it. When he isn't able to avoid a confrontation, his first reaction will be to adapt and to change.

Looking at Allen's temperament, we see that all his personal planets, except for Saturn, are below the horizon in the Northern Hemisphere, indicating that he will tend to be more introverted than extroverted. All his personal planets except for Venus, on the other hand, are in the Western Hemisphere of his chart, which indicates that he will tend to be more reactive and relationship-oriented. The strongest emphasis in his chart is in Quadrant II, which is both introverted and relationship-oriented.

Part 3: Essential Dignities

Planet	Ruler	Exalt.	Trip.	Term	Face	Detri.	Fall	Score
☉ (in ♐)	♃	☋	♃	♀	♂	☿	☊	–5 p
☽ (in ♒)	♄	—	☿	♃	☽+	☉	—	+1
☿ (in ♐)	♃	☋	♃	♃	♂	☿–	☊	–10 p
♀ (in ♎)	♀+	♄	☿	☿	♃	♂	☉	+5
♂ (in ♑)	♄	♂+	☽	♄	☉	☽	♃	+4
♃ (in ♐)	♃+	☋	♃+	♃+	♂	☿	☊	+10
♄ (in ♓)	♃	♂	♂	♀	♄+	☿	☿	+1
AS (in ♍)	☿	☿	☽	☿	☉	—	—	—
MC (in ♉)	♀	☽	☽	♂	♄	—	—	—
⊗ (in ♊)	☿	☊	☿	♀	♂	—	—	—

Part 4: Dispositor Tree Diagram

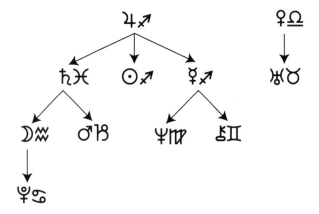

From the dispositor tree, we see that, like Meryl Streep, Woody Allen also has a fundamental split in his chart. In Allen's case, his relationship functions (Venus) are completely separate from the planets in the rest of his chart, which all report directly to a very dignified Jupiter in Sagittarius. Jupiter not only rules much of the chart, but also receives many of the other planets by triplicity, term, and face. Allen, then, will embody and express the expansive, generous, fun-loving, outgoing, philosophical, and spiritual nature of Jupiter in most aspects of his life. Mercury is also quite an important planet in Allen's chart, and receives almost as much dignity from the other planets and points in the chart as Jupiter does. If we add up the points that Mercury and Jupiter receive from the personal planets and angles, Jupiter gets a score of thirty-six, while Mercury gets a score of twenty-seven. (Remember, rulership is worth 5 points, exaltation 4 points, triplicity 3 points, term 2 points, and face 1 point. Jupiter gets 5 points every time it shows up in the rulership column, 4 points in the exaltation column, etc.)

Jupiter in Sagittarius is motivated to discover the ultimate truth in the universe. It experiences growth and expansion through exploring our individual relationship with the universe, through higher education, philosophy, religion, and spirituality. Allen will be very concerned with the "big picture," and quite passionate about his beliefs and ideas. Allen's Jupiter doesn't act alone, however, because it is also part of a Stellium in Sagittarius, and is conjunct both his Sun and his Mercury (which rules his Ascendant in Virgo). For Allen, it's not enough to simply explore his identity and place in the universe; he must also be able to understand it and communicate it to others. Is it any surprise, then, that the most common themes in Allen's film and writing career tend to center around man's battle with the universe? Allen's Sun is peregrine, so he will have taken a wandering and indirect path to discover his core identity.

Let's look at Allen's Mercury next. Here we have a prime example of how a debilitated Mercury in no way indicates a lack of intellectual ability. Allen's Mercury is both peregrine and in detriment, and yet he is renowned for his knowledge, intelligence, wit, humor, writing ability, and communication skills. Mercury's lack of dignity certainly hasn't hurt Allen! Let's look at how Mercury has expressed itself. Planets in detriment operate on the mental and emotional realms, and this often manifests as worrying about the affairs of that planet. Mercury in Sagittarius is very strong, but applies its strength in somewhat misguided ways. It's motivated to understand the ultimate truth, and yet seeks to do this by focusing on the details, rather than on the larger picture. Allen has virtually built his career on being a neurotic intellectual, continually worrying and obsessing about philosophy and religion, desperately trying to understand how to break these bigger concepts down into more easily digestible chunks; and, true to the mutable nature of Sagittarius, he always seems to be willing to adapt and adjust his fundamental beliefs.

Allen's approach to the world is though his Virgo Ascendant, which is ruled by his Mercury in Sagittarius. He will attempt to analyze and reason his way around the fundamental spiritual laws and mysteries of the universe. Even Allen's physical appearance reflects this bookworm, intellectual energy (Mercury rules the terms of the Ascendant, and influences his appearance).

As we noted when we looked at Allen's elemental balance, he has a noticeable lack of water in his chart. Allen's Moon is in Aquarius, and his Venus is in Libra. While Venus in Libra is quite strong, Libra is still an air sign, and both his Moon and Venus are going to prefer to operate on the mental and social levels, rather than on the emotional level. Allen will tend to live entirely through his head, and may in fact feel both threatened and uncomfortable with the idea of forming emotional connections that go too far beneath the surface. Sagittarius energy doesn't help this much at all. Sagittarius is very concerned with personal freedom and space, and will fight to break free if it feels at all confined; and Sagittarius' absolute dedication to the truth often results in a lack of tact, and a wake of bruised feelings.

Part 5: Aspects and Aspect Patterns

	☉	☽	☿	♀	♂	♃	♄	⚷	♅	♆
☽	☌ 4°31' A	☽								
☿	∠ 1°08' A	△ 1°12' S	☿							
♀	∠ 2°03' A	⊻ 2°00' A		♀						
♂				□ 3°12' A	♂					
♃	☌ 3°55' S		☌ 0°36' A			♃				
♄	□ 5°01' S		□ 0°29' S			□ 1°06' S	♄			
⚷	☍ 4°49' A							⚷		
♅							⚹ 1°49' S		♅	
♆	□ 7°38' A							□ 2°50' S	⊡ 0°29' A	♆
♇			□ 4°16' A	☍ 1°04' A				∠ 1°41' A	□ 5°00' A	

Aspect Patterns

Stellium

☉♐ ♃♐ ☿♐

Cardinal T-Square

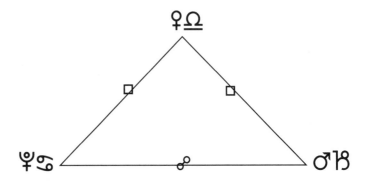

We've already looked at Allen's Stellium in Sagittarius, and have a good feel for how strongly his entire persona is influenced by the Sagittarius energy. Let's now take a look at Allen's Venus. As you will recall from his dispositor tree, Allen's Venus is off on its own, ruling only Uranus, and having no other connection with the rest of his Jupiter-ruled planets. Allen's Venus, however, is also the apex planet of a cardinal T-Square with Mars and Pluto, which presents more than a few interesting challenges of its own.

Venus in Libra will relate not only to Allen's interpersonal relationships, but also to his relationship to his art. Venus in Libra is motivated to express beauty, balance, and harmony in all things, and individuals with Venus in Libra are often attracted to the fine arts and to music. Venus in Libra tends to symbolize artistic expression that requires the use of tools—musical instruments, for example. While Venus in Taurus is often a very powerful creative force for singers, musicians tend to resonate more with Venus in Libra; and Allen's music is unquestionably an extremely important part of his life. We can also see the separation of his Venus from the rest of his chart when we consider that Woody Allen the jazz clarinet player is quite a different person from Woody Allen the comic and filmmaker. Allen the musician does not worry about his identity or his place in the universe. Allen the musician is expressing his true identity through the ordered, balanced perfection of music.

Allen's Venus, however, is the apex planet of a cardinal T-Square, which means that both his artistic expression and his interpersonal relationships are going to be quite important and prominent issues in his life. In order to understand how this pattern may operate, we need to look at the core issues and relationships of each of the planets and aspects.

Allen's Mars in Capricorn is exalted and therefore very strongly placed in his chart. Mars in Capricorn is one of the hardest-working, most productive energies in astrology. Since Allen's Mars is also in his fifth house of personal creativity and artistic expression, he is going to want to channel his focus, desires, anger, and aggression into his art. When we take the opposition to Pluto into consideration, Mars becomes far more powerful. The opposition aspect is one that lends perspective and requires balance. Mars opposite Pluto taps into the transformational, destructive energy of Pluto, and at the same time is consciously aware of how much power is at its disposal. Allen will tend to be very sensitive to issues of control, particularly when he feels that others are trying to influence or control him. These situations will trigger his Mars energy, and he will defend himself, ideally by channeling his anger and energy into building something that will make it far more difficult for others to control him.

The issues relating to the Cancer/Capricorn axis are also important here. Allen, remember, is rather uncomfortable with deep emotional connections. We can safely say that Pluto in Cancer will tend to bring up deep emotional issues, specifically issues about how we form emotional connections, how we nurture others, and how we allow ourselves to be nurtured. Capricorn energy is about being self-reliant, while Cancer energy needs to be open to the support and assistance of others. Whenever Allen feels pressure from Pluto to form an emotional bond, his first reaction will be to respond by putting up a wall and defending himself, asserting that he does not need anyone's support. Allen's nodes are also in Cancer and Capricorn—another indication that learning to balance and integrate these energies is one of his key lessons in this lifetime.

With Venus square Pluto, Allen will be extremely aware of the power dynamics in his relationships as well. Squares aren't nearly as conscious as oppositions, however, and as important as relationships may be to him, they're also going to feel a bit threatening as well. Venus square Mars indicates a fundamental difference between the things Allen is attracted to (Venus), and the ways in which he goes after the things he wants (Mars). This friction, however, is certainly one of the energies that fuels Allen's creative drive.

All three planets, Venus, Mars, and Pluto, are in cardinal signs, and what this pattern amounts to is a rather significant and ongoing identity crisis. This identity crisis is distinct from Allen's Sagittarius quest for the truth—and, in fact, it is Allen's cardinal T-Square that ultimately drives his creative expression. The Mars/Pluto opposition brings up Allen's core issues about autonomy, individual identity, and forming emotional connections with others, and he tries to resolve this conflict through his Venus in Libra, seeking balance and harmony both in his art and in his relationships.

Love and Relationships

Lastly, let's take a broader look at the other factors that will tend to influence Allen's romantic relationships. We've already established that Allen is not comfortable with emotions, and this can tend to become an issue in romantic relationships, where most people come to expect a certain amount of bonding on the emotional level. Both Allen's Venus and Moon are in air signs (and trine each other), and both are in hard aspect to Pluto in Cancer (Venus square Pluto, and Moon quincunx Pluto). Allen will not feel safe being pressured to open up emotionally. He will prefer his relationships to remain on a more abstract, social, intellectual level.

Allen's Descendant is in Pisces, and his Saturn in Pisces is conjunct the Descendant. Pisces on the Descendant tends to be attracted to partners who are very spiritual and compassionate, and who also tend to have poorly defined emotional boundaries. Saturn, of course, relates to forming and maintaining good interpersonal boundaries, but Saturn in Pisces has a rather difficult time of it. This combination has a very passive-aggressive feel to it. On a conscious level, Allen wants a partner with whom he can share an emotional connection— but only to a point! Saturn will tend to put up some rather abrupt boundaries, which most likely tends to be extremely confusing to Allen's partners. Allen will tend to attract partners who want to merge with him and become a part of his life, and he will seem to invite this energy. His partners will then start forming emotional bonds with Allen, until they cross a line and Allen feels like they're trying to control him, at which point he will put up a wall and retreat to the mental/emotional plane.

Allen's Vertex, which is not shown in the illustration, is in Capricorn, conjunct his Mars. The Vertex relates to our unconscious attractions in relationships, and Allen's Vertex ties directly into the engine that drives his creative and professional life. It's hardly surprising that three of Allen's relationships have been with actresses he had worked with—and with whom he continued to work during the course of the romantic relationship.

Some Last Words of Advice and Encouragement

First of all, I want to acknowledge that you have made it through this book! We've covered a tremendous amount of information in a relatively brief amount of space. Please trust me that if you actually read the entire book, you have absorbed much more information than you think you did. You may not feel that you can sit down and interpret a natal chart on your own right away, but this will come with time and practice.

Learning astrology is exactly like learning a foreign language. First, you learn a new alphabet, some simple words, and the fundamentals of grammar. As you become familiar with the basics and learn new words, you are able to form more complex sentences. Eventually, you will find that you have a strong enough understanding that you can begin to hold simple conversations, and actually translate your own concepts and thoughts. But you can't learn a foreign language from a book—it's not a passive activity. You actually have to practice it on your own, and speak and write it on a daily basis until you become comfortable with it. If you truly want to learn astrology, you're going to have to practice speaking it every day.

The best advice I can offer you when faced with a chart to interpret is to remember to stick with the basics. Follow the approach that we've used in the examples. Find the context of the chart first by looking at the elements, the modalities, and the quadrants. Look at the essential dignities and the dispositor trees. Try to find a context for the chart.

In appendix B, I've listed many of the national astrology organizations. These organizations often have local chapters, and you may also have local and regional astrology organizations near you. I encourage you to join an astrology organization and attend the meetings whenever possible. Novice astrologers are always welcome, and being able to share ideas and interact with other astrologers is the best way to become a better astrologer yourself.

If you're serious about astrology, you're probably going to want to get a computer and an astrology program or two. In appendix C, I've listed some of the better computer programs available.

Although you can find many books that offer interpretations of planets in signs and planets in houses, before you go to see what someone else has to say, try to reason things out yourself. My goal here was to provide you with all the tools that you will need to be able to come up with your own unique interpretations. You now understand the words and the sentence structures of the language of astrology. In order for it to become more familiar and comfortable to you, you simply have to start speaking and writing it yourself.

Appendix A

Natal Chart Interpretation Worksheet

Name   _____

Date and Time of Birth   _____

Location of Birth   _____

Part 1: Elements and Modalities

Element/Modality	Personal Planets	Personal Points (Angles)	Outer Planets
FIRE			
EARTH			
AIR			
WATER			
CARDINAL			
FIXED			
MUTABLE			

Part 2: Temperament

Hemisphere	Planets	Quadrant	Planets
Northern (Houses 1–6)		1st Quadrant (Houses 1–3)	
Southern (Houses 7–12)		2nd Quadrant (Houses 4–6)	
Eastern (Houses 10–12, 1–3)		3rd Quadrant (Houses 7–9)	
Western (Houses 4–9)		4th Quadrant (Houses 10–12)	

Comments:
Summarize Temperament and Fundamental (Elemental) Personality

_____

_____

_____

_____

_____

_____

_____

_____

_____

_____

_____

_____

_____

_____

_____

_____

_____

Part 3: Essential Dignities

Planet	Ruler	Exalt.	Trip.	Term	Face	Detri.	Fall	Score
☉								
☽								
☿								
♀								
♂								
♃								
♄								
AS						—	—	—
MC						—	—	—
⊗						—	—	—

Part 4: Dispositor Tree Diagram

Comments:
Essential Dignity/Dispositor Breakdown of Chart

_____

_____

_____

_____

_____

_____

_____

Comments:
Interpret and Synthesize Sun, Moon, Ascendant, and Part of Fortune

_____

_____

_____

_____

_____

Part 5: Aspects and Aspect Patterns

Aspect Patterns

Part 6: Synthesize Chart Themes

- Analyze Nodal Axis.
- Look for Themes in Elements/Modalities/Dignities.
- Look for Key Personal Planets—Who is the boss in the chart?
- Look for Aspect Patterns (if any).
- Look for Stationary Planets (either Retrograde or Direct).

Comments:
Summarize Chart Themes, Overall Impression, and Context of Chart

_____

_____

_____

_____

_____

_____

_____

_____

_____

_____

_____

_____

Part 7:
Interpret the Planets by Sign, House, and Dignity

Start with Personal Planets and Points: Sun, Moon, and Ascendant are the most important.

Part 8:
Interpret the Aspects and Aspect Patterns

- This can be included while working through the individual planets, or done separately.

- Begin with the most exact aspects in the chart—they are the most important by far.

- Try to work through the connections one at a time and get a feel for how each planet interacts with the other planets.

Part 9:
Explore Specific Life Areas and
Questions/Concerns of the Client

In each of these examples, you will look at the house ruler (by sign, house, and dignity), any planets in the house, and any planets aspecting the ruler of the house. All of these will have an impact on the affairs of the house in question.

- WORK/FINANCES: Look at second house (Resources and Money), sixth house (Job and Daily Routine/Work Environment), and tenth house (Career/Life Path). Pay particular attention to the rulers of the houses and how they interact with each other.

- LOVE/RELATIONSHIPS: Look at Venus by sign, house, aspect, and dignity to understand the client's relationship styles. The Moon shows safety/emotional/need issues. The Descendant and any planets in the seventh house show the type of person the client finds attractive on a conscious level. The Vertex shows what they're looking for on an unconscious or subconscious level. The fifth house is love affairs and the seventh house is committed relationships (i.e., marriage). Look at the relationship between the ruler of the fifth house and the ruler of the seventh house to see how easy the client may find it to take a relationship from the fifth-house arena to the seventh-house arena.

- PARENTS AND CHILDREN: The ruler of the fourth house represents the Father; the ruler of the tenth house represents the Mother (both in the experience of the client). The relationship between these two planets, their respective strengths and debilities, and, in particular, any aspect between them will show how the client perceived their parents and the patterns and models on which they will be basing their own relationships. Children are seen by the fifth house and the ruler of the fifth house.

Appendix B

Astrology Organizations, Resources, and Web Pages

Astrology Organizations

I've provided a list of some of the major astrology organizations in the United States and abroad. These groups are committed to the practice and profession of astrology, and their efforts over the years are greatly appreciated. Many of these groups offer education, training, and professional certification programs as well.

Kepler College of Astrological Arts and Sciences

Kepler College of Astrological Arts and Sciences is the only college of astrology in the Western Hemisphere authorized to issue bachelor and master degrees in astrology. Kepler is located in the Seattle, Washington, area in the Pacific Northwest, and it's curriculum is broken down into correspondence coursework and 7-day on-site symposiums conducted on the campus of Seattle University.

The father of modern astronomy, Johannes Kepler, based his life work on the synthesis of arithmetic, astrology, astronomy, geometry, and music. Unwilling to segregate his studies, he gave life to mathematics; to astronomy, a soul; and to astrology, scientific reason. It is to his holistic vision of an implicate order in the universe that Kepler College has been dedicated.

Kepler College's mission statement is to gather the best scholars, teachers and communicators for its faculty, and foster an atmosphere of philosophical diversity and academic freedom. The college is committed to providing a sound, liberal, intellectual, and humane basis for the study and practice of astrology through an integrated, interdisciplinary curriculum, combining the study of astrology with traditional liberal arts as well as computer applications and new, theoretical models in science and philosophy. In this way, the college will prepare today's practitioners and future generations of astrologers as writers, teachers, counselors, and researchers.

Kepler College is the single most important advancement in astrology in the twentieth century. To learn more about Kepler College of Astrological Arts and Sciences, visit their website at http://www.kepler.edu.

National Council for Geocosmic Research (NCGR)

NCGR is an educational organization whose prime purpose is to explore the interaction between the Earth and the cosmos from both scientific and symbolic perspectives. NCGR recognizes many legitimate paths of discovery. Collaboration between traditional and nontraditional modes of inquiry is essential. NCGR directs its energies to supporting education and research into geocosmic studies. The word "geocosmic" pertains to correspondences and cycles that relate earthly events with celestial phenomena.

NCGR counts among its 3,000 members many leaders in the geocosmic field—a membership group spanning six continents. To facilitate a global exchange of ideas, NCGR has reciprocal membership agreements with the Astrological Association of Great Britain, the Astrological Lodge of London, and the Federation of Australian Astrologers. NCGR members can join these organizations at their less expensive domestic rates, and members of the above three organizations may join NCGR at the U.S. resident rate. Through a network of chapters located all over the United States, Canada, and Mexico, NCGR seeks to bring together people who wish to share and learn. Local chapters host speakers and study groups, and some chapters convene conferences. Many publish their own newsletters. The chapters are as individual as the people who belong to them. You may affiliate with a chapter by contacting the membership secretary or chapter president. The best way to learn more about NCGR is to check out their web page at http://www.geocosmic.org.

NCGR is committed to education and offers a comprehensive program of Astrological Certification Examinations available in the United States. The examinations are offered at the various NCGR conferences, or can be arranged through your local chapter. The examinations must be taken in order, and the previous level's exam must be successfully completed before the next exam can be taken.

At the time of this writing, NCGR does not have a certification track that emphasizes classical astrology. However, Terry Lamb, along with other classical astrologers involved with NCGR, is working diligently to create and include a testing and certification track that emphasizes classical astrology.

American Federation of Astrologers (AFA)

The American Federation of Astrologers was born (incorporated) at Washington, D.C., May 4, 1938, at 11:38 A.M. EST. Its purposes are clearly set forth in section 2 of its constitution, in the following words:

(a) To encourage and promote the science and the art of Astrology through research, teaching, lecturing and practice;

(b) To advocate freedom of thought and speech concerning Astrology and to develop and promote a correct professional status for Astrology;

(c) To assist all persons engaged in educational, scientific, or humanitarian efforts, such as teachers, graduates, lecturers or writers on Astrology, whose work is beneficial and who are duly qualified as adjudged by this Federation, and who are not acting in "willful offense against public policy;"

(d) To develop ways and means of eradicating illiteracy and disassociating those whose work in the name of Astrology is misleading to the public;

(e) To establish as high a standard of professional ethics for legitimate Astrologers as now exists in other educational professions.

The American Federation of Astrologers offers three levels of astrological certification (Associate, Professional, and Teacher), and publishes a great number of astrological books.

The American Federation of Astrologers does not specifically emphasize or encourage the use of classical astrology, and classical techniques are not included in any of their examinations.

For more information on the American Federation of Astrologers (AFA), you can write them at P.O. Box 22040, Tempe, AZ 85285-2040, call them at (602) 838-1751, fax them at (602) 838-8293, e-mail them at AFA@msn.com, or visit their web page at http://www.astrologers.com.

Astrological Association of Great Britain (AA)

The AA was formed at 7:22 P.M. on 21 June 1958 in London by a group of astrologers from the Astrological Lodge, which itself had been founded by Alan Leo in 1915. The two most prominent members were John Addey, who originated the theory of harmonics, and Roy Firebrace, the sidereal astrologer and founder of the magazine *Spica*. They were backed by Charles Carter and many other prominent Lodge members, including Joan Rodgers, Margaret Hone, and Ingrid Lind.

The founding members' main purpose was to bring astrology out of the fringe and into society's mainstream. John Addey contributed his profound understanding of Platonic philosophy, in which the stars and planets reveal the passage of time, and time itself allows the unfolding of the ideas that emanate from the First Cause, or Creator, and his flare for statistical and mathematical research. At the same time, the full implications of modern work in depth psychology had transformed the average astrologer's understanding of astrology, which was now seen very much as a means to character analysis and as an aid to counseling and therapy: the future was no longer to be predicted, but changed.

The AA currently has about 1,600 members, 1,000 in the United Kingdom, and the rest around the world. Most members keep in touch with the AA via its four publications. The principal publication is the *Journal,* published six times a year, and respected around the world as a forum for high-quality debate and discussion. The current editor is Robin Heath, and past editors include Suzi Harvey, Zach Matthews, Joan Rodgers, and John Addey himself. Occasional guest editors take responsible for special issues, and in the recent past Nick Campion and Charles Harvey have prepared mundane issues (Nick also edited a history issue), and Jane Ridder-Patrick edited a medical issue.

The AA also publishes *Correlation,* an academic level semi-annual journal on astrological research edited by Rudolf Smit, a *Newsletter* containing information, debate, and opinion, and the *Medical Astrology Newsletter,* the only journal in the world devoted to medical astrology.

The AA also organizes occasional seminars on all aspects of astrology. The highlight of the astrological year is, of course, the annual conference, which is always held on the weekend following the first Friday in September, beginning on the Friday and concluding on the Monday with a choice of postconference events.

To learn more about the Astrological Association of Great Britain, visit their web page at http://www.astrologer.com/aanet/index.html.

International Society for Astrological Research (ISAR)

ISAR is dedicated to encouraging the highest standards of quality in astrology through actively promoting accuracy of data and the reporting of sources; networking with other organizations to provide the best educational resources available worldwide; sponsoring valuable research to build upon the body of scientifically founded evidence relevant to astrology; actively supporting thoughtful dialogue in the field of cycles related to human activity, including the correlation of astrological signatures to current social, political, and economic phenomena and psychological issues.

You can contact ISAR by sending e-mail to Raymond_Merriman@msn.com, or by visiting their web page at http://www.isarastrology.com.

Centre for Psychological Astrology

Founded by Liz Greene and Howard Sasportas, the Centre for Psychological Astrology provides a unique workshop and professional training program designed to foster the cross-fertilization of the fields of astrology and depth, humanistic, and transpersonal psychology. The Centre for Psychological Astrology offers a professional training course in psychological astrology. The main aims and objectives are:

1. To provide students with a solid and broad base of knowledge both within the realm of traditional astrological symbolism and technique in the field of psychology, so that the astrological chart can be sensitively understood and interpreted in the light of modern psychological thought.

2. To make available to students psychologically qualified case supervision along with background seminars in counseling skills and techniques that would raise the standard and effectiveness of astrological consultation. It should be noted that no formal training as a counselor or therapist is provided by the course.

3. To encourage investigation and research into the links between astrology, psychological models, and therapeutic techniques, thereby contributing to and advancing the already existing body of astrological and psychological knowledge.

For more information on the Centre for Psychological Astrology and their course offerings, visit their website at http://www.astrologer.com/cpa.

Astrology on the World Wide Web

Astrological Horoscopes & Forecasts— http://www.astro-horoscopes.com

This is my website. My mission with this site is to maintain one of the most comprehensive resources for astrological information anywhere on the web. Needless to say, it's grown considerably since it was first launched in July of

1996. Be sure to check out the "Ask Kevin" section where I answer questions about astrological techniques and practices, and browse through the "Ask Kevin Archives" where you can read past questions and answers. If you'd like to schedule a consultation with me, you can do that in the "Services" section.

Astrodienst Atlas—http://www.astro.ch/cgi-bin/ atlw3/aq.cgi?lang=e

This is perhaps the most useful astrological resource on the web. It is the ACS Atlas database available for use online. You can find the correct longitude, latitude, and time zone information for anyplace in the world, and you can even view a variety of charts online, all for free.

Astrology Organizations

Kepler College of Astrological Arts and Sciences—http://www.kepler.edu

National Council for Geocosmic Research—http://www.geocosmic.org

American Federation of Astrologers—http://www.astrologers.com

International Society for Astrological Research—
http://www.isarastrology.com

Astrological Association of Great Britain—
http://www.astrologer.com/aanet/index.html

Centre for Psychological Astrology—http://www.astrologer.com/cpa

Classical Astrology Links and Resources

Dr. J. Lee Lehman's Web Page—http://www.leelehman.com

Archive for the Retrieval of Historical Astrological Texts—
http://www.robhand.com

Project Hindsight/The Golden Hind Press—
http://www.ProjectHindsight-TGHP.com

Just Us & Associates—http://www.horary.com

Astrolabe Software (Solar Fire)—http://www.alabe.com

Matrix Software (Win*Star)—http://www.thenewage.com

Appendix C

Astrology Software

Astrology Software for the Macintosh

Time Cycles Research: IO Edition, IO Horoscope, IO Forecast, IO Relationship, Star*Sprite, Others

Being, as I am, a die-hard Macintosh user, I didn't have a lot of choices when it came to astrology software. It's a good thing the software that I do use is so powerful.

For most of my charts and reports, I use astrology software provided by Time Cycles Research. For over ten years, they have been publishing astrology software exclusively for the Macintosh, and I've been extremely pleased with the quality and power of their programs. These programs are geared toward the professional astrologer (or at least toward the very serious student), and range from about $150 to about $300 each.

Although Time Cycles Research programs are excellent, they do not offer any classical astrology features at all.

Time Cycles Research can be found on the web at http://www.TimeCycles.com, or toll-free by phone at (800) 827-2240.

Macintosh Software Recommendations

Unfortunately, there isn't a lot of astrology software available for the Macintosh. On a professional level, the only software available is made by Time Cycles Research, and while I'm a huge fan and long-time customer, their programs simply do not come close to the features available in the Windows-based programs. If you're looking for programs to calculate basic charts and perhaps to generate some very well-written interpretations, Time Cycles is definitely the way to go. If, on the other hand, you plan on practicing professionally and want to have all of the tools of a professional astrologer at your fingertips (including traditional reports and dignities, a variety of 90° dial options, and dynamic reports that can include transits, progressions, and directions), you're going to have to either invest in a PC, or else do what I did, which is buy a copy of Connectix VirtualPC and use it to run a Windows astrology program (such as the one I use, Astrolabe's Solar Fire).

For God's sake, though, don't give up your Macintosh!

Astrology Software for Windows

Astrolabe: Solar Fire 5

Solar Fire 3, by Astrolabe, was named Best Astrological Program of 1995 by *American Astrology's* software critic, and given exceptionally high marks by the *Mountain Astrologer* as well. The most current revision as of this writing, Solar Fire 5, is even better. Astrolabe also has an extensive selection of astrology software for Windows, including Solar Spark, Solar Maps, and JigSaw. I am and always will be a die-hard Macintosh user, and generally avoid everything Windows. However, I'm also a professional astrologer who does a great deal of work with the traditional techniques, so I've had to make a few compromises—namely, to purchase a copy of Virtual PC so that I can run Windows on my Macintosh and use Solar Fire as my program of choice.

Solar Fire continues to be the cutting-edge astrology program available today. Its feature set is far too extensive for me to even begin to list; however, and perhaps of the most importance to those of you who are learning interpretations from this book, Solar Fire has reports and layouts that include a wide variety of essential dignity and almuten reports and tables. These can be customized to fit your individual preferences, and you can even create multiple settings depending on the type of chart you wish to work with, and use a different set of points and conditions when working with natal charts, for example, than you use when working with horary or electional charts.

You can visit Astrolabe's web site at http://www.alabe.com, call them for a catalog at 1-800-843-6682, or e-mail Astrolabe at astrolabe@alabe.com for more information and to request a catalog.

Matrix Software: Win*Star

Win*Star is the flagship of the Matrix Software line, and it is jam-packed with features. It has many, many different chart display options and wheel styles, and can do just about anything from transits, progressions, and synastry, to dials, astro-cartography, midpoint trees, and graphical analysis of planetary strengths and dignities using three different systems. I found the interface rather clunky, and the program is not very easy to navigate; however, Win*Star certainly has more than enough features to justify its price tag.

Matrix also offers a selection of DOS programs, atlases, and report writers (although they do have a very strict and limiting usage agreement as to how you can actually sell their charts and reports). Check out their web page at http://www.thenewage.com for more information, or call 1-800-PLANETS for a free catalog.

Other Software Options

Although you have a great many different astrology programs to choose from, the most well-known and well-respected professional programs, at least from the standpoint of working with classical astrology, are Solar Fire and Win*Star. Either of these programs will provide you with easy-to-configure reports and charts and can include tables of essential dignities for any chart, saving you the tedious work of having to fill out the dignity table yourself.

No program, however, will generate a dispositor tree, so that you'll still have to do on your own—for now, at least. I'm going to make sure that Astrolabe knows that this is a feature that many classical astrologers would find useful in Solar Fire 6.

Bibliography

Arroyo, Stephen. *Astrology, Psychology and the Four Elements.* Sebastopol, California: CRCS Publications, 1975.

Arroyo, Stephen. *Chart Interpretation Handbook.* Sebastopol, California: CRCS Publications, 1989.

DeVore, Nicholas. *Encyclopedia of Astrology.* Totowa, New Jersey: Littlefield, Adams, & Co., 1976.

Hand, Robert. *Horoscope Symbols.* West Chester, Pennsylvania: Whitford Press, 1981.

Lehman, J. Lee. *Classical Astrology for Modern Living.* Atglen, Pennsylvania: Whitford Press, 1996.

———. *Essential Dignities.* West Chester, Pennsylvania: Whitford Press, 1989.

Lilly, William. *Christian Astrology.* Issaquah, Washington: Just Us & Associates Publishing, 1647. Reprinted 1997.

National Council for Geocosmic Research. *NCGR Education & Curriculum Study Guide Level II.* Published by NCGR, www.geocosmic.org.

Rogers-Gallagher, Kim. *Astrology for the Light Side of the Brain.* San Diego, California: ACS Publications, 1995.

Wakefield, June. *Cosmic Astrology: The Religion of the Stars.* Tempe, Arizona: American Federation of Astrologers, 1968.

Zolar. *The History of Astrology.* New York, New York: Arco Publishing Company, 1972.

Classical Astrology Internet Resources

Kevin Burk's website, Astrological Horoscopes & Forecasts
(http://www.astro-horoscopes.com)

Dr. J. Lee Lehman, Ph.D.

       (http://www.leelehman.com)

Archive for the Retrieval of Historical Astrological Texts

       (http://www.robhand.com)

Just Us & Associates

       (http://www.horary.com)

Project Hindsight/The Golden Hind Press

       (http://www.ProjectHindsight-TGHP.com)

Index